Mark Skousen's Complete Guide to Financial Privacy

Mark Skousen's Complete Guide to Financial Privacy

MARK SKOUSEN

Alexandria House

901 N. Washington St., Alexandria, VA 22314

ISBN 0-932496-07-5

Trade Distributor:
Caroline House Books
236 Forest Park Place
Ottawa, IL 61350

To My Parents

Contents

Acknowledgments

A recent Louis Harris poll showed that the issue of privacy ranked next to inflation as the single most important concern of Americans. As I have prepared this guidebook and presented numerous workshops and speeches on the topic of financial privacy, I have come to the same conclusion. Never have I seen so much attention paid to this question. I would guess that at least one-third of all the questions we're asked by subscribers to *Personal Finance*, Kephart Communications' financial newsletter, deal with financial privacy. American investors are deeply committed to individual liberty and are suspicious of government intrusion into all aspects of their lives.

In months of research on this urgent topic, I was surprised to learn that, until now, no single volume addressed the subject of *financial* privacy. Numerous books have been written on the question of *personal* privacy, but nobody has offered a practical guide to financial privacy. Thus, the research required many long hours of correspondence, interviews, and investigative reporting.

A long list of experts on financial privacy helped by providing facts, opinions, and insights. I particularly wish to thank the following individuals:

Robert Kinsman, author of several titles on Swiss banks and tax havens, for reviewing the manuscript and writing the introduction. Bob is a highly respected writer in the field of foreign investments.

Robert Ellis Smith, editor and publisher of *Privacy Journal*, for allowing me to examine his extensive files on privacy issues.

Douglas R. Casey, consulting editor of *Personal Finance*, for his numerous insights on a wide variety of investment topics.

Adam Starchild, for reading the manuscript and offering invaluable tips and advice. Adam is one of the few investors who have first-hand knowledge about tax havens, corporate finance, and privacy.

Jerome F. Smith, president of Economic Research Counsellors, who made several insightful suggestions on improving the work.

Howard Ruff, editor and publisher of *Ruff Times*, for numerous suggestions. Howard has been deeply concerned about the erosion of privacy in our personal and financial affairs.

Otto Roethenmund, vice-president of Deak-Perera International, for some very interesting stories about confidentiality in the world of international banking.

Walter Perschke, publisher of the *Numisco Letter* and a coin and commodity expert, for his emphasis on privacy in hard-money investments.

Robert Stankey, an official in the enforcement division of the Treasury Department, for answering questions and allaying fears about the Bank Secrecy Act of 1970.

I also wish to offer appreciation to Steve Beckner, Eugene Latham, Harry Browne, Ted Nicholas, and Joel Skousen for helpful suggestions. A few other individuals who contributed immensely will remain anonymous at their request.

Special thanks go to my wife, Jo Ann, for her excellent editing skills, and to Marilyn Staudaher for typing the second draft. Richard E. Band, managing editor of *Personal Finance*, has been extremely valuable in editing the manuscript before it went to the typesetter. Thanks, also, to Ronald G. Reddall of Santa Maria, California, for proofreading the final copy.

Special appreciation goes to my publisher, Robert D. Kephart, for stimulating my interest in this topic and providing financial and moral support.

Finally, I wish to express thanks to the hard-working staff at Kephart Communication, Inc., for seeing the book through to its final publication; especially Janet Fouse, Kathy Powell, Becky Geanaros, Phyllis Tankel, Lauren Boyd, Kay Mancini, Pattie Altizer, Cathy Taylor, Wayne Waybright, and Grace Kimberlin.

Someone cautioned that I would be sacrificing my own privacy by publishing this book, and perhaps I have. But, to paraphrase Benjamin Franklin, "Those who would give up essential publicity to purchase a little security, deserve neither publicity nor security!"

MARK SKOUSEN

Foreword

John Stuart Mill once poignantly defined freedom by observing, "The only freedom which deserves the name is that of pursuing our own good in our own way." If one aspect of "our own good" is money, and I believe it is, Mill's definition of freedom must include financial freedom. Yet many would thwart us from doing what we wish with our money—from pursuing "our own good in our own way." Governments, neighbors, and sometimes even family members interfere with our money matters. That is why we need financial privacy. Mark Skousen wrote this book because he understands the vital connection between financial privacy and our total freedom.

Skousen doesn't dwell on theory, however. This book is clear, practical, and highly readable. Skousen points out how our financial privacy has been eroded in recent years. Consider that legislative marvel known as the Bank Secrecy Act of 1970. That law, you'll recall, requires banks to copy or microfilm all of our checks (strictly speaking, the Act requires that those over $100 be copied, but banks find it easier to copy them all), and demands that the copies be served up to any government agency upon request. The Act also mandates automatic reports to the Treasury of any cash transfers over $10,000, as well as any large extensions of credit, other than mortgages, and any movement out of the United States of more than $5,000. The law is a crippling blow to financial privacy.

But you know all that. What you probably don't know is that one can sidestep these regulations—legally. Skousen identifies the ways. That's what I mean by practicality.

Here you'll also find a wide-ranging discussion of unusual techniques for preserving your money privacy. Should you do business under a registered company name? Skousen will help you decide. He explores the advantages of second or third bank accounts, and the kinds of transactions for which they're useful. When to use cash equivalents such as money orders, cashier's checks, and travelers checks—even money market funds.

All of this, and a great deal more, is put together in a readable, step-by-step format that will interest anyone caught in the toils of Big Brother government or prying relatives, friends, or salespeople; anyone who is concerned to keep his money matters to himself. In short, almost anyone with capital can profit from reading this book.

In writing two books on Swiss banks and another on foreign tax havens over the past five years, I've discovered that the subject of financial privacy has attracted increasing interest. I ascribe this to pressures from an all-enveloping government, an impersonal computerized society, and a legal system that has bound normal means of doing business in knots.

The new interest in financial privacy can also be attributed to any increasingly desperate desire to avoid taxes. And here the line between legality and illegality begins to blur.

To exploit the best available means to become a more private, independent person is to further a legitimate cause. To use the same means to evade taxes or perpetrate fraud immediately puts you on the wrong side of the law.

A case in point: let's say you decide to transact business under a registered company name. As Skousen rightly points out, this is perfectly legal in the absence of an intent to defraud. Order publications, merchandise, or equipment under this name to keep your true name off mailing lists, to run a private marketing test, or to deter eavesdropping credit investigatory firms, for example. Legitimate. Use it to skip a bill, omit taxable income from your return, or promote mail fraud, and you're worse off than not having used that name at all. Merely using the name could be evidence of intent to defraud. In the case of taxes, that brings criminal charges, not just interest penalties.

If you study this book carefully, you'll find dozens of ways to improve your personal financial privacy for wholly legitimate reasons. This book is quite valuable enough for those reasons. Extend them to illegalities—the temptation may be there—and you'll probably have defrauded yourself. Take Skousen's (and my) advice: don't.

I salute Mark Skousen for addressing, in the honest manner of all his work, this difficult and delicate subject.

By the time you've finished this volume, I believe you will salute him, too. This is a book whose time has come.

ROBERT KINSMAN
San Francisco, California

1

What Have You Got to Hide?

Privacy from government is perhaps the most important
thing in life right now.

Harry D. Schultz

If a privacy-seeker were asked, "What have you got to
hide?" he might respond, "None of your business."

The struggle over financial privacy can be summed up
in those two phrases. It's a modern war fought between two
major forces—those with a ferocious appetite to collect data
on every detail of a person's life, the government being the
chief offender, versus those individual citizens who seek an
independent course free from unwarranted intrusion. It's a
war between social regimentation and individual freedom.
The outcome of the war is still uncertain, but many individual battles have been won and lost.

A hundred years ago, financial privacy was not an issue.
A person had a name, and perhaps an occupation, to identify him. There was no social security number to be used in
every aspect of business life. No one carried credit cards
and few had checking accounts. There were no lengthy income tax forms to be filled in with revealing and intimate financial affairs. Recordkeeping was extremely limited. As
the Privacy Protection Study Commission observes, "The
records of a hundred years ago tell little about the average
American, except when he died, perhaps when and where
he was born, and if he owned land, and how he got his title
to it. Three-quarters of the adult population worked for
themselves on farms or in small towns. . . . No national military service was required, and few programs brought individuals into contact with the federal government." Con-

1

gress established the Privacy Protection Study Commission
in 1974 to find out how privacy had been compromised over
the years and what changes in the law needed to be made
to reestablish privacy among Americans.

Big Brother and the Open Society

In the 20th century we have become a brash, uninhibited
Bare-All Society. Communications and technology have
granted the government and large corporations the power
to intrude on every aspect of our personal lives. We live in
an age where the public wants to know everything about
everybody. "Tell it like it is," is a common slogan. Nothing
is too sacred to be discussed in front of millions of armchair
Americans watching television or listening to the radio,
whether it be the intimate details of a divorce, a financial
scandal, a family tragedy, or the president's hemorrhoids.

Today the casual acquaintance asks, without a hint of embarrassment, "What's your salary? How much did you pay
for that car? How much did you sell your house for?" A
decade or two ago, such questions were not asked, let alone
answered.

Fortunately, many people are becoming aware of this
growing monster and are greatly concerned about the
"secret files they keep on you," as one writer put it. Citizens
of all political persuasions are beginning to feel uneasy
about the mischief these bank, credit, medical, and other
records could do.

While the recommendations of the Privacy Protection
Study Commission are still being considered in Washington,
not much seems to be forthcoming that would substantially
reduce invasion of privacy in this country. The machinery is
still well established to keep Big Brother's prying eyes
attuned to your movements, your motives, and your money.
A decade ago people decried the feeling that they were
being treated like numbers instead of individuals. But the
feeling today has changed. For privacy's sake, it might be
better to maintain a low profile, to become an anonymous
face in a crowd of millions so as to keep from being selected,
honored, or singled out as being different, radical, maverick,
or dissident . . . to keep from being harassed or placed under
suspicion by the government.

Five Reasons for Financial Privacy

You need to act now to preserve your financial privacy. It's quite possible that you will suffer financially if you fail to take certain precautions. And once you've lost your monetary assets, you lose a great deal of freedom—to travel, to buy and sell, and to influence your community and the world.

There are significant reasons for protecting your capital assets from unwarranted intrusion. Historically, there have been at least five reasons why financial privacy was important, if not essential, to financial well-being.

1. *Political, religious, and racial persecution.* Over the centuries, hundreds of groups have found themselves out of favor with those in power and have suffered financially as a result. Jews, blacks, Protestants, and many other groups have borne the brunt of persecution—which extended from the confiscation of their property to the taking of their lives. Examine your own life. Have you ever been in a minority position, differing from the majority in politics, religion, or racial heritage? Perhaps you were only verbally attacked or socially outcast; but in the future, could it get worse—could your house be burned, your property pillaged, your life threatened? If so, wouldn't it be wise to keep a little money outside the country or hidden away just in case you had to leave suddenly?

Some people with a long history of persecution have thought so. Take an Austrian man named Schultz (not his real name) who was a Vienna coffee merchant during the 1930s. He was a Jew who foresaw the coming troubles with Hitler and the anti-Semitic drive. So on a trip to Latin America, he made arrangements with his business associates to overbill him, that is, to charge him higher-than-market price, for coffee shipped to Austria. The excess payment was then transferred to a secret Swiss bank account.

When Hitler annexed Austria in 1938, Schultz was prepared. Instead of facing intolerable harassment and eventually a concentration camp or even death, he was able to leave Austria on one of his trips to Latin America, never to return. Along with his family, he crossed the border into Switzerland and eventually had his money transferred to Mexico. After obtaining a visa to the United States, he emigrated to New York. Schultz was no longer a prosperous man, but he and his family were at least safe and had some money to start their new life.

Many other Jews made similar arrangements and escaped the holocaust, but unfortunately, too many Jews in Germany and other European countries didn't have the foresight to make the proper preparations.

2. *Oppressive government, confiscatory taxes, and war.* This second reason is often interrelated with the first. The government has often had a hand in the persecution of political, religious, or racial groups.

Jews, Pilgrims, mystics, lepers, and numerous other groups have suffered persecution, isolation, and even death—often by government edict. The American colonists, and later the French peasants, felt it was worth risking all to revolt against unreasonable taxation. And less than 40 years ago in our own country, many Japanese citizens found themselves in concentration camps for acts of war committed by their relatives across the sea.

Certainly war or the threat of war brings on a litany of government regulations, including restrictions on the movement of money and people. Price controls, rationing, foreign-exchange controls, blocking of foreign accounts held by banks and brokers, confiscation of property, and high taxes are typical ploys by the government to control people's lives in time of war—often with the support of the majority. During this wartime period, public outcries are made against those who consume too much gasoline or food or other essentials; in other words, the government persecutes the financially independent. During World War II, for instance, all countries engaged in some form of economic restrictions and austerity. The U.S. government froze German and later even Swiss assets in the United States. In another instance, during the 1956 Suez crisis, Egyptian accounts were blocked in American and British banks. In 1980, President Jimmy Carter froze Iranian assets in the United States.

Because many governments around the world are vulnerable to a coup d'etat—especially in Latin America—smart investors and even politicians have held money outside the country or in hidden caches in case of social troubles or a sudden revolution. In America and Europe, a growing concern has been the increasing power of intransigent government to control people's economic lives. A further concern in Europe has been the possibility of a Soviet or Eurocommunist takeover, which has precipitated a discreet transfer of investment funds into real estate, securities, and other assets in the United States.

War also invariably means the conscription of all young male citizens of a country (and in the future, perhaps female citizens as well), who may be forced to engage in an "immoral" war. During the Vietnam War, thousands of young Americans went unwillingly to war or federal prison. Others went underground, some to Canada, and a few ingenious souls assumed new names and new lives to evade the draft. I am not suggesting that wars are not worth fighting, but there is no doubt in my mind that some future conflicts will be highly questionable, both morally and politically, creating the need to hide yourself and your money.

Foreign-exchange controls have been a common phenomenon in both war and peace. As a matter of fact, 80 percent of the world's countries today have currency-exchange laws. Below is an interesting chart demonstrating that at present only 22 countries have no exchange controls:

COUNTRIES WITHOUT EXCHANGE CONTROLS

Bahrain	Liberia	Switzerland
Canada	Mexico	United Arab
Germany (West)	Netherlands	Emirates
Guatemala	Nicaragua	United Kingdom
Honduras	Oman	United States*
Hong Kong	Panama	Venezuela
Kuwait	Qatar	Yemen Arab
Lebanon	Saudi Arabia	Republic

*International transfers in excess of $US 5,000 must be reported to the government but are not restricted in any way.

COUNTRIES WITH EXCHANGE CONTROLS

Algeria	Chad	The Gambia
Argentina	Chile	Ghana
Australia	Columbia	Greece
Austria*	Congo, People's	Grenada
Bahamas*	Republic of	Guinea
Bangladesh	Costa Rica	Guyana
Barbados	Cyprus	Haiti
Belgium-Luxem-	Denmark	Iceland
bourg	Dominican Republic	India
Benin	Ecuador	Japan*
Bolivia	Egypt	Iran
Botswana	El Salvador	Iraq
Brazil	Equatorial Guinea	Ireland
Burma	Ethiopia	Israel*
Burundi	Fiji	Italy
Cameroon	Finland	Ivory Coast
Central African	France	Jamaica
Empire	Gabon	Japan*

Jordan	Papua New Guinea	Thailand
Kenya	Paraguay	Togo
Korea	Peru	Trinidad and
Lesotho	Philippines	Tobago
Libyan Arab	Portugal	Tunisia
Republic	Rhodesia	Turkey
Madagascar	Rwanda	Uganda
Malawi	Senegal	Upper Volta
Malaysia*	Sierra Leone	Uruguay
Mali	Singapore*	Western Samoa
Malta	Somolia	Yemen, People's
Mauritania	South Africa	Democratic
Mauritius	Spain	Republic of
Morocco	Sri Lanka	Yugoslavia
Nepal	Sudan	Zaire
Netherland Antilles	Swaziland	Zambia
New Zealand	Sweden	
Niger	Syrian Arab	
Nigeria	Republic	
Norway	Taiwan	
Pakistan	Tanzania	

*These countries are normally considered free currency areas. However, all have minor controls on currency movements. For most, but not all purposes these countries can be considered free of exchange controls. (Courtesy *World Money Analyst.*)

The United States does not now restrict foreign-exchange movements, but it has done so in the past and is likely to impose restrictions in the future. Under the Bank Secrecy Act of 1970, you are required to report to the U.S. Treasury if you carry over $5,000 in cash or negotiable instruments across the border. Banks are supposed to keep a file for checks over $10,000 going abroad. Finally, when filling out your tax return, you are required to list any foreign financial accounts you hold. Many foreign-exchange experts regard these regulations as forerunners of foreign-exchange controls. Certainly the reporting requirement can be used to ferret out citizens who have money abroad. Legal blackmail or harassment may result. Hitler made the holding of a foreign bank account illegal and subject to the death penalty (for which three Germans were executed in 1934).

For a number of reasons, government officials may not want to see billions of dollars leaving the United States. One principal reason is that it would be a clear sign of the country's weakness and, as in Latin American countries, if it became known that business or even government leaders were stashing away millions in foreign lands and Swiss bank accounts, the country might face a bonafide revolution. So leaders in power will do all they can to restrict monetary outflows.

The war against gold is another example of government's determination to support artificially its depreciating currency. Even today, when the official monetary role of gold is supposedly declining, many governments restrict the ownership or export of gold bullion or coins. For over four decades, the United States had laws on the books forbidding the ownership of gold bullion and bullion coins (Krugerrands, Mexican 50 Pesos, etc.) by Americans. It was even illegal to purchase gold outside the United States. Finally, these laws were rescinded. Since 1975, Americans can legally own and trade gold in any form without restriction. Privacy becomes an issue here because no one is certain whether the government will again declare war on gold, ordering Americans to turn in their gold, perhaps below market price (as happened in 1933). Under such circumstances, Treasury agents will no doubt be on the lookout for lists of coin buyers. Consequently, gold buyers often pay in cash, money orders, or other "bearer" instruments to maintain their anonymity.

Confiscatory taxes are becoming a greater and greater reason for maintaining financial privacy. Although tax rates in the United States average less than in most Western European nations, the tax bite is continuing to grow for most Americans. This is because of the progressive tax structure —federal taxes alone take up to 70 percent of income—combined with rapid inflation, which pushes income earners into higher tax brackets even though in real terms their standard of living remains the same. Citizens across the country are starting to protest this stifling tax structure. The tax revolt is real. It has two dimensions: the official dimension at the ballot box, where citizens are voting against real estate taxes and bond issues, and the "underground" dimension. As taxes reach unbearable heights, more and more Americans transact business off the record—in the "subterranean economy," as Professor Robert Gutmann of Baruch College calls it. Gutmann concludes that over $200 billion of income goes unreported annually. He observes, "We should admit that the increasing public contempt for the tax system and government regulation is causing the subterranean economy to grow more rapidly." The cash economy will continue to grow. Unless Congress acts to slash taxes across the board, high taxes and inflation will create a whole country of lawbreakers—people who underreport their incomes in an effort to survive.

Despite the growing popularity of the "underground economy," I want to make it clear that I am *not* advocating illegal tax evasion. True, some of the techniques outlined in my guidebook may be used to evade federal and local taxes. But that is far from the purpose of this work. Besides, why should you risk tax evasion when there are still many ways to legally avoid taxes? The techniques of financial privacy are quite helpful in achieving the goal of *legally* minimizing your taxes, and should be used accordingly. By maintaining a low profile, for example, it should be possible to avoid a tax audit and other menacing invasions of your financial affairs.

3. *Gossip and other threats to your reputation.* Have you ever been the subject of unkind gossip because someone else didn't like your lifestyle, your personality, your children, or some such thing?

Your reaction might be, "So what? What has that to do with my financial affairs?" Actually, it may have quite a bit.

Take the story of James Millstone, assistant managing editor of the *St. Louis Post-Dispatch*. A credit-investigating firm had gathered some damaging information on Millstone as a result of an interview with one of his neighbors. The report stated that he was a hippie with a beard and long hair, could be a drug user, and failed to discipline his children. Because of this report, Millstone's credit rating was almost ruined and his automobile-insurance company was considering canceling his policy. When Millstone learned of the false credit report, he sued. In the end he was vindicated, but only after spending four years and $4,000. In this case, the false report was based on a single neighbor who disliked Millstone and had been feuding with his children.

You must be careful what you say and do in front of neighbors, friends, and business acquaintances. Even your doctor, sworn to protect patient privacy, can be a source of consternation. Recently, a doctor's discharge report to an employer contained a statement that the patient might have difficulties handling money. Although this was not a medical judgment, it kept this person from advancing in the firm.

Many celebrities—entertainers, political leaders, corporate heads, millionaires—use an assumed name or a corporate name to disguise the kinds of investments they make. Often there is a stigma attached to a certain kind of investment and a person of some renown or reputation may wish to keep such financial activities undisclosed. For example, suppose a well-known physician in the community wishes to own part or whole interest in a local tavern. If known, such an investment might be frowned upon by the community, which could hurt his business and his standing in the community. So he invests through a company name.

Finally, thousands of Americans every year suffer from an unsavory past. Bankruptcy, draft evasion, or a criminal record can bring bad publicity. Many seek to start a new life by covering up their past through devious means. Several methods of switching one's identity have been suggested. One is the fraudulent use of a dead infant's birth certificate to take on a new identity, complete with a new social security number, new credit cards, and bank accounts. In most parts of the country, the basic system of establishing an alias and starting a new life still works. Because of the illegal nature of this "deep cover" operation, I will not discuss it further in this book. In most cases, I would not regard the purpose of a new identity as legitimate. Often the person who wants to change his identity is trying to conceal a past fraud, theft, or bankruptcy. In general, he is running away from problems that should be resolved, no matter what the consequences.

4. *Divorce, family disputes, and lawsuits.* From a practical point of view, this may be the most frequent reason for maintaining financial privacy. Innumerable battles have been waged in the courtrooms of the world over divorces, wills, and other money matters. Lawsuits involving large amounts of money are quite frequent between relatives. Medical doctors, especially surgeons, have recently been besieged with expensive malpractice lawsuits threatening to damage them monetarily. The propensity to sue at the drop of a hat seems to be increasing dramatically, and the target is anyone who appears to be wealthy—the fellow with the "deep pocket."

In a divorce suit, private investigators are often hired to check on the real financial situation of a spouse to determine if wealth is being hidden in the form of real estate or cash in a safe-deposit box or secret Swiss bank account. Your personal activities can also have a strong bearing on the final settlement in a divorce case. The story is told of a woman who sued her wealthy husband for half a million dollars on grounds of incompatibility. She hired a detective to see if her husband was carrying on an affair with another woman, knowing that if he was, she could probably receive a far greater sum in court. Her suspicions were confirmed and she immediately amended her suit to $2 million; she had a new ground: adultery. The husband was furious about the discovery (and the request for more money) and he retaliated by hiring a private investigator to check on his wife's sex life. Sure enough, she was seeing another man. His lawyer confronted her with this knowledge and the lawyers agreed to reduce the suit to the original half million dollars. No doubt this is an unusual case, but it demonstrates the lengths parties will go to to bolster their own financial status, particularly when personal revenge or vindication is involved.

The case of "honor bonds" is another example of the need for privacy when family relations are deteriorating. "Honor bonds" were bank certificates issued in bearer form—the bank records only the bond's serial number, not its holder, who can remain anonymous. The IRS prohibited such bonds in 1979 because interest payments on the bonds may not be reported to the IRS. The agency feared that such bonds would be used for tax evasion. (Now the banks must ask for the name and address of the purchaser and redeemer.) Actually, there are legitimate reasons for using these private "honor bonds." In one case, for example, a lady interviewed by the press said that she purchased the bond to hide money from her husband, who was physically and mentally abusing her.

5. *The increasing threat of robbery.* People who exhibit their wealth by driving around in big, flashy automobiles and living in mansions run a high risk of being robbed. Crime is increasing rapidly in the United States and the rewards are high in expensive residential areas. Thieves are becoming more sophisticated and even expensive alarm equipment is not always a deterrent. Professional robbers often check the obituaries and society pages to learn when people will be away at a funeral or on a long trip. Some thieves allegedly rent mailing lists of high-income investors and then find out when they are not at home.

As society grows more discontented and crime increases, it pays to keep your financial affairs as confidential as possible. This means you should maintain a low profile—perhaps a home less stylish than you might like, or an older car, or a post office box instead of your home address for mail. Why tempt thieves to take advantage of your property and belongings?

Sometimes you can actually save money by lying low. Many times, if a merchant knows you have money, he will try to charge you more. A man dressed in ordinary clothes who looks middle class may get a better deal on a new car than the man who comes in with an expensive set of clothes and the air of a millionaire. In economic jargon, it's called price discrimination and it happens all the time. A major university recently supplied financial information on one of its students to his landlord, who immediately raised the rent. Although this was definitely a case of unauthorized access to confidential information (a growing problem today), it proves the point.

What Records Do They Keep on You?

The average American has about 50 files on him. These records include all kinds of government and business records. Among the records kept by government:

- Motor vehicle licenses and registrations
- Professional licenses
- Social security (taxes paid and benefits received)
- Welfare payments
- Federal, state, and local tax returns
- Medical histories (public hospitals)
- School records
- Unemployment compensation
- Birth, marriage and death certificates
- Military and veteran's benefits
- FBI and police records
- Court records
- Deeds
- Passports
- Census records

In the business world, the following may keep records on you:

- Insurance companies
- Employment agencies
- Doctors (including psychiatrists)
- Credit bureaus
- Banks and financial institutions
- Brokerage houses and investment funds
- Car dealers, mail-order firms, mortgage companies, and other places where you do business

- Clubs and organizations
- Genealogical bureaus
- Churches

According to one study, 72 percent of the time you are the one who provides the data for these files. Clearly, the solution, if you desire financial privacy, is to keep silent. But that is easier said than done. In many cases, you will be forced to give personal data on penalty of law, particularly when the government is doing the asking. Many Americans particularly resent the census as an invasion of privacy—and they take precautions to make sure they are not around when the census taker drops by. But if you are applying for credit, you will have to provide a lot of information. Otherwise, no loan. So there is really no way to completely avoid having records made of your life unless you plan to live like a hermit. Fortunately, there are ways to minimize invasion of privacy. The purpose of this book is to provide you with a wide variety of tactics to suit your personality and desire for privacy.

Insurance is a major area where you reveal personal and financial information. Aetna Life and Casualty Co. is in the forefront of insurance companies concerned about protecting privacy. A recent release by Aetna stated the company's policy as follows:

> We'll ask you for the information we need, and no more. We'll tell you what data we're after, how we intend to get it, and from whom. If we turn you down, we'll tell you why. (And we won't turn you down just because someone else has.) If you think we have misinformation, just ask what we've got. We'll tell you the nature and substance of all underwriting information in your file. (Except medical information, which we'll give your doctor.) If you say some part of it is wrong, we'll reinvestigate—and respond. And we'll go out of our way not to pass on information about you without permission.

The Computer Threat

The computer has worked miracles in the free-enterprise system. It has boosted productivity and spawned countless new consumer products. But it is not without its drawbacks. The prime concern of many civil libertarians is that the computer, like the giant all-seeing television in George Orwell's *1984*, will be used for political, religious, or other harassment by the people in power. Already congressmen and other leaders have raised doubts about data-processing networks proposed or already installed by the FBI, the IRS, and the Federal Reserve. The Carter administration recently scuttled an $850 million nationwide computer to monitor taxpayers—for now anyway. Congress objected to a new FBI data network because the system "might contribute to the growth of federal social control or become an instrument for subversion of the democratic process." Recently, the Federal Reserve ignored critics and went ahead with its plans to establish a national electronic banking system that would handle transfers of funds for bank customers. So the battle is still being fought.

David F. Linowes, Chairman of the Privacy Protection Study Commission, which Congress commissioned to investigate the issue of privacy in America, has stated, "The truth is that a piece of silicone the size of the head of a pin can store 2,000 pieces of information. So, physically, storage is meaningless. There is already available a computer system that could store a 4,000 word biography of every man, woman and child in this country, retrievable in a matter of seconds."

Not only could computers keep this kind of personal data on individuals, but the kind of purchases and the physical whereabouts of individuals could be monitored through the use of checkless electronic transaction reports, especially when banks, retail stores, credit bureaus, employers, and the government have all put their files on one grand system.

Experts in computer technology were once asked to come up with the most effective surveillance system that a government could use to spy on its citizens. They came up with an electronic funds-transfer system. No other system provides a better way for the government to know how you spend your money and your time, and where. Electronic funds transfer can be used to reconstruct an exact profile of the way you live—and all of this will be available at the push of a button.

The World's Most Famous Private Man

The most extreme example of a man who treasured his privacy was Howard Hughes. Of course, Hughes was not truly a private man because his fame grew with his untiring efforts to remain in complete seclusion.

Reporter James Phelan, in his book, *Howard Hughes: The Hidden Years*, describes Hughes' secluded life as follows: "Howard Hughes' greatest invention was—his Secrecy Machine. Unlike his great flying boat which barely got off the water, his Secrecy Machine functioned almost flawlessly for fifteen years . . . Only a very rich man could afford such a Secrecy Machine, and only Howard Hughes wanted and needed one . . . He hid women, business transactions, old planes and cars, his thoughts, his whereabouts, what he looked like, the uses to which he put his money, praiseworthy or disreputable . . . In an age that exploded into personal openness, self-revelation, letting it all hang out, he believed in tucking it all away." His private life, which was revealed in detail after his death, was bizarre. For years he would seclude himself in a completely blacked-out room where he would handle his affairs, watch movies over and over again, let his hair grow long, and make unusual demands on his staff. There was always an air of mystery about his desires, his motives, and what his next move would be. He coveted this seclusion so much that he forfeited a $145 million lawsuit rather than make a personal court appearance.

Of course, such secrecy is not what most of us are in search of. If we tried to be the private person Hughes was, we would be far away from a truly secluded existence. Like Hughes, we would probably become a celebrity. Our aim is to mix in with the average Joes of this world so that we are no longer noticed as being peculiar or publicly known. No longer will we be known, say, as a maverick who stashes away gold, stockpiles food, or collects firearms. Only in complete confidentiality will we have the power to survive when times turn difficult.

After reading over all these reasons for financial privacy, you may ask yourself: "Is this a paranoid view of what the government or my neighbors might do to me?" It's an understandable feeling because in most instances the "horror stories" we've related seem to be either a thing of the past or an exception to the rule. Yet we live in extraordinary times and no one can foretell the future with certainty. Each person must choose what degree of privacy he wishes to maintain. I'm not suggesting that everyone follow every single piece of advice offered in this guidebook—some things are just not suited for certain individuals. But there is no doubt that you are currently compromising your own privacy in subtle ways, and without knowing it.

This book will help you identify those areas and then correct them.

Drug Dealers, the Mafia, and Tax Evaders

It must be admitted at the outset that many of the privacy techniques found in this book have been used by illicit drug dealers, the Mafia, tax evaders, embezzlers, prostitutes, and other underground elements of society. This does not mean that I have written a manual for illegal activity—that would be tantamount to saying that a cookbook causes heart attacks, cancer, obesity, and other food-related illnesses. On the contrary, I have already outlined at least five distinct, legitimate reasons for financial privacy: persecution, government tyranny, threats to your reputation, lawsuits, and theft. The purpose of this guidebook is to help the concerned citizen to maintain his privacy—legally and ethically.

The risks of tax evasion are high, moreover. Even though you may regard the taxation of your hard-earned dollars as illegal and unconstitutional confiscation of your property, you may have guilt feelings—knowing that you have broken the law and Treasury agents could secretly be on your trail. More importantly, are you willing to face the legal consequences of being caught—interest charges, penalties, fines, and a possible jail sentence? Could you live with that?

In addition, if you have an undeclared foreign account, how can you bring your untaxed earnings back into this country without arousing suspicion? This is a major question in the tax evader's mind. Discretion is essential if you want to maintain your privacy. You can keep your money abroad, compounding interest, building up a nice little nest egg. But what will you do with it? Perhaps you can spend some of it when you travel overseas. Or maybe you plan on letting it sit in a foreign bank until retirement, when you will move abroad and live off the money. But the minute you decide to bring it back into the United States to invest or consume, you have a problem of concealing the money. Even if you can bring the money back undetected, you must invest or spend it quietly and unobtrusively. You can't all of a sudden start living like a king, buying big, expensive cars and another colonial-style mansion, or opening up a $100,000 brokerage account, without raising eyebrows or creating curiosity.

2
Keeping Your Bank Account Confidential

Where stands our total freedom in the absence of financial freedom?

Robert Kinsman

One of the first steps to financial privacy is keeping your bank account confidential. Banking services—checking and savings accounts as well as loans—seem almost indispensable in today's highly mobile society. Your checking account offers a convenient way of keeping track of income and expenses. It pemits you to pay for goods and services in person or by mail and it is a relatively safe place to keep idle money.

But unfortunately, your bank account is also vulnerable to official government snooping. This was made possible through the Bank Secrecy Act of 1970—a misnomer if there ever was one. And, as we shall see, your bank account is a revealing account of your financial situation and your personal life.

The Bank Secrecy Act of 1970

Officially called the Financial Recordkeeping, Currency, and Foreign Transactions Reporting Act of 1970 (Public Law 91-508), the Bank Secrecy Act requires banks to photocopy deposit slips and the front and back of all checks drawn for over $100. But since it would cost too much to sort checks to comply with the law, banks routinely micro-

17

film all checks regardless of value.* Banks are required to maintain records of any extension of credit in excess of $5,000 (except real estate mortgages). The law mandates the reporting of "cash" transactions (deposits or withdrawals) in excess of $10,000.

Banks are required to ask for your social security number or taxpayer identification number before a new checking or savings account can be opened. The bank is to make a list of customers who fail to supply the number within 45 days. This list, which includes names, addresses, and account numbers, must be available for inspection by the Treasury Department if called upon. There are some exceptions to this requirement: ambassadors, ministers, foreign attaches, representatives of international organizations, foreign students, and foreigners temporarily residing in the United States. But for the average American citizen, the number is required.

Naturally, the cost of photocopying billions of checks is tremendous—a spokesman for the American Bankers Association says that this provision of the law has cost over $1 billion since its inception! But the government feels there is a purpose in it. According to official word, the Bank Secrecy Act was established to fight "organized and white-collar crime," which is a noble enough goal. But some civil libertarians see it as "legalizing government espionage of American banks, businessmen, and ordinary citizens." In the words of Supreme Court Justice William Douglas, "I am not yet ready to agree that America is so possessed with evil that we must level all constitutional barriers to give our civil authorities the tools to catch criminals."

Several government agencies, particularly the Treasury Department, the Securities and Exchange Commission, and the FBI, have taken advantage of this Bank Secrecy Act to pry into bank accounts of *suspected* criminals and tax evaders. On the surface the average law-abiding citizen could find no objection to such action. But such excessive, unrestrained powers can lead to abuses.

Take the case of Bill Kaysing, a young "activist" student in the early 1970s. For a period of time he served as a writer and publicist for a black group in the Santa Barbara area. One morning Kaysing walked into his local bank only to find

---

*Detroit Bank & Trust Co. is the only bank I know that does not microfilm checks of $100 or less—at considerable savings, according to a spokesman!

that the bank vice-president was leafing through his checks. He thought it a little abnormal, but he didn't object and went about his business. Months later, he realized that he was under surveillance by the FBI for working with the black group.

So he went through his checking account to determine what his profile might have looked like to the federal agents. Some of his checks were written to: a gun store (he liked to target-shoot), a Southern legal aid society (a donation on behalf of a man in prison), the black group (to repay a debt), and several similar organizations and stores. Kaysing comments, "Taken as a group, the expenditures would appear to be very suspicious, especially the check to the gun store. Was I supplying the blacks with guns and ammunition? Was I a bleeding-heart liberal attaching himself to a revolutionary cause?" Apparently his motives were misinterpreted, because two years later he was investigated by the FBI, even though his only interest was to be helpful to a worthy cause.

According to the American Civil Liberties Union, there is a long list of cases where political information has been sought by government surveillance of bank records: in the early 1970s, the FBI monitored the checking account of a "left-leaning public affairs think tank" called the Institute for Policy Studies; New York banks "routinely" turned over to the FBI financial information on politically active customers, including Jane Fonda and Benjamin Spock. By sifting through his bank records (without his permission), the White House "plumbers" discovered that Daniel Ellsberg was going to a psychiatrist. Richard Stark, a California artist favoring "radical" political causes, came across a memo accidently placed in his monthly statement: "This memo is to authorize you to read checks to the FBI before sending the statement to the customer."

The IRS has zealously rifled the bank records of tax evaders. But on occasion it has also abused this power, threatening taxpayers who are vocally opposed to wasteful government and confiscatory taxation. Take the late Karl Bray, a leader in the tax revolt, who wrote a popular booklet called *Taxation and Tyranny*. He had a popular radio talk show in Salt Lake City, but when he started talking about tax revolt and inviting "radical" guests to speak, the IRS pressured the management into firing him. Later, when sales of his book were brisk, the IRS took Bray to court for tax evasion and issued a summons for his bank account,

which included the microfilm of checks of people who had
purchased his book on taxes. Leaders of the tax-revolt movement allege that the IRS used this list to choose names for
federal income tax audits.

Little Privacy in Bank Records

Several individuals and groups, including the American
Civil Liberties Union, have challenged the constitutionality
of the Bank Secrecy Act, but in each case the Supreme
Court has ultimately ruled in favor of the government.
The most famous case is *U.S. v. Miller*, decided April 21,
1976, a fateful day for financial privacy. Mitchell Miller
was charged with selling unlicensed and untaxed whiskey,
and under a grand jury subpoena his bank was forced to
turn over copies of his bank accounts, without his knowledge, to Treasury agents. Miller argued that the bank's
policy of microfilming checks, as required by the Bank
Secrecy Act, was an infringement of his Fourth Amendment
rights (the Fourth Amendment prohibits "unreasonable
searches and seizures" of private papers). The Supreme
Court ruled that Miller had no "expectation of privacy" in
his bank account and that bank records are actually the
property of the bank, not the individual customer. As Justice
Lewis F. Powell, Jr. stated: "The depositor takes the risk,
in revealing his affairs to another, that the information will
be conveyed by the person to the government."

Civil libertarians, financial experts, and many newspaper editors strongly criticized the Supreme Court decision. The *Washington Post* said that it made "financial
privacy something of a joke." The Final Report of the Privacy Commission observed, "The *Miller* case said, in effect,
that government no longer has to operate within the stric-
tures of the Fourth and Fifth Amendments when it wants to
acquire financial records pertaining to an individual; that
what were once his private papers are now open to government scrutiny. What amounts to mere curiosity will suffice
as justification if government agents want to see them."
This, coming from a report commissioned by the government
itself, is particularly frightening.

Several important consequences resulted from the *Miller*
decision.

Fortunately, some legislative action has been taken
to reduce wholesale government inspection of bank records.
The state of California, for example, includes in its consti-

tution the "inalienable right" to personal privacy and, since 1972, requires that authorities must show probable cause of a criminal act *before* gaining access to bank records.

The 1976 Tax Reform Act requires that the IRS notify an individual when a summons has been served on his bank (or any other third party, such as credit card companies), thus giving the individual the opportunity to intervene. At first, Treasury bureaucrats objected strenuously to this new imposition. Attorney General Griffin Bell argued before the House Ways and Means Committee that this "radical departure from existing laws [will] stultify the IRS's every investigative move." So far, however, this has not been the case. During the first three months of operation, 8,732 IRS summonses of personal information were issued, and in only 365 instances did taxpayers challenge the summons. In only 22 of those instances did the taxpayer successfully intervene in a bank-record summons, and so far, all of these have been resolved in the government's favor. The Justice Department was crying wolf when it predicted that the IRS would be "stultified"; government snooping really hasn't been restricted much at all. As the Privacy Commission notes, "While it may deter baseless investigative activity, [it] gives the individual little with which to impede IRS access . . . To be sure, the individual may go to court, but when he gets there he has nothing to say, because he has no legal interest to defend or to balance against the government's desire for the record."

Finally, in late 1978, Congress passed the Financial Institutions Regulatory Act, which essentially overturned a portion of the Supreme Court ruling in *U.S. v. Miller.* The law now states that government investigators must notify an individual and give him the opportunity to challenge the search before his records are turned over to the government. Banks, savings and loan associations, and credit card companies are covered by the new law. The restriction applies to all government agencies, except the Securities and Exchange Commission, which was exempted for two years only.

IRS Summons—Easy Access to Your Records

A search warrant, a subpoena, and a summons fall into different legal categories.

It's important to recognize the distinctions. A search war-

rant is a court order to seize materials. It is governed by
the Fourth Amendment. A subpoena is a legal order for
papers and is signed by a court clerk. A summons, however, is simply an order signed by an administrator.

The IRS has authority to issue its own administrative
summons or "pocket" summons, which requires that you
or some third party (such as a bank) must produce the documents in question within 10 days, often at your expense.
Note that these are not subpoenas issued by a federal court
or grand jury, but fishing licenses issued by and for the
selfsame agency. The FBI snoops around even more freely
than the IRS—FBI agents are often allowed to examine "in-
formally" a financial institution's records without pro-
ducing any kind of summons or subpoena, simply by flashing
a badge.

The April Game, a book written by an experienced IRS
agent, demonstrates how the IRS exercises similar power:

> Four times out of five, when I walk into a bank and flash
> my credentials, I get to see anything I want to see. Some
> banks are so cooperative that they border on the servile.
>
> When they don't want to cooperate, it is seldom diffi-
> cult to change their minds.
>
> "You won't show me the records?" I asked the plump
> little banker.
>
> He had pale-blue eyes, and he had a habit of blinking them
> rapidly. He looked almost as though he were about to burst
> into tears. "I'd really rather not," he said. "I'd like to check
> with some other people around here first. I don't quite know
> what our position would be in a situation like this . . ."
>
> I nodded, than made a production of pulling a small black
> notebook and pen out of my inside breast pocket. "May I
> have your full name, sir?"
>
> That got him. It almost always does. There is hardly an
> American citizen above the poverty level whose tax con-
> science is so completely clear that he isn't scared of being
> audited . . .
>
> He mumbled, "Well—um—maybe we can—um." He scur-
> ried out of the room. A few moments later he was back, brim-
> ming over with cooperation. "My secretary will show you
> any records you want to see," he said, "But just to protect
> myself—in case my customers get mad, you know—may I
> ask you to serve me with an official summons first?"
>
> It was a common request, quickly arranged.

The 1978 Financial Institutions Regulatory Act will go
a long way toward curtailing the fishing expeditions of the
IRS and other government agencies.

What Does Your Bank Account Reveal?

How personal is your checking account? How much information can someone uncover by digging through your bank records?

Go through a couple of months of checks you've written—it will be a worthwhile exercise. You'll be astonished at how much your monthly bank statements reveal about your activities: places where you shop and dine, names of friends and relatives, your church or favorite charity, organizations you belong to, political affiliations, and clubs. Look what the government surmised from Bill Kaysing's checking account! David F. Linowes, who chaired the Privacy Commission, states: "Information in a checking account lists the organizations a person belongs to, the contributions he makes. It is a reflection of his political beliefs, and will even tell who the person's friends are. Should this information get into the wrong hands, it could be used for harassment purposes, for criminal activities." He foresaw the possibility that the Federal Reserve, which supervises the clearing of all checks, could become a "lending library" of information for other government agencies.

Electronic fund-transfer systems are a matter of concern to the Privacy Commission and to civil libertarians. The Federal Reserve has already publicly announced that it is going ahead with plans to establish a centralized clearinghouse that will transfer funds electronically. A nationwide electronic banking system—the next step—would probably require a "personal identification number" (fortunately, not your social security number, since several states have already passed laws forbidding its use for this purpose), which could easily be turned to sinister purposes. Such a system could possibly be used to track the movements of individuals. As with credit cards, the transactions could be traced to specific "points of sale." Combined with the Customs nationwide computer system, electronic funds transfer would give the government a master system to control the personal and financial lives of all Americans.

Robert Ellis Smith, who follows these trends in his excellent newsletter, *Privacy Journal* (P.O. Box 8844, Washington, DC 20003, $45 a year), states: "You have nothing to hide? Your canceled checks, remember, record the names of your doctors and hospitals, the publications you read, the relatives you help, the religious and charitable activities you support, the volume of business you give your liquor store and the amount you spend on transportation (including whether you consume more than your share of gasoline). Remember, also, that some of your cancelled checks include your physical description, and if you're unfortunate enough to shop in certain places, they may also have your thumbprint. the information in canceled checks can be a mirror of your whole life, a reflection you do not want seen by the wrong set of eyes—like those of a government or commercial investigator who adds two and two and gets five." Supreme Court Justice William O. Douglas was right when he observed: "Financial transactions can reveal much about a person's activities, associations, and beliefs."

Smith maintains that a checking account may be a *distorted* mirror of your life. "The amount of money that passes through my liquor store in my personal checks, for instance, is not a true reflection of the amount of liquor I consume, nor is the amount of money I pay to a major oil company a true reflection of the amount of gasoline I consume, nor is a check to a particular publisher evidence of my reading tastes. I often get extra cash at my liquor store and I often buy products other than gasoline with my major oil credit card. The magazine subscription may be a gift or a means of staying informed on both extremes of an issue. I don't want strangers drawing conclusions about me based on what's reflected in my canceled checks, that I am a big drinker, that I am an owner of a gas guzzler that consumes more than my share of energy, or that my political views are identical to those of a magazine that I have paid for."

How to Preserve Banking Privacy

Now that you realize how public your private bank account is, what can you do about it? To eliminate the possibility of intrusion on your bank account, consider the following practical methods:

1. *Negotiate a contract with your bank that sets down the ground rules.* Robert Ellis Smith suggests that you insist that the bank notify you whenever a third party asks to see your records. Also, reserve the right to see and correct any records the bank might keep on you. In his new book on *Privacy* (Doubleday, $10), Smith offers a basic contract to draw up with your bank:

    1. The bank recognizes a responsibility to protect the privacy of information and records relating to the financial transactions of its customers, and adopts and promotes

a general policy of nondisclosure of identifiable records to all third parties.

2. The bank pledges specifically that none of its employees will, on a mere demand or request unsupported by legal process or the written consent of the customer, provide any government or nongovernment party with access to any identifiable records or information concerning the undersigned customer.

3. The bank further pledges that before complying with any formal subpoena, court order, or statutory duty to disclose such information, it shall make a reasonable effort to communicate such demand to the customer within two days of its receipt by the bank. Within legal limits, the bank shall not comply with such a demand until the customer has had an opportunity to respond, within 14 days of receiving notice. The mailing of a copy of the subpoena, court order, or statutory duty to the customer's current address shall constitute a reasonable effort to communicate the demand to the customer.

4. The bank and customer hereby agree to the above declaration and will uphold it to the fullest extent possible.

5. This agreement shall not extend to the examination and audit of the operation of the bank in accordance with applicable state and federal banking laws, provided that no auditing or examining agency shall use the records or information for any purpose other than regulatory or statistical purposes. Nor shall the auditing or regulatory agency disclose to third parties any identifiable records about the customer, except under the terms of this agreement.

6. The customer will not be treated in any manner different from other customers, because of this agreement, in bank services, charges, or rates of interest.

_____   _____
Date   Customer

                                 _____
                                 Bank Officer

Although the 1978 Financial Institutions Regulatory Act requires federal agencies to notify you if they are examining your bank records, this contract will still be valuable to prevent unapproved disclosure to commercial interests, credit bureaus, and state governments.

Does a contract with your bank violate the principle of maintaining a low profile? Perhaps. But your chief aim is to uncover the bank's policy on third-party requests for your

records, and to find out to what extent the bank will preserve the confidentiality of your financial dealings. Of
course, the difficulty lies in finding a cooperative bank.

Smith also maintains that you are not required to list
your social security number to open a checking account or
a safe-deposit box, or to apply for a loan. It is mandatory
for a savings account because the bank must report interest
earnings to the IRS, but no such interest is earned on most
checking accounts. The Bank Secrecy Act, however, requires
that banks make every "reasonable effort" to obtain a
taxpayer identification number or social security number
within 45 days of the opening of a new account. Moreover,
a list is to be made of all customers who fail to supply the
bank with the number. This list contains the names, addresses, and account numbers of such customers, and the bank
must make that information "available to the Secretary of
the Treasury when directed." In practice, the bank retains
the list and will turn it over to the Treasury only if a request
is made, which is seldom. Incidentally, if you don't tell the
bank your social security number, it's usually easy for the
bank to get it by calling the local credit bureau.

The prospect of being put on a "blacklist" of unidentified
customers no doubt deters many who would like to keep
their banking private. However, a spokesman for the American Bankers Association told me that he is convinced many
people simply report a fictitious social security number
because the government has no program of checking the
accuracy of the numbers. What's more, the social security
number is an imperfect identifier. The Privacy Commission
reports that several million individuals have more than one
social security number. In addition, one number may sometimes be used by more than one individual—as in the case
of a son who uses his father's number when he starts
working. (This isn't supposed to happen, but a surprising
number of young workers do use their parents' numbers.)

2. *Use your local checking account for routine deposits
and expenditures only.* Some have recommended that you
discontinue your checking account completely, but this becomes far too cumbersome and time-consuming. Imagine
the time and expense of making all payments in person, with
cash, or purchasing multitudes of money orders or cashier's
checks week after week. And what happens if one or two
bank checks or postal orders get lost in the mail? It could
be a very burdensome task to continue such an austere program.

Instead, compromise. Use your checking account for ordinary or routine expenses. These might include mortgage or rent payments, utility bills, and car loans. Ordinary deposits, such as your weekly paycheck, should be made as well. Very little of your personal life is revealed by such a conservative use of your checking account.

Sensitive purchases or deposits should be made outside your normal checking account. These might include contributions to religious or political organizations, purchases of gold and silver coins, opening of a foreign bank account, mail order purchases of books, firearms, and other personal products, loans to friends or relatives, and investments.

Go through the past six months of your canceled checks and determine for yourself what you would consider ordinary or routine, and what you would regard as sensitive or just plain nobody's business.

The same applies to deposits, which are also photocopied by the banks and subject to inspection. Deposits can also reveal much about whom you deal with socially and financially—so care should be taken. In addition, deposits may imply income. Even though in reality it may not be income—it could be repayment of a loan, reimbursement for travel, or a gift, or you could simply be switching your own money from one account to another—the IRS may consider it income for tax purposes unless you can prove otherwise. It would be prudent, therefore, to deposit only those incoming checks that are taxable. If you do make deposits of nontaxable items, make sure you state the source of the deposit.

Alternative Checking Accounts

So what do you do about money received from or paid to sensitive sources? One solution would be to consider the use of alternative checking accounts. Not all checking accounts are the same. Some may be more difficult to trace, and therefore may be used in conjunction with your regular local account for additional privacy. Let's look at some examples.

1. *Another local checking account.* This may be used for cashing third-party checks or conducting other transactions, such as the purchase of money orders or cashier's checks. In this case, I recommend that you open up such an account with a balance of, say, $500 and leave it idle. You can then use this checking account to cash sensitive third-party checks. Since you have an account

with the bank, and a sizeable balance, there should be no
problem in cashing a check. Do not deposit the check. Cash
it, receiving in return cash, a money order, or a cashier's
check. Most likely, you will be required to list your account
number on the back of the check, but the check will clear
through a general bank account. There will be no reason
for this check to appear in your own account, unless the
check is returned for insufficient funds (a "bounced" check).
Another possibility is to have a friend deposit your check
in his business account, and pay you in cash.

2. *An out-of-state checking account.* You can use an out-
of-state checking account for anything purchased (or paid
for) by mail. Regular monthly bills can be paid this way.
Often local merchants will accept out-of-state checks if you
have your home address and telephone number printed on
the check for identification purposes (although this, again,
could compromise your privacy, unless you maintain a post
office box). Incidentally, if you use an interest-paying checking account such as a NOW account in New England, be
aware that your account number is reported automatically
each year to the IRS because of the interest you earn.

3. *A money-market fund.* Money-market funds are no-
load mutual funds (no sales or redemption fee) that invest in
highly liquid money-market instruments such as Treasury
bills, bank certificates of deposit, and commercial paper.
These funds pay daily dividends in most cases and offer
free check-redemption services. In essence they act as in-
terest-bearing checking accounts. From the point of view
of privacy, they are useful because all checks that clear
through the fund are maintained in a single account—not
in the name of each customer, but in an "omnibus" account
under the name of the money fund. Consequently, the checks
you write are "lost" among the thousands written by thousands of shareholders. This provides a considerable measure
of privacy. It would be highly impractical for a government
or private investigator to check through the whole file for
your checks. It might be done, but only at great expense of
of time and energy. It would be worthwhile only in a case
of genuine wrongdoing involving substantial amounts of
money.

Again, keep in mind that your money-fund account becomes known to the government because a dividend statement is automatically sent to the Treasury Department.

Another important point to remember is that a money-
fund check must be drawn for at least $500, so use such an

account for large expenditures. Minimum requirements
to open an account varies from $1,000 to $5,000. Some
funds keep the checks—they are not returned. More complete information on money-market funds can be found in
my book, *The Insider's Banking & Credit Almanac* (available from Alexandria House Books, 901 N. Washington St.,
Alexandria, VA 22314, $14.95). The list of funds offering
check-writing privileges includes:

Dreyfus Liquid Assets	Scudder Managed Reserves
600 Madison Avenue	10 Post Office Square
New York, NY 10022	Boston, MA 02109
Fidelity Daily Income Trust	Capital Preservation Fund
35 Congress Street	459 Hamilton Avenue
Boston, MA 02103	Palo Alto, CA 94301

To completely avoid having your account reported to the
government, consider the tax-free municipal bond funds
that offer a check-writing privilege:

Federated Tax-Free	Warwick Municipal Bond
Income Fund	Fund
421 Seventh Avenue	Drummer's Lane
Pittsburgh, PA 15219	Valley Forge, PA 19482

Again, checks must be for $500 or more. The reason your
account should remain anonymous is that municipal bond
dividends are tax-free and need not be reported by the fund
or yourself (unless you earn capital gains).

   4. *An overdraft checking account.* These are checking accounts established by the bank or credit card company that
loan you money automatically when you write a check for
more than the amount in your account. In the case of credit
cards, the company may issue its own checks that clear
through a local bank or it may work in conjuction with your
regular checking account. In either case, it is important for
privacy's sake to use an overdraft account that is separate
from your regular checking account. Of course, these
checks, like many others, are photocopied—but the point is
that they are at least not as noticeable as your regular
checking account. As with the money market funds, credit
card checks are photocopied under a single account in the
name of the credit card center, not of the individual cardholder. However, specific records are kept on extensions
of credit beyond $5,000.

5. A Foreign checking account. A foreign checking account also provides a useful, though limited, way to keep your financial affairs private. If you make many purchases outside the United States (for example, books, investments, or real estate), or if you transfer funds from one foreign bank to another, such as a Swiss bank, then a checking account in Canada, Mexico, the Caribbean, or Europe might be advantageous.

All the Canadian banks offer U.S.-dollar checking accounts, and some even pay interest. Canada has a law similar to the Bank Secrecy Act in this country—all checks are microfilmed and can be turned over to Canadian authorities for inspection or to the U.S. government in cooperation with an IRS investigation. You're under a legal obligation to report the account's existence to the U.S. Treasury Department, and if you earn interest on your Canadian Account, the amount earned is reported and may be made available to U.S. tax authorities (for privacy, stick with non-interest-bearing checking accounts).

Mexican banks also offer U.S.-dollar checking accounts—and their checks are not copied. Mexico has no tax treaty with any government and it is against the law to reveal any information to a third party about someone's Mexican bank account. Safety may be a problem, however, since there is no federal insurance to cover bank failures. (Consequently, Mexican checking accounts may be best for simply transfering money confidentially to safer money havens.)

U.S.-dollar checking accounts are also available in the Bahamas, Bermuda, and other Caribbean islands, as well as in Europe. Many European banks have what are known as multicurrency checkbooks, which permit you to write checks in any of the major currencies of the world. Any bank that offers this service is a great candidate for your foreign checking account. Names and addresses of Swiss banks are mentioned in the chapter on foreign bank accounts. These banks operate under the Swiss bank secrecy law, but as I will explain later, the recent tax treaty with the United States breaches this secrecy under certain circumstances.

The two drawbacks to foreign checking programs are that (1) the U.S. government becomes aware of your account when you declare it, and (2) a foreign checking account may be impractical to use here in this country. You can't possibly use it as a daily expense account. Merchants, coin dealers, bankers, and other businesses will be reluctant to accept payment from a foreign account, especially if you present the check in person. You may be able to pay by mail, however. The greatest value of a foreign account may be for making deposits and expenditures outside the country. Using it to make routine payments here at home could raise suspicions. From a practical point of view, you may also find that you will be charged extra for using a foreign account because banks are notorious for charging a few extra dollars to clear a foreign draft.

The Case of the Vanishing Check

One of the most ingenious ways to keep the government from snooping on your financial transactions is by using nonreproducible checks or ink. Your checks cannot be photocopied. A firm called Liberty Graphics (P.O. Box 3614, Charlotte, NC 28203) offers bank checks on dark red paper, which is "least reproducible while being legible to the eye." The checks are expensive, five cents each in quantities of 500. You send the firm a personal check and they make a perfect copy using special red paper.

However noble Liberty Graphics' aims may be, the Treasury Department is not far behind. Recently, Treasury issued a warning to the nation's banks about the red checks: banks that honor them may be in violation of the Bank Secrecy Act. I am aware of some banks that have already refused payment on the red checks because they couldn't be microfilmed. And more are likely to do so. Indeed, I would discourage the use of red checks for the simple reason that they may tip off the IRS and increase the possibility of an audit. Remember, your goal is to blend in with the crowd, to become anonymous.

Liberty Graphics is not to be undone. The firm also offers special light-green and light-blue pens that don't reproduce well under microfilm. Again, there's a drawback. The endoresement on the back of the check will most likely be written with an ordinary blue or black pen, which defeats the purpose of the light-ink writing. Nor will it help if you write a check out to "cash," as some have suggested, and endorse it on the back to the payee in order to avoid detection. Remember, banks microfilm both sides of all checks.

The Company Checking Account

One final method of maintaining privacy in a checking account is through a registered trade name. We will encounter this technique in many forms throughout this book because the registered company name provides a flexible, low-key way to preserve privacy within the bounds of legality.

The typical company is given a name that readily identifies the owner. His initials may appear in the name of the company, or it may be formed from a composite of the partners' names. The company may even carry the full name of the owner. But the company set up to provide privacy will take a name that is completely unrelated to that of the person who sets it up. It might be the ABC Company or the Alpha-Omega Company. It's up to your imagination.

Your company must be registered, either at the county or state level, or both. The name should not conflict with company names already registered, or incorporated. Your fictitious company name is perfectly legal as long as you register it and use it without intent to defraud. *Intent* is a key word when you use an assumed company name. If your intent is aboveboard and legal, then the use of the assumed name is legal. If your intent is faudulent and illegal, the use of an assumed name is illegal and fraudulent.

This is the common law verdict on the use of assumed names. However, many states have laws on the books that declare *unregistered* assumed names to be *prima facie* evidence of fraudulent intent. So, I repeat, you must register your company name to remain aboveboard. Moreover, under no circumstances should you use an alias or assumed name on the signature card. This, too, could be regarded as fraud. A stage or pen name is appropriate only when the bank knows your true identity, and there is a real purpose for the assumed name.

To eliminate as much legal paperwork as possible, you may wish to remain unincorporated. Registering your company will require a taxpayer identification number or social security number. Creating a company name will not escape the attention of the IRS. But it will, in general, provide some measure of privacy from unwarranted intrusion.

After you have registered your company name, select an appropriate address, such as a post office box or mail drop, that will reenforce your privacy.

One word or warning: when you register a company name at the county courthouse, it becomes a public record. As a result, companies are often inundated with phone calls and solicitations through the mail from insurance companies and other salesmen. To avoid this problem, you might use the address of your attorney, or some other disinterested party. But definitely use a post office box to ward off *direct* solicitation.

Your signature is the final important part of the company checking account. Some people have considered making the signature *illegible,* a common practice in Europe. (Swiss bankers, in particular, are famous for their scribbles, making it impossible for outsiders to know their true identity.) There are pros and cons to illegible signatures, however. True, you gain privacy, but you also increase the chances of forgery. Unless your illegible signature is distinct and standardized, you could lose all your money if your checkbook were stolen. So if you do decide to sign with a scrawl, make sure you practice well. You can minimize the risk of forgery by maintaining a low balance at all times in your checking account. Use your account to pay bills, and make deposits sufficient to cover the checks you write. Also, the bank and government agents are less likely to show an interest in your account if the balance remains a paltry hundred dollars or so.

Now, let's take a look at the company checking account. If someone were to take a look at one of your checks, he could learn very little about you or your operation. The name of your company reveals nothing about what you do. The address is a post office box in a nearby town that offers no information about where you actually reside. And the signature is illegible—so the identity of the company's real owner is concealed.

You should also be careful how you use this company checking account. Although it can be used to purchase anything on the market, you would be wise to avoid making deposits from your personal checking account that would reveal your real name. Deposit cash, or checks signed by a third party and made out to your company.

Warning: A note of caution. Although you may establish a registered company checking account, as outlined above, do not—I repeat, do not—do business with or invest your money in a company that operates a similar program! Ironic as this advice may seem, it may save you from becoming a victim of fraud. On the one hand, your intentions in setting up an anonymous account may be completely aboveboard; you want to preserve confidentiality when investing or making purchases. On the other hand, there have been numerous cases of fly-by-night operators working out of a small office or a post office box, soliciting money from the unwary. All of a sudden, the whole operation disappears, and you've lost thousands of hard-earned dollars overnight. Such schemes are common. They spring up wherever quick fortunes are promised—in diamonds, coins, real estate, insurance contracts, repairs, or construction. They all seem to have similar characteristics: a high-sounding fictitious business name, a post office address, and an operator with no legitimate credentials or references. Avoid these questionable enterprises at all cost.

Credit Cards

There are several alternatives to a checking account for transacting business; they include credit cards, money orders, cashier's checks, travelers checks, and last but not least, cash.

Credit cards serve as a convenient alternative for buying merchandise and services. With over 400 million cards in the hands of Americans already—VISA, Master Charge, American Express, or any of the oil company, department store, or travel and entertainment cards—they seem destined to continue growing in popularity.

Unfortunately, the government has the right to subpoena credit card records just as it does bank records. All it needs to do, to gain access, is to serve an administrative summons on the credit card company. An administrative summons, or in-house subpoena, is backed only by the threat of judicial enforcement, but without any actual legal penalty if the credit card company doesn't comply. Now, of course, the government must notify the credit card customer that it is requesting his records.

Some credit card companies have had a policy for some time of notifying customers of government investigations. In November 1976, Citibank of New York inserted the following clause in its Master Charge agreement: "Your performance of this agreement may be reported to credit reporting agencies. No one else will be given such information without proper legal process or your prior written approval. We will try to notify you by phone or by mail of any court order in order to give you an opportunity to object to it."

American Express has also introduced a new policy of informing its cardholders of a government or court subpoena before turning over the records, thus allowing the cardholder to fight the subpoena if he desires. American Express states:

American Express has always been scrupulous in protecting the privacy of the information held in its files. In 1975, under subpoena, we released information on the records of only 469 out of over seven million Cardmembers. Even though this is a rare occurrence, we want to take this opportunity to let all Cardmembers know our policy, which has been further strengthened thanks to the work of the Privacy Protection Study Commission.

When Cardmembers' records are subpoenaed, we will respond as required by law. However, we think Cardmembers ought to know about it, and in all instances, we will tell them promptly, unless we are specifically prohibited from doing so by a court order. We will wait the full length of time allowed by the subpoena before providing the information in order to allow Cardholders the opportunity to contest the subpoena if they so wish.

But remember, credit card records are still available to the government and therefore their use cannot be recommended if absolute privacy is desired, unless you restrict the use of your credit card to nonsensitive items. (Recently, the IRS examined the credit card records of a lady to prove that her expenses far exceeded her reported income.)

One other possibility remains: obtain a credit card outside the United States, such as an American Express, VISA or Master Charge in Britain, Mexico, or Canada. Credit card companies are reluctant to open accounts outside their operating area, but special arrangements might be possible with valuable customers. Obtaining your credit card records from a foreign company would be much more difficult for the U.S. government, and perhaps impossible. Remember, however, that your credit card program would be in a foreign currency—if you can, choose a weak foreign currency, such as the British pound or Canadian dollar, since you will be billed in a currency that declines in value as you put off payment. Such a plan is quite possible for Americans residing in Europe. The Canadian American Express company will keep your account in the currency of your choice.

Another suggestion is to use your foreign company, to apply for a *company* credit card in the foreign jurisdiction. In most cases, the credit card company will bill you in the currency of your choice.

Money Orders

Money orders are useful for making payments in specific amounts, either in person or by mail. They are one of the most discreet ways of transferring funds or paying bills, with a number of advantages over a personal check.

Money orders are available almost anywhere—you can buy a money order up to $1,000 from most banks; up to $200 from drug stores, supermarkets (Safeway, Seven-Eleven), and financial companies (American Express, Thomas Cook, Deak-Perera); and up to $400 at any U.S. Post Office. Charges run anywhere from $1.00 to $4.00 per money order, although they are often free of charge with "package plans" at local banks.

Company policy varies considerably on the use of money orders. Traditionally, you have been able to purchase money orders without giving your name at banks and most other places. However, one friend tells me that recently his bank adopted a new policy on money orders, requiring the customer to fill in his name, address, and zip code at the teller's window, which then goes into the bank's files. This may become a trend someday. But you can still purchase blank money orders from supermarkets, the post office, and financial companies. After obtaining them, you can sign the money order in an illegible scrawl, and fill in the required address with your town and state only.

Money orders still leave a trace, nevertheless, and eventually come back to the issuing company or bank. They are not filed according to the purchaser's name, however. In order to assure privacy, it is suggested that you limit your purchases to two or three money orders at any one place, and do not make regular purchases anywhere.

Here are some other suggestions on the purchasing of money orders:

Avoid purchasing a money order immediately after withdrawing money from your bank account. Many banks will routinely note your account number on the bank's copy of the money order.

Avoid banks that insist on typing the name of the recipient on the money order. (Money orders are different from cashier's checks, which must be typed up by the bank.)

Sometimes the bank teller will ask where the money order will be sent. This is routine, done for the convenience of the recipient. The bank may have a correspondence bank near the recipient. If you say Europe, for example, the bank might issue a money order drawn on a European bank. Instead of revealing the true identity of the money order's destination, you might suggest that the money order be drawn on a New York bank (or on the West Coast, San Francisco).

Finally, bear in mind that if you need to send more money than the maximum available with a single money order, you can purchase as many money orders as you wish. You can buy several money orders and put them in the same envelope for mailing.

Cashier's Checks

Cashier's checks are available at most banks and are made out to whomever you choose. Cashier's checks are not certified checks but bank drafts, signed by the bank manager. You may pay for them with your own money, either by cash, personal check, or travelers check. Use cash to maintain complete privacy. If you purchase the check with cash, you probably won't be asked for identification.

Be careful that you obtain a cashier's check that does not include your name on the face of the check. Many banks will print your name above or next to the payee. Banks will tell you that they do it for your own safety, in case the check is lost. Yet the practice is optional and many banks will omit printing your name if you request it. (If the bank insists on a name, consider giving them your company name instead.) In some cases, you can ask for a "no payee" check, which leaves off the name of the person or firm the check is written to. If you're planning to mail the cashier's check abroad, make sure the check isn't made out to cash or bearer. Otherwise, you would be required to report it as an international transaction if it's for more than $5,000. You would also have to file a Treasury Report if the cashier's check was made out to cash in excess of $10,000, even if you intended to use the check domestically.

Cashier's checks can be made out for any amount, unlike money orders. International checks over $10,000 are supposed to be filed separately by the issuing bank, available for inspection by Treasury. However, a Treasury spokesman insists that a subpoena is needed to see the records of checks over $10,000 going abroad.

Travelers Checks

Travelers checks serve as an excellent substitute for personal checks or cash and are readily accepted for payment nearly everywhere in the United States and the world. Numerous companies and banks offer travelers checks: American Express, Citibank, Bank of America, Thomas Cook, Deak-Perera, and Master Charge among them.

More and more banks are offering free travelers checks

as part of a package deal—including the more popular brands like those issued by American Express, Citibank, and Bank of America. Most banks gain up to 60 days floating period before the checks are redeemed, and a short-term investment of this cash often exceeds the commission loss. Some banks have offered special discounts on the 1 percent commission charge—such as a $2 charge no matter how many travelers checks you buy.

Several lesser-known brands of travelers checks, issued by Thomas Cook or Barclays Bank, are also being offered free of charge. Thomas Cook travelers checks are free of commission when issued through an affiliate sponsor, such as the American Automobile Association (AAA). Barclays Bank travelers checks are free at most of the sponsoring banks in the New York metropolitan area. Of course, you should have no problem cashing these travelers checks at offices of Thomas Cook, Deak-Perera or at Barclays Bank in New York. But in many cases, you'll want to use them in place of a personal check at a local store or at a hotel or restaurant. If they don't recognize these kinds of travelers checks, they may request another form of payment. This lack of recognition is probably one reason these travelers checks sell at face value. (Barclays travelers checks are ideal, though, if you're planning to spend them in Britain or on the Continent: Barclays Bank is the biggest banking establishment in the British Isles, with thousands of branches.)

"Do-It-Yourself" Travelers Checks

A few banks in the United States have introduced a rather bizarre form of travelers checks, called "Do-It-Yourself" travelers checks, where you can write out the exact fare on your travelers checks. The bank guarantees payment of each check, up to a limit, of course. In this way, out-of-town stores and restaurants are more likely to accept payment because they don't have to give you cash as change. You may incur a small service charge on the checks you write and if you write a check for more than you have in your checking account, the excess automatically becomes an overdraft loan.

The First National Bank of Boston offers a similar program for corporations to take the place of cash advance travel and reimbursement programs. It is called the "Corporate Bancardcheck System," P.O. Box 2016, Boston, MA 02106. Corporate officials and executives who travel take with them blank "Bancardchecks" travelers checks, which they use to pay for each expense item—lunches, hotel bills, airfare, and so forth. There is no need to sort out personal and business expenses or to rely on credit cards or cash advances. The checks are guaranteed by the First National Bank of Boston, just like travelers checks. So both the company and the traveling executive benefit. The company doesn't have to tie up reimbursement and cash advance programs, so cash flow is improved.

Blank Travelers Checks

To use travelers checks, you must sign them, and since a second signature is required whenever you purchase something by travelers check, you probably won't be using travelers checks to pay by mail. Of course, if you wanted, you could simply sign the second signature and treat the travelers checks just like cash. But you run the risk that the recipient will not accept the already signed checks or that persons opening the mail will steal the checks and cash them.

There is a new method by which you can purchase completely blank travelers checks. In the past, you were required to sign your travelers checks at the teller's window when you purchased them. This was a time-consuming and often annoying requirement, particularly if you happened to be in the bank behind several travelers checks purchasers. Now many banks require that you sign a bank copy on which is recorded the serial numbers of the checks. You can avoid even this signing by purchasing American Express travelers checks at their special dispensers found in several U.S. airports, At present, American Express has installed these special machines in 16 major U.S. airports. Travelers checks up to $500 may be purchased through these machines; the customer's checking account is debited electronically. The fee is the regular 1 percent of the value of the checks. No one is there to make sure you sign the checks, so although your signature is on file with the credit card company, you can leave them blank. In essence, they are just like cash. But remember, if they are lost or stolen without being signed, it will be difficult, perhaps impossible, to get your money back.

American Express travelers check dispensers are available 24 hours a day, so they are a great way to get immediate "cash" for emergencies. All you need to take advantage of this service is your American Express card and a special four-digit number issued by the company after you have supplied certain information and given permission to American Express to withdraw money electronically from your checking account to pay for the travelers checks.

One of the best ways to minimize the expense of purchasing travelers checks, money orders, and cashier's checks is to take advantage of a local bank's "package plans." These package plans usually offer "free" money orders, travelers checks, safe deposit boxes, and overdraft protection for a fixed monthly charge, such as $3 a month. Often savings and loan associations offer free money orders and travelers checks if you establish a savings account with them. If you plan to use a lot of these quasi-cash checks, this is the route to go.

How to Raise Cash

Nothing is more anonymous and readily acceptable for payment than cash. True, each dollar bill has a serial number, but the bills are not marked, or attached in any way to the bearer, except in the case of a bank robbery or other illegal activity. Cash is the supreme way to pay bills and purchase merchandise if you wish absolute anonymity. Unfortunately, for most people the risks of carrying large sums of cash overshadow this advantage. Nevertheless, there are ways to reduce this risk. Therefore, the use of cash in everyday transactions should not be dismissed lightly.

A Strange Phenomenon

The use of cash for confidential transactions is growing spectacularly in this country. There are several evidences of this phenomenon. First, a recent Congressional study showed that $85 billion in cash is being held outside the banks, which turns out to be an "unexplainable" $1,545 for every American family! The question is, do you know any family holding $1,545 in cash around the house? If not, where is all that cash? (Cash registers? The Mafia?) Who is hoarding it, and why?

Another mysterious occurrence is the $100-bill "shortage." In 1977, Daniel S. Greenberg wrote an unusual story for the *Washington Post* entitled, "Who Uses All Those $100 Bills, Anyway?" Below is a reproduction of the article. It is worth reading carefully.

WHO USES ALL THOSE $100 BILLS, ANYWAY?

By Daniel S. Greenberg

Let us examine the $100-bill explosion. Though little-known and poorly understood, this fiscal phenomenon suggests some important and peculiar goings-on in American society.

While it is rare to encounter $100 bills in ordinary day-to-day dealings, this is not because they are rare. To the contrary, $100s are plentiful and are also the fastest-increasing denomination in American currency. According to the latest Currency and Coin Report of the U.S. Treasury, they already account for an astounding one-third of the total value of U.S. money in circulation, though they make up only about three per cent of all bank notes in current use.

Their prevalence simply reflects demand. The banks in the Federal Reserve System tell the Fed what they need to serve their customers, and the Fed places their orders with the Bureau of Engraving and Printing.

Thus, the national stock of $100 bills is growing because people want them. But why should this be happening at a time when extended use of checks and credit cards is supposedly creating a "cashless society"? And where are all those unseen $100s, of which nearly 290 million are in circulation? Who's doing what with the so-called century notes? Attache cases stuffed with hot money immediately come to mind. But the clues, scant though they are, since the matter has only recently aroused scholarly and official interest, suggest possibilities beyond the obvious one of criminal transactions.

First, let there be no doubt about the trends and numbers. The $100 bill is the biggest growth item in the money business, outdistancing even the popular $20 in terms of increased dollar amounts ordered from the printers. Between 1960 and 1971, the value of money in $100 bills rose by 122 per cent, compared with 89.6 per cent of all money in circulation; at present, the figure is nearly 33 per cent. What's going on?

Inflation creates demands for the convenience of bigger denominations, but, then, some of that demand is countered by the ubiquity of credit-card systems. And, of course, organized crime, with its need for record-free transfers of large sums of cash, would rather tote one $100 than five $20s.

But among the few persons who have looked systematically at the $100-bill explosion, other possibilities are noted. For example, George E. Cruikshank, editor of the Morgan Guaranty Survey, thinks that part of the boom in $100s reflects a mattress-deposit mentality that, in turn, arises from widespread distrust of established financial institutions. A lot of people, he says, are tucking cash away at home because they worry about bank stability and also don't want anyone to know what they have. Anecdotal support for this assessment, he says, is to be found in reports from retail shops in strike-bound industrial towns. After the paychecks stop, idle workers start making purchases with big bills—presumably withdrawn from home storage.

A 1975 government-sponsored study by Arthur D. Little, Inc., estimated that in 1972, when $61 billion was in circulation, roughly $25 billion could be accounted for in business cash registers, banks and U.S. currency held abroad. The balance, at least $36 billion, works out to about $800 in cash on hand for the average family of four—a sum that is considerably at odds with the acknowledged cash-on-hand resources of most families of four. The report expressed doubt about any such evenness in currency distribution. It also stated that "it would appear that a significant fraction of cash either is immobilized or moves in other than normal channels."

Concerning the $13.2 billion in $100 bills at that time, the study added, "Most of these do not move actively in normal flows of cash; thus, perhaps 20 per cent of all cash in possession of individuals does not enter normal channels."

These findings raise interesting questions. If big bank notes play an important role in illicit dealings and a relatively minor one in normal commerce, why do we need big bank notes? Could the Mafia get along on $20s?

What economic consequences arise from the immobilization of billions in cash, which, after all, amounts to an interest-free loan for government and erosion-by-inflation for the home "depositor"?

Finally, anyone who claims we need $100 bills in the economy should first pass a severe test: Whose picture is on the big bank note?   (©1977 *The Washington Post*)

What has caused the $100-bill phenomenon? Something more than just Mafia activity or a "mattress-deposit mentality." Cash is the most discreet way to transact business.

Cash dealings have created what Robert Gutmann calls "the subterranean economy." Dr. Gutmann estimates that "in 1976, the subterranean economy—business that transactors either didn't want recorded or didn't want taxed—generated an illegal gross national product of $176 billion. The figure is still rising steadily as rising tax rates and the ever-increasing burden of governmental regulation drive more of our total economy underground."

Dr. Gutmann elaborates: "Who participates in the subterranean economy? Anyone who receives cash in a business transaction has the option of joining. Cash transactions are common in certain kinds of businesses—e.g., retailing, personal services, and the classic illegal and quasi-legal activities. Restaurants, car-washing establishments, garages, bars, and small retail shops, in particular, lend themselves to tax avoidance through cash transactions. Certain types of transactions—payments to casual labor, payments for part-time work, payments of bribes—also commonly involve cash."

The conclusion is clear—whether for legal or illegal purposes, the cash society is growing. Strictly from the point of view of privacy in your personal and business transactions, cash provides an excellent means of payment.

How can you raise large sums of cash quietly and unobtrusively? If you withdraw money from your checking account, checks made out to cash will be noted and microfilmed. A check made out to your bank may be less noticeable, though recently banks have been requiring customers to endorse such checks on the back. If you take out a portion of a deposited paycheck, your deposit slip will show the amount of cash received.

Some have recommended that you cash checks frequently at gambling casinos under the pretense of being a heavy gambler—while pocketing some or all of the cash received!

There are more discreet ways. Third-party checks can be cashed at your local bank (where you have an *idle* checking account) by endorsing them on the back rather than depositing them. Microfilmed records of the canceled check will not be recorded on your idle account. This works with any kind of check you receive. Of course, the bank usually puts your account number on the back.

You can always cash a check at the bank where it's drawn. For example, you can obtain cash for your paycheck by taking it directly to the local bank where your company has its payroll account. Postal money orders can be cashed at your local post office. The postal employee will probably require identification, which will be noted on the back of the money order. But the money order is then filed—and not under your name—so your money order becomes one in a million.

You can have your company reimburse you for travel or other expenses in cash. Or you could occasionally cash small checks at work, making the check out to your company name, perhaps using your out-of-state account.

You can go to the grocery store and sometimes cash a check for more than the amount you purchased, receiving the difference in cash.

Another way is to endorse a check over to a friend, who can cash the check at his bank—and give you the money.

The local pawnbroker's shop is a place to cash in your valuables quickly, though often at a wholesale price. (Pawnbrokers are also a source of quick, confidential cash loans, albeit at high interest rates.)

So you see, there are numerous ways to obtain cash. If you have gold or silver coins, you can insist on being paid in cash when you sell them at a coin shop. The same applies anytime you sell small items—say, at a garage sale. Invariably, the proceeds from garage sales are not taxable or reportable because you sell home belongings for less than you paid for them. You then pocket the cash—free and clear.

Anytime you deal in large amounts of cash, you run the risk of theft. The safekeeping of your funds becomes an important issue. Money belts are an unobtrusive way to carry large sums of cash. If you hold large amounts at home, consider unorthodox places to hide the money. Also consider the use of a home safe or a safe deposit box. You can even bury your cash in the ground. Don't keep your money all in one place—diversify your holdings. See Chapter 10, "Safekeeping Your Valuables." Remember, however, that the IRS is suspicious of cash and may ask how you got it and if you paid taxes on the money.

One-hundred-dollar bills are the highest denomination currently available. In earlier years, the Treasury issued denominations of $500, $1,000, and even $10,000. Those days are long gone. The Treasury discontinued such series in an effort to keep people from being able to carry large sums of cash in small compartments without being noticed. Perhaps inflation will someday force the Treasury to reissue the $500 series. At any rate, if you find yourself overloaded with small bills, consider turning them in for $100 bills while they're still available. It is not unusual to find temporary shortages of $100 bills at local banks. Remember, though, anything over a $20 bill is still conspicuous.

Sending cash (or any bearer instrument) through the mail is not always safe these days. What surprises me, though, is that it is still done and on a scale that would really surprise you. An acquaintance in Europe who handles discretionary accounts for American customers told me that he often receives large envelopes, stuffed with dollar bills, completely unregistered and uninsured! Apparently, many people are still taking a chance in a frenzied effort to maintain financial anonymity. It is not illegal to send cash in the mail, of course, but to avoid the risk of losing the money, you'll need to register and insure the contents. (You are required to report to the Treasury if you send more than $5,000 cash out of the country.) Of course, very little first class mail gets permanently lost, so sending out small amounts of cash may not involve much risk.

Your Savings Account

A typical savings account at your local bank is not only a poor investment in today's inflationary climate; it is not very private. You must release your social security number, and your account number and interest earned are reported each year to the IRS. Some tax evaders have been known to open up accounts with phony social security numbers. Then they change savings accounts at the end of the year to avoid reporting the interest. This game is hardly worth the return, especially as inflation worsens. You should have money close to home for emergencies, but only a minimum of your financial assets should be in a savings account.

Contrary to rumors, there is no special form that the bank fills out and sends to the Treasury when you open a savings account with more than $10,000. That report is called for only when you take more than $10,000 *cash* out of your savings or checking account at any one time—something you should clearly avoid.

3
Your Foreign Bank Account

It is very easy to awaken resentment against people who not only have money, but also the boldness to send that money abroad via more or less legal channels, in order to protect it against all manner of domestic insecurity . . . It is vital that people and their means of existence—that is, capital—still have the chance to move about internationally, and when absolutely necessary, to escape the arbitrariness of government policy by means of secret back doors.

Wilhelm Roepke

Why keep money outside the country? Why have a foreign bank account? And if you do have a foreign account, which is the best country?

There are legitimate reasons for maintaining financial accounts outside the United States. In Chapter 1 ("What Have You Got to Hide?"), I mentioned persecuted individuals who survived only because they moved their money beyond the grasp of a totalitarian government. While the United States is more tolerant than other countries of individuals with dissenting views, it is not impossible that financial and social persecution of supposedly "radical" individuals could occur here. This is especially true during war or economic crisis—no one knows to what lengths the powerful Washington bureaucracy will go to achieve social conformity and economic stability. By holding funds outside the country, you achieve freedom from this power and influence. How much and how secure that freedom is depends on where you put your money.

But it is not only from the government that you are hiding your wealth. Money held in a foreign bank, trust, or other financial institution may go undetected and untapped if you are involved in a court case—a divorce, malpractice, or other potentially expensive suit. Often, private investigators are hired for the purpose of ferreting out secret accounts abroad. But if you've made the proper preparations and placed your money in the right place, the search will be in vain and your money will remain intact.

Another reason for opening a foreign account is that there are numerous opportunities around the world for the smart investor to make a sizeable return on his money. There is no sense in taking the nationalistic, provincial view that money-making opportunities exist in America and nowhere else. While the stock market is stumbling in New York, it may be booming in Mexico, Paris, Bonn, or Hong Kong. The same applies to real estate, bonds, and collectibles.

Critics have countered, "The United States is the last bastion of freedom in the world. If it collapses, just think what things will be like in Europe, Latin America, and the rest of the world! No thanks, I'll keep my money in the States." A world-wide economic catastrophe may well come to pass—but we haven't reached that point yet. If it does come, undoubtedly the signs of the times will be apparent, giving you plenty of time to bring your money home. And I'm not suggesting that you hold a majority of your assets outside the country, but rather a modest amount, based on your investment desires and your need for diversification and privacy. It's a way of hedging your bets.

The Bank Secrecy Act—Again

I previously discussed the Bank Secrecy Act of 1970, which imposed photocopying and reporting requirements on the nation's banks. The act also requires the reporting of money taken abroad, as well as the reporting of certain foreign accounts. All financial institutions are required to keep records for five years of transfers of over $10,000 into or out of the United States. If someone carries across the border more than $5,000 in cash, travelers checks, or "bearer" securities, he must report this to customs. Finally, you are required to report certain foreign financial accounts to the Treasury Department. Form 1040 (the federal income tax form) asks specifically if you have a foreign bank account, trust, or corporation. If you answer "yes," you must fill out Treasury form 90-22.1.

Such reporting requirements alone indicate that the government wants to discourage people from placing funds abroad. Interestingly enough, when Congress first considered the bill that later became the Bank Secrecy Act, Treasury officials wanted to make secret foreign accounts illegal, and would have limited the amount of money you could take out of the country in any one year to only $10,000! According to the Treasury, the Bank Secrecy Act is aimed at frustrating "organized and white-collar criminal elements who use secret foreign accounts to conceal substantive violations of drug smuggling, securities, and gambling laws, as well as untaxed income...."

Many critics believe that another reason for the Act is to make it easier for the government to impose foreign-exchange controls. Congressman Steve Symms (R-Idaho) recently wrote on this subject for *Inflation Survival Letter* (now *Personal Finance,* 901 N. Washington St., Alexandria, VA 22314, $65 a year). He observed:

A WARNING ABOUT FOREIGN-EXCHANGE CONTROLS

By Steven D. Symms

Is it possible in the foreseeable future that the U.S. government could outlaw the ownership of foreign currencies, securities, and bank accounts by U.S. citizens? I believe the machinery to implement such a policy may already exist. The desire to use that machinery may not be too far away.

In 1970 Congress passed legislation requiring detailed reports and recordkeeping by banks and other financial institutions of all transactions. These records are available to U.S. government agents in compliance with a subpoena or summons. The expressed intent of Congress is that these records should be available for criminal, tax, and regulatory investigations and proceedings.

One provision of the law requires all banks to make a microfilm or other reproduction of each check, draft, or similar instrument received for deposit or collection, together with an identification of the party for whose account it is to be deposited or collected.

Still another provision states that: "Transactions involving any domestic financial institutions shall be reported to the Secretary (of the Treasury) at such time, in such manner, and in such detail as the Secretary may require if they involve the payment, receipt, or transfer of U.S. currency, or such other monetary instruments as the Secretary may specify, in such amounts, denominations, or both, or under such circumstances, as the Secretary shall by regulation prescribe."

This theoretically gives the Treasury Department power to require that almost every financial transaction of any kind be reported. Presently, the regulations call for any transaction of over $10,000 in cash to be reported within 45 days to the Internal Revenue Service. Thus, if you deposit or withdraw over $10,000 in cash the bank is required to report this transaction in detail to the IRS.

Another far-reaching provision involves reports of exports and imports of monetary instruments. Anyone who transports monetary instruments between any place within the United States and any place outside the United States, in an amount exceeding $5,000, must file a detailed report with the Customs Service of the Treasury Department *before* the export or import is made. The report is to include, among other things, the origin, destination, and route of the transportation.

For the purpose of the currency export-import reporting law, the term "monetary instrument" means cash, travelers' checks, or bearer-type instruments. A cashier's check or personal check made payable to a specific person or entity would not have to be reported (a record of this would automatically be made as a result of the recordkeeping law); however, a check made out to cash *would* have to be reported. Transportation of gold and silver would not have to be reported.

In addition, of course, it is required that all foreign bank accounts be reported to the Treasury annually.

A Standby Mechanism

Although the government would probably deny it, I believe that all of these reporting requirements are standby mechanisms for the enforcement of foreign exchange controls. A careful examination of Public Law 91-508 will reveal that wide latitude is granted to the Secretary of the Treasury in the making of regulations. Should exchange controls be imposed, the government will already have access to most of the necessary records to ferret out all those who do not voluntarily divest themselves of contraband currencies, securities, foreign bank accounts, etc.

The obvious question remains: How likely is the U.S. government to impose foreign exchange controls on the American people? No one can foresee the future, but the past and current trends are not comforting. Most sources of "establishment" opinion would dismiss the idea of controls. But then they said the same thing about wage-price controls. History shows that exchange controls, like regulations outlawing gold assets, are always imposed suddenly, when least expected. As Harry Schultz once said, "History repeats itself because every generation refuses to read the minutes of the last meeting."

As the direct tax burden rises to the limits of political toleration, monetary inflation and credit expansion become necessary to perpetuate the political shell game of bribing the voters with their own tax dollars. In order for the politicians to maintain control during prolonged periods of inflation, it becomes necessary to deny any alternative to the official currency. Hence, the prohibition against private ownership of gold from 1933-1974.

The Present Situation

In the present situation, foreign "hard" currencies can serve essentially the same purpose as gold for protection of the purchasing power of one's assets. As you probably know, the purchasing power of the Swiss franc has increased relative to the U.S. cost of living during the last seven years.

As more and more people come to realize that certain foreign currencies offer protection from inflation, the flight of U.S. dollars out of the country in exchange for Swiss francs, German marks, and other "hard" currencies will become an increasing problem for the present political establishment. In all likelihood foreign exchange restrictions would be applied selectively with only certain currencies—the sound ones—being banned initially. This would be done "for the public good" to protect us from "international currency speculators." Such action would not be out of character for an Administration that tells us that it's the rising gold price that is hurting the dollar.

In a similar vein, prohibitions against ownership of foreign securities would not be out of the question. There are already moves in Congress and elsewhere to prohibit American investments in South Africa. The same enforcement mechanisms could be applied against foreign securities as well as against foreign currencies.

The possibility of controls remains. The likelihood of their imposition will grow in correspondence to the need that you and other investors feel to abandon the dollar. It will be at the time that you want most to get out that you will be prohibited from doing so.   (©1978 Personal Finance)

Now that we have established several significant reasons for a secret foreign bank account, let's look at the various opportunities that are available around the world.

Bank secrecy laws exist in many countries, most of them patterned after the Swiss. We will examine in detail the laws pertaining to Mexico, Switzerland, the Bahamas, and other tax havens.

Mexico: A Secret Account South of the Border

Mexico has a bank-secrecy law patterned after Switzerland's. So far Mexico has not succumbed to political pressure from U.S. authorities to relax its secrecy standards.

It is unlawful for any Mexican bank, broker, or bank counselor to reveal any information about a bank client to a third party. "Third parties" include the IRS, the Securities and Exchange Commission, and all other agencies of the U.S. government. The Mexican government has no tax treaty with any other country, so confidentiality is maintained.

Mexico, of course, is not known for its economic or political stability; Switzerland is. But it is interesting to note that in the recent past, U.S. government agencies, in particular the IRS and the SEC, have made tremendous efforts to sequester records of American clients. In one case, the SEC sought to obtain the names of clients holding accounts with an American investment counselor in Mexico, who strongly suspects that the SEC's purpose was to give the names to the IRS. Despite a federal suit and the eventual signing of a "consent decree" by the American investment counselor in Mexico, the list of clients was never released.

In an effort to cut down on tax evasion by Americans who place funds south of the border, the United States offers investors a choice of tax credit or a tax deduction on the interest withheld by the Mexican government for taxes. Like Canada, Mexico levies a withholding tax on nonresidents. The rate is 21 percent of the total interest earned each year. Any taxes paid in Mexico can be offset against your U.S. tax bill, or deducted from your gross income (if you itemize your deductions). At first glance, it looks as if the IRS is simply being fair in letting you deduct taxes paid to a foreign government. Actually, though, you must divulge the existence of your Mexican financial account to get the tax break—information the United States could never obtain so easily without giving a financial incentive. Unquestionably, many American tax dodgers feel that secrecy is worth more than the tax deduction or credit.

There are several ways for Americans to invest confidentially in Mexico. Banks offer two kinds of savings plans, peso accounts and U.S. dollar accounts. In both cases, interest rates are considerably higher than in the United States. Yields on peso time deposits (*after* Mexican taxes) vary from 12 to 24 percent, depending on time to maturity. Yields on dollar deposits now exceed 14 percent.

Peso accounts pay much higher rates of return because of the risk of devaluation and the possibility that the bank will go under. As long as foreigners, particularly Americans, view Mexican peso investments with suspicion, the banks will continue to offer high rates to attract funds. Even at the high rates of 24 percent a year, however, I cannot recommend peso time deposits as an investment. The rate of inflation continues at a double-digit level in Mexico and the political situation is uncertain, especially as election time approaches. There are positive factors, such as the increasing oil production in the southeast of the country. But overall, Mexico will probably face several additional minidevaluations over the next few years.

Dollar deposits are a much sounder investment, with returns over 15 percent after Mexican taxes. A peso devaluation would not affect the value of your investment. The only other consideration is the safety of the bank, and as long as it is a government-authorized bank, you shouldn't have to worry. Several banks have run into financial trouble over the years, but in each case the government simply took them over. Not a single depositor lost any of his money to bankruptcy (though American investors lost heavily during the 1976 devaluation). As long as this government policy continues it takes the place of federal deposit insurance.

One more suggestion: stay with the shortest maturity for dollar deposits, which is in three-month certificates. Interest rates are rising in Mexico, especially for dollar accounts, so it's best to keep the account as liquid as possible.

For full information in English on peso and dollar deposits, write to the following banks:

Banco Banamex   Banco Metropolitana
Isabel la Catolica 39   42B-3
Mexico 1, D.F.   Mexico 1, D.F.

Banco Somex   Bancomer
Paseo de la Reforma 213   V. Carranza 44
Mexico 5, D.F.   Mexico 1, D.F.

Incidentally, the postage to Mexico City is the same as in the United States—15 cents for first-class mail. To maintain your privacy, use your post office box to receive bank information.

Mexican banks also offer investment-portfolio management, gold depositories, and real estate deals. When it comes to investments, privacy cannot be the single factor. You must also consider the questions of stability and capital preservation in times of inflation and economic trouble. The high peso returns beat inflation, but they may be subject to devaluation. The dollar returns just barely keep up with inflation—but perhaps that's all you can hope for in today's risky climate. You could speculate on the *bolsa* (the Mexican stock market), which has been strong recently. Customer-confidentiality law in Mexico covers stockbrokers as well as banks. Or consider a Mexican gold-coin portfolio held by a Mexican bank in a trust account. For consultation on Mexican accounts, contact Eugene Latham, Apartado Postal 1339, Mexico 1, DF, Mexico.

Canada

What about Canada as a nearby financial refuge? Many Americans have placed funds and gold in Canadian banks and depositories in an attempt to escape government control of their financial assets. Lindsay Semple has written in *Inflation Survival Letter:* "The level of secrecy adhered to by Canadian banking is about on par with U.S. banks, although a Canadian account certainly would be more inaccessible to prying U.S. authorities than U.S. banks . . . It is possible that a bank account in Canada could be overlooked or that Canadian authorities would refuse to yield the contents, thereby leaving assets at the individual's disposal. Additionally, because of the geographical proximity of Canada, an individual with money already in Canada would find it easier to move to Canada, if only temporarily, in case of social upheaval in the United States." How closely Canadian tax authorities work with U.S. authorities is unknown. But there have been instances where the Canadian government has violated the trust of Americans who held gold bullion in Canada (the case of C.V. Myers being the most prominent). The Bill of Rights, cherished in the United States, is not Canadian law, unfortunately. So, if you hold assets in a Canadian bank, you're at the mercy of the bank's or government's policy, which could change dramatically in a monetary crisis.

Switzerland: Bastion of Bank Privacy

No guide on financial privacy would be complete without a detailed discussion of Swiss bank secrecy.

Unlike many other countries with bank-secrecy laws, Switzerland has a long tradition of financial freedom and confidentiality. It has always been the Swiss attitude that your money is your own business and no one else's, not even the government's. The gnomes have learned over many long centuries to respect hard work and the economic blessings of capitalism. The Swiss revere honesty, private property, political neutrality, a stable currency, and the inalienable right to privacy. Banks in other countries that imitated the Swiss "were hothouse corporate refuges and storage banks," according to T. H. Fehrenbach. "They did not grow out of a solid banking philosophy and national ethic like Swiss institutions. Some who organized and ran them more often loved than respected money, and they would take any kind of money . . . Unlike the Swiss, the other exotic banks did not stem from a national consensus, nor did they have an honest, hard-working, stable society behind them. Most of them have always been on shaky ground, and the customers know it."

Fehrenbach summarizes the popularity of Swiss banking: "Very little of the money that fled to Switzerland was ever criminal money; it was frightened capital. More modern governments than not have proved themselves inept at management, shaky from war, or thoroughly untrustworthy in tax or social policy. In a world without war, with limited and reasonable taxation even of the rich, with liberal economic policies, with stable politics and sound money—in short, if all the world were like Switzerland—many Swiss citizens who came to sit behind impressive bank desks might have gone on making cheese."

Swiss Bank Secrecy Act of 1934

Swiss banks are regulated under the Swiss Bank Secrecy Act of 1934, as revised in 1971. The original law was passed to protect foreign account holders from Nazi persecution. Unlike the Bank Secrecy Act in the United States, the Swiss act really does promote secrecy. One of the most important articles of the act states as follows:

> Whoever knowingly as member, official, or employee of a bank, as auditor or assistant auditor, as member of the Banking Commission, as official or employee of its staff, violates the obligation of secrecy or of professional secrecy or who causes or attempts to cause its violation . . . is liable to a fine up to 50,000 Swiss francs or to a prison term not exceeding six months. Both penalties can be imposed concurrently. If the fine is due to negligence, the penalty is a fine up to 30,000 Swiss francs.

The Swiss penal code contains several important provisions. Not even the Swiss government can gain access to bank records, except in criminal cases clearly defined in the statutes. Moreover, the sentence of up to six months for violating bank-secrecy laws pertains to each piece of information divulged. If twenty different bank accounts were revealed, the violator would be subject to 10 years in prison and a fine of 1,000,000 Swiss francs. Thus, the law is really very strict. Finally, the penal code makes it a crime to reveal a "business secret" to a third party without permission.

U.S.-Swiss Tax Treaty

The 1934 Bank Secrecy Law made a few specific exceptions. These allow disclosure in cases involving certain criminal acts *as defined by the Swiss penal code.* Forgery, robbery, and kidnapping are some of the crimes, but the list does not include tax evasion. In one case, a Swiss bank refused to cooperate with U.S. federal agents investigating the concealment of $75,000 in stolen Treasury bills, which the Swiss regarded as an economic rather than a social crime. The Swiss have, on the other hand, cooperated in cases involving forged checks. Essentially, as a SEC official once commented, "Swiss bank secrecy can be pretty much what they want it to be. If they want to divulge information, they will find a way to do it." But the Swiss seldom want to.

The Clifford Irving affair in 1971-72 is good evidence of

this. Author Clifford Irving has presented an "authorized" biography of Howard Hughes to McGraw-Hill. It later turned out to be a hoax. By Irving's instructions, an advance of $650,000 was paid to the account of "H. R. Hughes" at Swiss Credit Bank in Zurich. Prior to this deposit, a mysterious woman, later to be identified as Irving's wife, Edith, opened an account under the name, "Helga R. Hughes," with a phony Swiss passport. After the $650,000 was safely deposited in the Swiss bank account, Edith Irving withdrew the money and deposited it in another Swiss bank, the Swiss Bank Corporation, for portfolio management under the fictitious name Hanna Rosenkranz.

When Howard Hughes became aware of this forthcoming biography, his attorneys vehemently denied that any such book had been authorized; they asserted, moreover, that Hughes had no account at Swiss Credit Bank. His attorneys then requested an affidavit from the Swiss Credit Bank stating that Hughes did not have an account there. After debating whether it would breach bank secrecy to reveal that someone did not have an account, the Swiss Credit Bank acquiesced to the request. But the bank would not inform McGraw-Hill who opened the "H. R. Hughes" account. "Private bank information," the bank officer replied.

McGraw-Hill finally approached the Swiss cantonal court in Zurich and asked it to compel the bank to reveal the identity of the mysterious "Hughes" account. The court agreed that the account was opened through falsification and a Swiss crime had been committed. Responding to the court's decision, Swiss Credit Bank revealed the account holder as Helga R. Hughes, whom local newspapers identified as Edith Irving. As a result, the Irvings were charged with fraud and subsequently imprisoned.

Erosion of Swiss Bank Secrecy?

There is considerable debate going on over the new Swiss-U.S. tax treaty, officially called the U.S.-Swiss Mutual Assistance Treaty, which went into effect in January 1977.

First of all, several investment advisers argue that major inroads have been made against Swiss bank secrecy. Gary North, editor of *Remnant Review*, states that the new treaty could be used to investigate tax rebels, laetrile users, and "upper echelon" criminals—in other words, virtually anyone the government wishes to prosecute. In the article below, Gary North spells out the reasons for his concern:

The Erosion of Swiss Bank Secrecy

By Gary North

The new treaty provides access by U.S. Justice Department investigators to the Swiss bank records of suspected criminals. If a man is suspected of committing a crime that is listed in the two-page schedule (35 different types of crimes are listed), American authorities can request that Swiss authorities turn over the man's bank records. Unless the Swiss claim national sovereignty (e.g., security), lower Swiss authorities must comply. The bankers have no choice whatsoever.

Certain crimes are exempted from the treaty at the insistence of the Swiss authorities. These are essentially financial crimes: income tax evasion, customs-duties violations, securities-investment transactions, and foreign-currency exchange. This compromise disappointed the American negotiators. The Senate's Committee on Foreign Relations states explicitly that the original goal of the Americans was to stop just these kinds of activities. The American authorities discovered in the 1960s, the committee reports, "that Swiss bank secrecy was furnishing protection for a variety of illegal activities. The most important of these are the avoidance of American securities laws, evasion of American taxes, and the financing of organized crime activities." In short, violations against SEC laws, IRS rules, and criminal violations. The order of importance is not an accident.

Officially, the Swiss seem to have retained secrecy for those involved in commercial activities that are frowned on by U.S. bureaucrats. But there is a gaping loophole in the treaty. If the Americans can convince the Swiss Ministry of Justice and Police that they are chasing a member of organized crime who is in the upper echelon, then the Swiss government can force Swiss bankers to turn over the records to the Americans, even if the only crime is income tax evasion (Article 6, Section 2; Article 7, Section 2).

The "technical analysis" provided by the American negotiators is highly revealing. Who is a member of the "upper echelon" of organized crime? Minor members are not included. Say the American interpreters: "Assistance would not ordinarily be required in investigations or proceedings involving minor members or associates of the group. Such persons would not normally utilize facilities in a foreign country, such as banking facilities." It does not take a genius to see what the Americans understand by "upper echelon" criminals. Anyone who has a bank account in Switzerland, unless he is Swiss, is prima facie an upper echelon man.

There is another aspect of the treaty which could be significant in the future. Section 30 of the schedule of listed crimes includes a series of criminal activities that could easily be applied to the American tax rebellion movement. "Offenses against laws (whether in the form of tax laws or other laws) prohibiting, restricting, or controlling the traffic in, importation or exportation, possession, concealment, manufacture, production, or use of: (a) narcotic drugs, cannabis sativa-L, psychotropic drugs, cocaine and its derivatives; (b) poisonous chemicals and substances injurious to health; (c) firearms, other weapons, explosive and incendiary devices; . . ." This is the language of the treaty, not the "technical analysis," which is only opinion. The "technical analysis" is even more explicit:

"The exclusion for fiscal offenses does not apply to offenses with respect to taxes on bookmaking, lotteries, and other gambling when conducted as a business, or to criminal offenses with respect to taxes on narcotic drugs, on poisonous chemicals and substances injurious to health, or on weapons, explosives, and incendiary devices, as described in item 30 of the schedule. The exclusion is similarly inapplicable to attempts or conspiracies to violate such tax laws and to persons who are accessories to the violations of such tax laws."

The phrase, "conspiracies to violate such tax laws," is the key. There is a continuing rumor that the next step of the IRS in its war against tax rebels is to declare a conspiracy. This will eliminate the problem that the IRS has had in the courts, namely, the singling out of tax rebels for audits. The courts have not always been willing to permit nonrandom tax audits of tax rebels. But if the "conspiracy" charge can hold up in court, then it will undoubtedly be tested in Switzerland. (Guns, dope, and poisons [laetrile?]: the anti-Establishment is caught.)

The Swiss authorities are staying conspicuously silent. The question will arise soon enough. Will Swiss authorities buy the "conspiracy" argument? If they do, the end of Swiss banks as an American haven is in sight. In fact, the new treaty already exposes a major chink in the Swiss armor.

I would think that banks in other tax havens are likely to do a lot more business after January 23, 1977.

One problem for Swiss depositors is the difficulty of obtaining accurate information on the extent of the changes. Bankers have a built-in incentive to downplay its importance. The embassy will say as little as possible. If a man withdraws his funds now, will the records remain? I am afraid the records are permanent. They are now vulnerable.

If the Swiss Ministry of Justice and Police is able to convince Swiss political authorities that it is more important to stop international crime than to preserve the Swiss monopoly of banking secrecy—and law enforcers obviously have a basic hostility to any closed vaults that would inhibit their investigations, including Swiss law enforcers—then the assurances of your friendly Swiss banker really don't mean very much. The records will be opened.

This doesn't mean that Swiss bank secrecy is dead. It means that it could be killed in the future by Swiss authorities who have already signed treaties that create gaping holes in the tradition of secrecy. The once sacrosanct idea of banking secrecy is no longer sacrosanct in Switzerland. Bureaucrats and politicians in Switzerland are beginning to act like bureaucrats and politicians everywhere else. This is an ominous sign. Those who rest confidently on the tradition of Swiss banking secrecy may very well be resting on a weak reed—or worse yet, on a sword. The scabbard is wearing thin.   *(©1977 Inflation Survival Letter)*

Other critics are even harsher than North. Col. E. C. Harwood, who was attacked by the Securities and Exchange Commission for establishing "unregistered" gold accounts for American customers in Switzerland before the 1974 legislation allowing Americans once again to own gold, concludes that "agents of the United States have obtained almost unfettered dominion, direction, and control over the Swiss government and its agencies. You can forget what you have read about Swiss banking secrecy." Adam Starchild argues that civil disputes, including bankruptcy, divorce, and lawsuits, can force open a Swiss bank account. Swiss bank secrecy has been eroded, according to Starchild. In fact, as a result of the Swiss-U.S. tax treaty, "it is actually easier for U.S. authorities to look at a Swiss account than for Swiss authorities to do so." On the other hand, Charles Stahl, editor of *Green's Commodity Market Comments*, maintains that Swiss bank secrecy has gone too far:

Over the past 43 years, the Swiss bank secrecy has been used for many legitimate resons, but it has also been a 'blessing' for those with money that needed laundering, for tax evaders, and for many multinational corporations to pass bribes, overbill and underbill, depending on the circumstances, in order to retain funds in Switzerland . . . More than 20 years ago we wrote a pamphlet in defense of the Swiss banking secrecy; but the destructive effect that it has had on the morality of business and to a great extent on the poor financial conditions of many Third World countries, whose leaders have been stashing away billions of dollars in Swiss banks, has convinced us that the time is ripe for the Swiss bank secrecy law to be changed. In the end, it may benefit not only many foreign nations, for which the drain of capital fleeing to Switzerland is disastrous, but the Swiss themselves as well. No bank can demand adherence to high principles of conduct from its employees when the bank's main business is to help depositors violate the laws of their own countries.

Perhaps the change in the bank-secrecy law that Stahl recommends has already come through the U.S.-Swiss tax treaty.

Several authorities dispute Gary North's gloomy view of Swiss bank secrecy—in particular, Harry Browne and Robert Kinsman. In his excellent book, *Harry Browne's Complete Guide to Swiss Banks* (Kephart Communications, Inc, 901 N. Washington St., Alexandria, VA 22314, $25) Browne argues that the new treaty changes its bank secrecy practices in only one way,"and that is the willingness of the Swiss government to help prosecute members of 'organized crime' on charges of tax evasion. Everything else in the treaty is redundant; it merely declares what has long been true—that the Swiss will prosecute cases of violence, forgery, larceny, etc." Moreover, declares Browne, the treaty's definition of "organized crime" is extremely narrow and specific. Browne analyzes the treaty and even reproduces it in full in an appendix.

Robert Kinsman, in his book *Robert Kinsman's Guide to Tax Havens*, dispels the view that the U.S. government now has the ability to break Swiss bank secrecy. Kinsman confirms what Browne says on the topic. "Tax evasion, which is not a crime per se in Switzerland, can now come under provisions of the treaty if crimes of gambling, narcotics, poisons, firearms, or an association with organized crime are also involved, *and* if the U.S. government requires Swiss government assistance to convict." However, Kinsman does raise the possibility that this treaty is "the camel's nose under the tent," because of Swiss willingness to change the rules.

Kinsman cites several recent cases where U.S. government authorities have succesfully "blackmailed" Swiss banks into opening their books. In the case of Col. E.C. Harwood and the American Institute Counselors of Great Barrington, Massachusetts, the SEC forced Swiss Credit Bank to audit the Harwood gold account held for American customers (none of whom, by the way, ever complained to the SEC about possible misconduct of the gold program!). When the Swiss Credit Bank refused, on grounds of the Swiss secrecy laws, the SEC threatened to freeze assets of Swiss Credit Bank in the United States. In response, Swiss Credit Bank deposited a $122 million letter of credit in the United States. Kinsman asks, "Can money or other assets falling under jurisdiction of a U.S. court act as a hostage to compel a break in Swiss bank secrecy, where existing laws would otherwise be insufficient?"

Finally, Kinsman responds to the rumor that the new tax treaty allows Swiss banks to reveal a secret account during a divorce suit. According to Kinsman, "Swiss authorities have little interest in providing exemptions to their fabled privacy. A husband may stash away funds in a Swiss account and even swear to its nonexistence in an American court (running risk of perjury, of course), and face little chance of being discovered. Even if the American court requested assistance of a Swiss court in determining bank balances, experts say it is doubtful if the Swiss court would find sufficient exception to banking secrecy to check all Swiss banks for the existence of family assets. Sequestering funds from relatives, including a wife, is not a crime in Switzerland." (However, as Kinsman points out, under certain circumstances Swiss law permits a husband to inspect a wife's account!)

In a recent interview, officers of Foreign Commerce Bank of Switzerland said that they take strong exception to the comments by North and E.C. Harwood that Swiss bank secrecy is eroding or falling apart. In fact, the bank officers were convinced that recent changes in the bank-secrecy laws have increased rather than diminished secrecy. They noted that under the former banking laws, any judge in a Swiss canton could issue an order requiring a Swiss bank to turn over records to the SEC or to IRS investigators. Under the new law, however, U.S. authorities must obtain, in addition to an order from the court, an order from the

Swiss National Police, which at present is disinclined to breach Swiss secrecy. Objecting to Harwood's statement about SEC infiltration, the bank officers replied, "We can assure you that no agents travel freely in Switzerland to receive whatever information they seek from Swiss banks."

Swiss Bank Secrecy: A Summary

Rumors will continue about this sensitive issue of Swiss bank secrecy. It is clear to me, however, that under the Swiss laws and the new tax treaty a Swiss bank can be forced to divulge bank account information. Below are the 35 offenses for which bank secrecy can be discarded:

1. Murder
2. Voluntary manslaughter
3. Involuntary manslaughter
4. Malicious wounding; inflicting grievous bodily harm intentionally or through gross negligence
5. Threat to commit murder; threat to inflict grievous bodily harm
6. Unlawful throwing or application of any corrosive or injurious substances upon the person of another
7. Kidnapping; false imprisonment or other unlawful deprivation of the freedom of an individual
8. Willful nonsupport or willful abandonment of a minor or other dependent person when the life of that minor or other dependent person is or is likely to be injured or endangered
9. Rape; indecent assault
10. Unlawful sexual acts with or upon children under the age of sixteen years
11. Illegal abortion
12. Traffic in women and children
13. Bigamy
14. Robbery
15. Larceny; burglary; housebreaking or shopbreaking
16. Embezzlement; misapplication or misuse of funds
17. Extortion; blackmail
18. Receiving or transporting money, securities or other property, knowing the same to have been embezzled, stolen, or fraudulently obtained
19. Fraud, including:
    (a) obtaining property, services, money, or securities by false pretenses or by defrauding by means of deceit, falsehood, or any fraudulent means;

(b) fraud against the requesting country, its states, or cantons or municipalities thereof;
(c) fraud or breach of trust committed by any person;
(d) use of the mails or other means of communication with intent to defraud or deceive, as punishable under the laws of the requesting country

20. Fraudulent bankruptcy
21. False business declarations regarding companies and cooperative associations, inducing speculation, unfaithful management, suppression of documents
22. Bribery, including soliciting, offering and accepting
23. Forgery and counterfeiting, including:
    (a) the counterfeiting or forgery of public or private securities, obligations, instructions to make payment, invoices, instruments of credit, or other instruments;
    (b) the counterfeiting or alteration of coin or money;
    (c) the counterfeiting or forgery of public seals, stamps, or marks;
    (d) the fraudulent use of the foregoing counterfeited or forged articles
    (e) knowingly, and without lawful authority, making or having in possession any instrument, instrumentality, tool, or machine adapted or intended for the counterfeiting of money, whether coin or paper
24. Knowingly and willfully making, directly or through another, a false, fictitious, or fraudulent statement or representation in a matter within the jurisdiction of any department or agency in the requesting country, and relating to an offense mentioned in the schedule or otherwise falling under this treaty.
25. Perjury, subornation of perjury and other false statements under oath
26. Offenses against the laws relating to bookmaking, lotteries, and gambling when conducted as a business
27. Arson
28. Willful and unlawful destruction or obstruction of a railroad, aircraft, vessel, or other means of transportation or any malicious act done with intent to endanger the safety of any person traveling upon a railroad, or in any aircraft, vessel, or other means of transportation
29. Piracy; mutiny or revolt on board an aircraft or vessel against the authority of the captain or commander of such aircraft or vessel; any seizure or exercise of

control, by force or violence or threat of force or violence, of an aircraft or vessel

30. Offenses against laws (whether in the form of tax laws or other laws) prohibiting, restricting, or controlling the traffic in, importation or exportation, possession, concealment, manufacture, production, or use of:

(a) narcotic drugs, cannabis sativa-L, psychotropic drugs, cocaine and its derivatives;

(b) poisonous chemicals and substances injurious to health;

(c) firearms, other weapons, explosive and incendiary devices, when violation of such laws causes the violator to be liable to criminal prosecution and imprisonment

31. Unlawful obstruction of court proceedings or proceedings before governmental bodies or interference with an investigation of a violation of a criminal statute by the influencing, bribing, impeding, threatening, or injuring of any officer of the court, juror, witness, or duly authorized criminal investigator

32. Unlawful abuse of official authority which results in deprivation of the life, liberty, or property of any person

33. Unlawful injury, intimidation, or interference with voting or candidacy for public office, jury service, government employment, or the receipt or enjoyment of benefits provided by government agencies

34. Attempts to commit, conspiracy to commit, or participation in, any of the offenses enumerated in the preceding paragraphs of this schedule; accessory after the fact to the commission of any of the offenses enumerated in the preceding paragraphs of this schedule; accessory after the fact to the commission of any of the offenses enumerated in this schedule

35. Any offense of which one of the above listed offenses is a substantial element, even if, for purposes of jurisdiction of the United States government, elements such as transporting, transportation, the use of the mails or interstate facilities are also included

Thus, Gary North could be correct in saying that the U.S. authorities could press for prosecution of politically "radical" Americans who maintain Swiss bank accounts. And the Swiss could acquiesce under a loose interpretation of Swiss laws. When there is a question of U.S. tax liability, the

United States will no doubt always argue that "tax fraud" has been committed, which is unlawful in Switzerland, rather than "tax evasion," which is not illegal in Switzerland. It is clear that major Western governments, including the United States, are doing everything possible to topple Swiss bank secrecy. But it won't happen unless the Swiss let it happen. Swiss bank secrecy has been eroded in some areas, but I still have a good deal of faith in the system. No one can guarantee that such a policy of secrecy for the average hard-money investor will last forever, but the Swiss have done a remarkable job for decades despite great odds.

To assure yourself of the greatest amount of privacy in Switzerland, many hard-money advisers feel that you should *not* deal with any Swiss bank that has a large amount of assets in the United States—bank branches, exchange memberships, customer-held securities, or other assets, that could be used for official blackmail by U.S. government agencies. Obviously, most Swiss banks have some kind of holdings in the United States, but you should deal with banks which minimize their American holdings. Avoid the largest banks—Swiss Credit Bank, Union Bank of Switzerland, Swiss Bank Corporation and others that fit into this category.

Which Swiss Account Is Best for You?

Unlike U.S. banks, Swiss banks feature a complete line of banking and investment services, including the buying and selling of securities, bonds, and commodity contracts. Following are the main services you would be interested in when dealing with a Swiss bank:

Checking ("current") accounts. These checking accounts are the most flexible in the world because you can have the account denominated in any major currency—Swiss francs, German marks, French francs, or British pounds as well as U.S. dollars. At the same time, they are "multicurrency" accounts because you can write a check in any currency you wish. When the check clears and is returned to the Swiss bank for final payment, the amount of the check is translated into the checking account denomination (e.g., Swiss francs or German marks) at the going exchange rate. No interest is paid on the account and most banks charge transaction fees and commissions.

Savings ("deposit") accounts. Most Swiss banks also offer savings accounts in the major world currencies. The minimum varies from $500 (at the three major Swiss banks) to $5,000.

Most of the banks allow withdrawals up to $2,000 on demand, but for larger amounts three months notice is often required. Interest is credited to your account on December 31 and is based on the average daily balance during the year.

The interest return varies from currency to currency. For the strong Swiss franc, the average return is only around two percent at present. But with the appreciation of the Swiss franc over the past several years, Americans have been earning over 20 percent a year on these accounts, in addition to the small interest return. So the Swiss banks have no problem attracting savings funds from foreigners despite the low interest return.

Like Mexico and Canada, Switzerland has a withholding tax—35 percent of the interest earned. You can obtain a refund of six-sevenths of the tax by submitting a special tax-refund form to the Swiss government. But note: by filling out this form, you furnish private bank information to the Swiss government. The Swiss bank does not reveal how much tax each individual account pays, nor does it reveal individual account holders' names. Instead, the bank totals the value of *all* its savings accounts, from which 35 percent is withheld and sent to the Swiss tax authority. So, if you wish continued anonymity, do *not* request a withholding tax refund. The withholding tax is only on the interest earned, not on any capital gain based on the appreciation of the currency.

Both savings and checking accounts have been subject to substantial interest penalties in the past if the balance in them reached a high level. The Swiss government imposed these penalties in the 1970s to discourage large inflows of flight money from politically unstable countries. But since the regulations were temporary, I won't go into details.

Custodial accounts. For a small service fee, Swiss banks will obtain banknotes of a specified country, put them in an envelope, and place the money in the bank vault for safekeeping. This envelope of money belongs to you, not the bank.

Gold and silver accounts. Swiss banks also offer accounts in gold bullion, silver bullion, and bullion coins. Minimum investment is usually $5,000 to $10,000. Fees are generally one percent for purchase or sale plus a small storage fee. No Swiss taxes apply. The gold or silver may be stored in Zurich, London, or elsewhere. You can borrow up to 50 percent on the account for additional purchases.

Investment portfolios. Swiss banks will buy U.S. silver coins, common stocks on major world exchanges (with temporary restrictions on Swiss securities), mutual funds, bonds, options, numismatic coins, real estate, life insurance, and any other investment vehicle you desire. They also offer safe-deposit boxes. If you ever had the need for "one-stop" banking, this is it.

Your foreign investments remain completely confidential under Swiss bank auspices. Swiss banks invest in U.S. securities under "omnibus accounts"—accounts held in the name of the Swiss bank, not of the individual customer. Only your account executive and you would know the kinds of securities you hold abroad.

Ultimate Privacy: The Numbered Account

The famous numbered account has had a bad press lately. Even those writers favorably disposed toward Swiss bank accounts have questioned the practicality of a numbered account at a Swiss bank. Harry Browne, for instance, insists that "there's little reason to ask for a numbered account unless there's at least $500,000 involved. And it's often pointless to try to open one by mail, because bank officers may want to size you up before granting your wishes in this matter." Browne also points out that some Swiss banks will not offer numbered accounts to Americans, or if they do, they may expect an American to sign a "waiver of privacy" that permits the bank to turn over account information to U.S. authorities if a legitimate request is made. (Do *not* sign any such waiver if you want complete privacy.)

Robert Kinsman is even more adamant: "The 'numbered account' is, with rare exceptions, a waste of both time and money." Kinsman also reveals that the top officials of the bank are not the only people who know the name of the customer behind the numbered account—perhaps the secretary who handles the correspondence, the customer's portfolio account executive, or the bank manager has access to this information. Moreover, Kinsman reports, in order to obtain a numbered account, which must be done in person, "the prospect will be asked to produce a passport identification and register the account in that name alone unless accompanied by others joining the account, also in person and with passports in hand." Swiss banks will no longer accept numbered accounts for corporations or for dummy names.

Finally, Kinsman says that the customs reporting requirement (you must report if you leave the country with more than $5,000 in cash) severely restricts the amount of money available to you for opening an anonymous numbered account, especially when many (but not all) Swiss banks require a fairly stiff minimum to open such accounts. As we shall see, however, there are ways to avoid the customs reporting requirement—for example, by taking rare coins, diamonds, and other nonreportable *commodities* out of the country (admittedly, an *expensive* way to transfer money). It is still possible to open a numbered account with the required minimum.

However difficult to establish, the numbered account should not be dismissed lightly, in my opinion. Consider the fact that numbered accounts are extremely popular among the Swiss themselves. According to an estimate by Harry Browne, 10 to 15 percent of all Swiss accounts are numbered!

A review of the history of numbered accounts would explain the European affinity for them. When Hitler came to power in 1933, Germany was in economic turmoil. In an effort to control the economy, Hitler's regime went after citizens who held money abroad, especially in next-door Switzerland. Thousands of Germans had sent funds to Switzerland in anticipation of the Hitler takeover. A law was promulgated making it illegal to hold foreign accounts on penalty of death. Still, most Germans refused to obey this ruling.

Many German accounts remained open in Switzerland. It became the task of the Gestapo to discover these illegal accounts and to punish offenders. Mail and cables were monitored and German bank records were carefully examined. Gestapo agents started showing up at banks in Zurich, simply to determine if certain people, especially Jews, had a Swiss bank account. Friendship, sex, and money were used to induce bank employees to reveal names of German account holders. Another method often employed was simply to make a deposit in the name of a suspected German national. If the teller accepted the money, it meant the German had an account.

This battle went on until 1934, when the Nazis publicly tried and executed three Germans for having secret bank accounts. As a result, the Bank Secrecy Act of 1934 was passed in Switzerland, making it a criminal offense to give any information on a bank account to a third party, including the Swiss government, even by accident. As could be expected, exceptions were granted, but they were strictly defined in the Swiss penal code, and excluded most financial or political crimes (violations of exchange controls, tax evasion, etc.).

The Swiss also instituted numbered accounts to protect German citizens, particularly Jews. A numbered, rather than named, account offered much-improved secrecy and protection against inadvertent remarks by employees, outright bribes, or phone deposits. Even if the account holder, under pressure from the German Gestapo, was forced to send instructions to withdraw his money, the request would be ignored unless the secret number was given. Under the numbered account, only the chief bank officers were supposed to have access to the names of the account holders, which were locked away in the bank manager's private safe.

Numbered accounts *are* impractical. They require great expense of time and money because transactions must be made in person or by methods previously authorized and recognized by the bank. But they do serve their purpose under unusual circumstances. A spy might be paid directly to a numbered account in Switzerland. A Latin American businessman might have an anonymous account as insurance against a coup d'etat. A Soviet dissident writer might have money from book royalties stashed away in his secret Swiss bank account, waiting for the time he will be allowed to emigrate. And there may come a time when unpopular political figures in the United States will seek financial asylum through a Swiss numbered account. The disadvantages must be weighed, but the benefits may someday exceed the costs.

On the practical side, how does a numbered account work? First, you will probably have to establish the account in person. Second, to maintain anonymity, you can make arrangements to have all correspondence opened only by the bank manager. Otherwise, normal signatures are not used—you will simply write your account number instead of signing your name. If you send instructions by cable, a special code may be devised. It becomes more complicated if you try to insure your foreign mail against theft, because you will have to reveal both the contents of the letter and the receipient.

How to Open a Swiss Account

You can use a Swiss bank for almost any investment you wish to make confidentially. I would recommend that you try the following banks:

Bank Indiana Suisse
50 Avenue de la Gare
1001 Lausanne, Switzerland

Foreign Commerce Bank
Bellariastrasse 82
8022 Zurich, Switzerland

Bank Leu
Postfach
8022 Zurich, Switzerland

Cambio + Valorenbank
Postfach 535
8021 Zurich, Switzerland

Uebersee Bank, A.G.
Limmatquai 2-K
8024 Zurich, Switzerland

By the way, Foreign Commerce Bank is part of the Deak-Perera Group, originally established by Nicholas Deak, a veteran expert on foreign currency markets. Deak has numerous foreign-exchange offices around the world, as well as banking services in the United States and other countries—which could subject his companies and banks to the same kind of "official blackmail" experienced by Swiss Credit Bank. Vice-President Otto Roethenmund believes, however, that such government pressures could be deflected. Deak has established each of its offices on an independent financial base, and each is separately incorporated. How much this will help in a pinch is still a matter of conjecture, since Foreign Commerce Bank actively promotes American accounts.

Private Swiss banks should also be considered when you choose a money haven. These are privately owned, unincorporated financial institutions. Most do not advertise their services because if they do, they are required to publish financial statements. The bank's services and wealth become a closely guarded secret and reputation is their chief advertisement. Since there is no federal deposit insurance in Switzerland, and since the government will be less likely to bail out a private bank than a large national bank, one of the most important factors you must study in choosing a Swiss bank is its ability to withstand an economic or banking crisis. You should also bear in mind that private banks are partnerships and that each partner has unlimited personal liability for funds invested in the bank. Accordingly, private-bank portfolio managers tend to take a more cautious attitude than do their counterparts in the national banks.

But without concrete financial statements in front of you, how can you adequately evaluate the stability of a private Swiss bank? The answer is, you can't. You can ask to see a financial statement, but it is very doubtful that you will get one. You must rely, therefore, on the long-standing reputation and experience of the bank in question.

On this interesting facet of Swiss banking, Robert Kinsman writes: "The private banks are not required to publish annual balance sheets as are the public banks. They do business in small, externally austere buildings, marked only with obscure brass plaques stating their presence. They are not permitted to solicit client business in any direct way. They discourage portfolios being brought to them under the substantial size of $250,000. . . . Friendship and references are the principal means through which the private bankers obtain their new clients. They represent the ultimate in privacy in a nation where privacy is both a legal and habitual watchword."

The future of the private banks is uncertain. The largest such bank, Julius Baer & Co., went public several years ago, but none have followed. If you're interested in pursuing this connection, I recommend the listing of private banks in *Harry Browne's Complete Guide to Swiss Banks* (available from Kephart Communications, Inc., 901 N. Washington St., Alexandria, Va. 22314 $25.)

One concern many international investors feel is the threat of war or other political events affecting the safety of funds stored in Switzerland and other parts of Europe. One private Swiss bank has an interesting solution. The bank has set up a subsidiary in Canada where account holders can repatriate their funds in the case of a war or other economic disaster in Europe. Clients are given numbered accounts so that, upon revealing the number in Canada, they can obtain their funds. Naturally, this private offering is available only to a select group of investors with substantial wealth (minimum investment is SFr 200,000).

As a matter of interest, many Swiss banks can make such an arrangement with their correspondent banks around the world, whether in Canada, the Bahamas, the Cayman Islands, or the United States. Simply write a letter instructing your Swiss bank that in case of war breaking out in

Europe, your account should be transferred promptly to a designated correspondent bank in North America.

Using the Tax Havens

I have previously mentioned the fact that several countries have imitated Swiss bank secrecy and, in some cases, have enlarged upon it. These countries are known collectively as tax havens—the Bahamas, Panama, the Cayman Islands, the Channel Islands, Andorra, and so forth. A few countries—notably Uruguay, Lebanon, and, surprisingly, Hungary—are not regarded as tax havens but have created favorable bank-secrecy laws. While these banks cannot be trusted for long-term banking services because they have relatively unstable economies, one friend told me that a Hungarian bank account would provide a great way to launder money; once the money went through Hungary, the tracks would end. From there, you could transfer the money to Switzerland without a trace. (But could you be blackmailed someday by a Communist government?)

Tax havens can be used (1) to hold funds abroad in a "hard currency" (Swiss franc, German mark); (2) to establish a trust for heirs or others; (3) to set up a foreign corporation for business purposes; (4) to acquire foreign real estate; (5) to invest in foreign stocks, bonds, and currencies; (6) to save taxes.

A word about foreign trusts. Although they no longer offer tax advantages, foreign trusts located in tax havens are excellent tools to keep your capital from potential lawsuits. This may be especially important to doctors subject to malpractice suits and high malpractice insurance premiums. By establishing a confidential trust arrangement abroad, doctors and other high-profile individuals can escape expensive litigation of their property.

Though tax havens can be used for a number of purposes, I will emphasize only the confidentiality of their services. These countries provide a host of bank-related services, including the formation of trusts and corporations, and the management of personal investment portfolios. The tax havens are concentrated in the Caribbean and Europe. Let's examine the most prominent ones.

The Bahamas

Located just 60 miles east of Miami, the Bahama Islands

offer easy access in addition to the other financial benefits of a tax haven. There are virtually no taxes in the Bahamas, and your privacy is respected. No financial information need be provided when a business is established. At least five shareholders must be registered, but these may be nominees provided by a local bank or trust company, so the names of the real shareholders need not be revealed. In essence, a corporation can be established in the Bahamas, without actual employees and without a principal officer living in the Bahamas. However, bearer shares are not permitted.

The Bahamas have a bank-secrecy law similar to the Swiss. Major Swiss banks have established branches in the Bahamas and, logically, these are subject to Swiss secrecy laws. The Bahamas law, passed in 1965, prohibits unauthorized disclosure of a customer's financial accounts to anyone, on penalty of a $2,400 fine or one year in prison or both. No one knows for sure, however, how well this measure is enforced. The Bahamas have no tax treaty with the United States.

As far as access and communications are concerned, the Bahamas are excellent. Air transportation is superior, as are telephone and telex communications (including direct dialing from the States). Douglas R. Casey says, "Unlike other countries you might consider (with the single exception of Canada), the Bahamas are practically part of the United States, but without sharing its government."

Of course, the Bahamas have long been under the scrutiny of the U.S. Treasury. As part of the Treasury's ill-fated Project Haven, tax agents used illegal methods to obtain records of secret bank accounts in the Bahamas. In particular, the briefcase of the deputy managing director of the Castle Bank and Trust Company of the Bahamas was illegally opened and searched by IRS agents in 1973 while the bank officer was in Miami. The agents discovered a list of 300 bank depositors, many of whom were subsequently audited and indicted for tax evasion. Ultimately, one of the courts threw out the evidence because the district court judge ruled that "the activities of the government agents . . . were outrageous. They plotted, schemed, and ultimately acted in contravention of the United States Constitution and the laws of Florida, knowing that their conduct was illegal. It is imperative to signal all like-minded individuals that purposeful criminal acts on behalf of the government will not be tolerated in this country and that such acts shall never be allowed to bear fruit." The Treasury has since dropped Project Haven, but the Bahamas remain a point of focus by the government.

Another interesting turn of events, as reported by the *Wall Street Journal* in April, 1980, was that the CIA squelched much of the Project Haven tax cases. Apparently the CIA used the Castle Bank and Trust Co. extensively for underground payoffs of Cuban covert activities, and revelations regarding these Castle Bank accounts would have significantly damaged CIA manuevers. One wonders how many other Bahamian banks are so favored by CIA activity. After all, Castle Bank was a relatively small island bank.

The Cayman Islands

Located south of Cuba and west of Jamaica—only a two-hour flight from Miami—the Cayman Islands also provide easy access to tax haven facilities. In 1976, the Caymans passed a new bank-secrecy law called the Confidential Relationships (Preservation) Law, which made it a criminal offense for a bank or official to misuse confidential information, whether within or outside the Caymans. Corporations organized in the Caymans may issue bearer shares. No annual shareholders report need be filed, nor do names of shareholders have to be maintained. One board of director's meeting must be held, but such a meeting can be arranged by local "alternate directors." All of these characteristics make it possible to set up a very private concern in the Caymans.

Cayman banks have been the subject of special Treasury investigations, along with Bahamian banks. In January 1976 the bank manager of Castle Bank of Cayman Islands was brought before a federal grand jury when federal agents found him at the Miami airport on a layover. The government tried to make the bank manager talk about account holders, but he invoked the Fifth Amendment and Cayman bank secrecy laws. The court ruled that Cayman's laws do not apply in the United States, but so far Treasury agents haven't managed to breach the wall of secrecy in the Caymans.

Bermuda

Bermuda is another well-known tax haven close to the

States. But while it may have the characteristics of a good tax haven, confidentiality is lacking. Bermuda has no tax treaty with the United States, but it doesn't have a bank-secrecy law either. This could pose serious problems in the future. You must file a multitude of privileged information and undergo close scrutiny to determine your reliability in the community before you can set up a foreign corporation. Costs are also much higher than in the States. Bermuda has also suffered recently from race riots, which may or may not affect the status of foreign trusts and corporations.

Panama

Panama has patterned its banking and corporate account procedures after the Swiss and other tax havens. Under Panamanian law, foreign corporations established there are not taxed on any income earned outside Panama. Bearer shares are permitted and shareholders' meetings can be held in any part of the world. Moreover, Panama has bank secrecy and no withholding taxes on interest earned. Some of the 100 banks in this financial center offer numbered accounts, just like Switzerland.

Panama's currency is the U.S. dollar. The country has a Colon Free Zone for duty-free purchases. It is also well known for its law on vessel registration, which does not require ships to fly under the Panamanian flag. It is surprising how much of a tax haven and free port Panama is, given the political troubles there and the socialist background of the country's leaders.

The Channel Islands

Sandwiched between France and England, the Channel Islands are easy to get to. Telecommunications are good. Trusts established in the Channel Islands provide considerable privacy; your name does not appear anywhere in the trust documents. However, in the case of a corporation, shareholders' names must be provided to the Bank of England, which has agreed to keep these names confidential— but for how long is anyone's guess. Bearer shares are not allowed, but "nominee shareholders" can be used in place of the real shareholders.

Liechtenstein

A small country couched between Switzerland and

Austria, Liechtenstein puts up what some tax haven experts call a "double wall of secrecy." You could establish a secret financial account with a Swiss bank and then have the Swiss bank transfer funds to a foundation, corporation, or trust in Liechtenstein, which also enjoys strict privacy. (Or *vice versa.*) A Liechtenstein fiduciary company can set up a *Stiftung*, which has the markings of a foundation/corporation. The founder of such trust arrangements does not require the traditional founder's rights to control or own the funds, at least officially. A Liechtenstein trust is a quasi-independent enterprise, carrying its own assets and liabilities, independent of the trustee. Privacy is maximized, but tax haven experts warn that the IRS, if it heard about the discretionary trust arrangement, could challenge it. The IRS could deem it arbitrarily a corporation, foundation, or trust, whichever yields the most taxes.

Ian Anderson, in his book *Making Money*, highly recommends the use of a Liechtenstein "establishment" if you have $100,000 or more of investment funds. This type of business entity can be formed by an individual, a group, a partnership, corporation, or a trust. Shareholders carry no personal liability and bearer shares are available. Expect to pay $5,000 to establish the company and up to $2,000 yearly maintenance. Once you have established your Liechtenstein company, "it can buy property without your creditors, friends, wife, husband, or anyone else knowing it. It can acquire works of art, rare antiques, or stock in other companies without the seller knowing the identity of the buyer. In short, it allows you to move through the financial world invisibly, totally insulated from the hordes of drones who might otherwise seek to be your 'partner.'"

Anderson suggests strict privacy in establishing your Liechtenstein company. Although your Liechtenstein director or lawyer is not, under penalty of law, to reveal any information about shareholders or founders, and the state does not know the names of shareholders, you should remain cautious. "First, pick a pseudonym," advises Anderson. "This will be your code in all contacts with your lawyer. Do not send any correspondence on your stationery; use no return addresses. It's best to contact your Liechtenstein representative by telephone or in person. Use a pay phone . . . arrange for your lawyer to accept collect calls . . . Arrange to have mail sent from a neutral tax country, like France, Germany, or Austria." The problem of how to deal with the U.S. tax authorities is uppermost in his mind: "As for taxes in your homeland, let your conscience be your guide." You cannot satisfy the law by simply paying taxes on your Liechtenstein profits—the IRS wants you to report the existence of the foreign account on Treasury Form 90-22.1 too. Of course, that would destroy the precious secrecy you're hoping for. International investors are in a box when they seek financial privacy.

Some financial advisers, including Mark Tier of *World Money Analyst*, argue that a Liechtenstein discretionary trust can legally escape the reporting requirement and even U.S. taxation. Why? Because the founder of the trust does not acquire the traditional founder's rights to control or own the funds, at least not officially. A Liechtenstein trust is a quasi-independent enterprise, carrying its own assets and liabilities, and independent of the trustee. Consequently, reasons Tier, the trust need not be reported as your foreign account, nor need you pay taxes on profits from the trust. Needless to say, Tier's argument is highly controversial. Whether he is technically correct or not is immaterial, in my judgment. The whole trust arrangement could be challenged as a "sham" by the IRS, which could argue that even though officially you do not own the assets of the trust, you established the trust and gained by it. Therefore, you must pay taxes on profits and report it as a foreign account. The penalties could be severe if the IRS so ruled (of course, the major hurdle for the IRS would be to discover the existence of the trust in the first place). From a practical standpoint, a Liechtenstein trust is unquestionably expensive.

If you desire expert advice on tax havens, write Robert Kinsman, P.O. Box 881, San Rafael, CA 94902. His consultation fees are high, but well worth it if you're a serious investor.

A few other countries offer interesting possibilities for financial confidentiality. Andorra, a small enclave between France and Spain, has strict bank secrecy, although corporations must be run by local Andorrans. Liberia, an African nation famous for its favorable shipping laws and "flags of convenience," uses the U.S. dollar as an official currency and permits bearer shares, with virtually no records of directors or officers of companies established there. During investigations of Liberian-registered ships involved in oil spills, U.S. authorities were often unable to track down the names of the ship's owners or officers, nor could they subpoena non-existent company records! And then, of course, there are a few other countries previously mentioned—Uruguay, Lebanon and Hungary—which offer bank secrecy. All of these lesser-known countries offer little long-term benefit to the privacy seeker, but may provide some advantages from time to time.

Once nations establish bank secrecy, it doesn't always mean that secrecy will be maintained. Just recently, banks in Denmark lost their account secrecy. A bank official in Copenhagen states: "The information that banks will be compelled to supply to the tax authorities includes account balances at the end of the year, interest credited during the course of the year, the name and address of the account holder, and his or her personal registration number . . . This information must also be provided in respect to foreigners, even though their balances in Denmark and the interest on them are free of Danish tax . . . The extent to which this information will be passed on to foreign countries depends on (tax) agreements."

How to Send Money Abroad

There are several alternatives available in setting up a foreign bank or other financial account without raising suspicions or alerting third parties. Let's examine these alternatives, both the advantages and the disadvantages.

By Mail

You can send a check, money order, or other form of payment through the U.S. Postal Service to open an account in Switzerland, Mexico, or any other area of the world. This is the cheapest and most common way to transfer funds. However, there are several tips to follow that will reduce the chances of unauthorized detection.

First, avoid the use of personal checks, no matter what the amount. Special records are kept on checks written in excess of $10,000. But even if the check is for less than $10,000, your bank microfilms the check and keeps it on record for up to five years—you leave records of a sensitive transaction. There is an exception to the $10,000 recording requirement: a bank need not record transactions with an established customer maintaining a deposit relationship with the bank, in amounts which the bank may reason-

ably conclude do not exceed amounts commensurate with
the customary conduct of the business, industry, or profession of the customer." But the bank must make a list of such
customers and keep it available for inspection at any time
by the Treasury. Banks are also exempt from microfilming
business accounts averaging more than 100 checks per
month, but few adhere to the exemption.

Money can also be sent by bank wire. The fee is about
$10. A wire may be sent by any commercial bank that works
through corresponding banks, or by a foreign exchange
dealer. You could also have your money-market fund transfer money by wire to your foreign bank, identifying the account by number only. You will have to notify the foreign
bank by letter that the money is coming and what the bank
should do with it. Unfortunately, bank wires also leave
records, which can be inspected.

Sending cash through the mails is done frequently, and
can be done fairly safely and confidentially in small amounts.
Another method of transferring funds is to send one municipal bond each day. The face amount for most municipal
bonds is $5,000. If they trade at a discount, you can mail
them abroad without reporting them to customs.

The best approach is to use money orders.

Money orders are useful in small amounts, up to $1,000
each, and you can obtain as many as necessary. After you
purchase the money order, you can fill in the name of the
bank without putting your own name on the money order.
The money order will eventually return to the United States,
but it will not reveal who sent the money order. You can also
register the letter containing the money order, giving your
name but not revealing the contents. If you insure the letter,
you'll have to disclose its contents. *Caution:* don't make your
money order out to "cash"—that would limit the amount of
money orders you can place in a single envelope. If the value
exceeds $5,000, the money orders would legally have to be
reported. But if the name of the bank is the payee, the money
orders will not be reportable as cash leaving the country.

Cashier's checks can be used for larger amounts and can
be sent in any amount, as long as they are not made out to
"cash." Make sure you obtain cashier's checks signed by
the bank manager, not you, and made out to the foreign
bank. Preferably, pay cash when purchasing a money order
or cashier's check—this will lessen the chances of revealing
your identity when you make the purchase.

When you mail the money, you can preserve your privacy by addressing the letter to your bank contact, such as the bank manager, and using the bank's post office box address. Your return address might be your own post office box. You might try using *no* return address, a practice used by Swiss banks, but in that case, you must be absolutely positive you have the correct address and the correct amount of postage!

By Wire

One little-known private technique of spending money abroad is through a Western Union money wire, which is transferred via the bank wire system of Chase Manhattan Bank, in New York. You can pay for the money wire with cash up to $10,000 without any reporting requirement to the government.

The sender is not required to identify himself or to sign any declarations. You simply fill out a Western Union form, and present it to the Western Union window clerk. The form asks for (1) the amount to be sent; (2) a message, if any; (3) the payee's address and telephone number. You can also request a "test question" for the payee before he can pick up the money. There is also a space for your name and address, but this is not required *unless* you want verification that the money arrived properly. It's also necessary if you wish to claim a refund. No proof of identity is required if you pay in cash. But I would say that the chances are quite small that the money could be lost when it's going to a large institution or Swiss bank.

The cost is relatively small for sending a Western Union wire. Cost is from $6.20 to $98.25 for a $10,000-money wire. That's as low as 1% of the money sent. Delivery normally takes within 5 hours.

Paying in Person

It's possible that you might want to deliver the money in person to open an account. This is a rather expensive alternative, but it might be appropriate if you're already planning on a vacation to the area. You may wish to travel across the border to Mexico or Canada and have a bank wire the money to your foreign bank. The only trace of the transfer will be on the books of the Mexican or Canadian bank. The transfer will not, as a matter of course, be reported to any U.S. authorities.

To avoid the customs reporting requirement, carry $5,000 or less in cash, travelers checks, or bearer securities. Or, for larger amounts, consider the use of commodities—rare coins, diamonds, and other highly marketable gems—which are not reportable at this time. Sell the commodities when you arrive in Mexico or Canada, and transfer the proceeds to your bank destination.

Courier Services

Money couriers are often available from international banks, foreign-exchange dealers, and brokerage firms. The best way to transfer money anonymously is to use the services of a U.S. branch (or corresponding bank) of the foreign bank, or a foreign-exchange firm. Have the bank or firm transfer the money in its own name, with separate instructions informing the foreign bank to place the money under your account number. You can pay the bank or company in cash or by other "bearer" means and give instructions accordingly.

A professional courier may be willing to take cash out of the country for you, but the fee is usually steep. One courier service quoted airfare plus $8 an hour. Others quote 2 to 5 percent of the money. The percentage take is often higher in countries where foreign-exchange controls are strictly enforced. The risk of your money being stolen is also high. These professional couriers maintain a low profile and do not advertise their services. Some of them are employed by the underworld. Others are lawyers, businessmen, or bank agents who make numerous trips abroad every year or the courier may simply wire the money abroad under his own name.

Foreign Business Transactions

One of the most popular ways to transfer money undetected is through business transactions with foreign companies. The "overbilling" method is frequently used under foreign-exchange controls. You ask the foreign company that bills you for a particular item to "overbill" you by a certain amount and when you pay the bill, that excess is transferred to a secret foreign bank account.

Once your account is established, you can use the other methods above to add to your account.

How to Bring Money Back

If you can't get your money back, why send it outside the country at all? At some point, you must consider ways to repatriate your money now lying in a foreign bank account. It's surprising how few, if any, books about foreign banking deal with this problem.

First of all, you can instruct your bank to transfer money to just about any bank in the world without returning the money directly to you first. You will need to alert the other bank of your plans, of course.

If this bank is in Mexico or Canada, and near the border, you might possibly travel by plane or by car and pick up the money in person. Or consider again the use of a bank agent, foreign-exchange dealer, or professional courier to deliver money to you in a discreet way.

An easy way to repatriate your money is to instruct your foreign bank or financial institution to send you small amounts over a period of time in the form of bank drafts written against its New York or San Francisco correspondent bank. Use the foreign check to pay off a debt or bill, deposit it in a little-known account, or have a friend deposit it in his account. Or cash the check at the New York or San Francisco correspondent bank.

Or you could instruct your bank to purchase and mail you bearer certificates, such as municipal bonds, which are negotiable in the United States. Make sure the value of the bonds is $5,000 or less to avoid customs reporting.

Another idea is to have your foreign bank mail a check to your local coin dealer. When the check arrives, you pick up the coins and the dealer cashes the check.

Finally, consider having your foreign bank wire you the money. The most private way is to have the bank send money by way of a "pay by identification" wire, whereby the carrier would not hand over the money until you identified yourself by passport number, driver's license, or other form of identification. Such arrangements are made all the time at vacation areas, where tourists frequently run out of money.

How to Move Gold into or out of the Country

Sometimes it's not just currency or checks that you want to transfer abroad, but gold or silver bullion, coins, diamonds, or other commodities. In many cases, when investors purchase gold or silver through a foreign bank, they wish to take possession of the bullion or coins in the United States. Quite a few foreign banks will, for a fee, send the bullion or coins to you by registered or insured mail.

Gold coins and bullion sent into the United States by mail must be declared to U.S. customs, even though there is at present no duty on gold or silver. If the gold is for personal use, the package containing the gold can be sent directly to your home without official inspection, although customs inspectors spot-check to make sure packages contain what they say they do. The declaration statement, made by the shipper, should list the type of item—in this case, "gold coins—personal use," and the market value. Fortunately, there is no central record-keeping of such declarations.

You would still have to declare the coins if you carried them into the country personally, although customs officials require only a verbal declaration. Even if the market value of the gold or silver exceeds $5,000, you're not required to report to the Treasury, since commodities aren't subject to the regulations.

To maintain confidentiality, you could rely on a courier service to deliver your coins, but the cost and risk would be quite high. You could also consider the possibility of having your foreign bank sell your coins or bullion; you would then repurchase similar coins in the United States with the proceeds of the sale. Although there may be tax ramifications, such a method may be cheaper and more private than having the coins shipped from some faraway country.

Perhaps the easiest and most confidential method would be to transfer the coins to your bank's office under the bank's name, thus maintaining your anonymity.

The same principles apply when you wish to take your gold or silver out of the country. If you have gold and silver in your possession that you would like stored in a foreign country, it would be a much better idea to sell your gold and silver at home, buying an equivalent amount through your foreign bank by mail. Banks in Canada, Mexico, Switzerland, and elsewhere provide custodial services for gold and silver at modest fees.

4
How to Deal With the Foreign Reporting Requirements

The greatest impediment to privacy of foreign accounts is the Bank Secrecy Act of 1970, which imposed reporting requirements on foreign-account holders. While the Act does not outlaw such accounts, it does require the reporting of any "foreign bank, securities, and other financial accounts" to the U.S. Treasury Department each tax year. Currency transactions across the border are also monitored.

A Treasury official told me that he didn't consider the Bank Secrecy Act a threat to the privacy of Americans at all. On the contrary, the Treasury was doing a great service to the public in fighting organized crime and drug dealers. In one instance, he was able to determine in 20 minutes that a man was a drug dealer after reviewing the suspect's currency-transaction reports. Since 1970, Treasury has sent 1,700 reports to the Drug Enforcement Administration for prosecution of drug dealers based on currency-transaction reports.

To give the "positive" side of the Bank Secrecy Act, I have obtained permission from *Reader's Digest* to reprint a most interesting story about how one underworld figure laundered his dirty money:

THE SWISS CONNECTION

By Nathan M. Adams

The illicit profits reaped by organized crime within the United States from the sale of narcotics, from gambling, loan sharking, and fraud, are huge—they may total $60 billion a year. Much of this money is smuggled out of the country and hidden within a maze of secret foreign bank accounts and overseas investments, where—until recently—it has been virtually immune from discovery, seizure or taxation.

If the flow of these dollars to their ultimate shelters can be traced, choke points can be established, to cut off this life-supply system of organized crime. Specialized task forces of agents, accountants, and intelligence analysts of such agencies as the Federal Bureau of Investigation (FBI), the Internal Revenue Service (IRS), and the Drug Enforcement Administration (DEA) have therefore spent long, frustrating months trying to document and unravel the trail of some of these transactions. Here is a step-by-step account of one important investigation.

His name is Alberto Sicilia-Falcon, but the gardeners who barber the lawns of Chapultapec called him, respectfully, "Don Alberto." His castle was built into the rock face of an overlook, towering above the other expensive homes in this posh neighborhood, high above the hardscrabble Mexican border city of Tijuana. A Rolls-Royce was conspicuous in the driveway. Campers and mobile homes bearing California license plates came and went at all hours of the night.

By 6 PM on the evening of May 18, 1973, Alberto Sicilia-Falcon had just concluded a lengthy meeting with his accountant (who lived in a bungalow on the estate) and several American associates. Now, alone, he crossed his luxurious living room and stared out through tall, sun-proof windows at the United States a few miles to the north. Slim, modishly dressed, 28, he could have passed for a successful rock-music entertainer.

In 1961 he had arrived penniless in Miami, a Cuban refugee. He worked as manager of a flower shop, as a clothing-store clerk, then, while taking university courses part-time, moonlighted as courier for a cocaine and mari-juana-trafficking organization. He learned fast. When his employers were arrested, he acquired their sources of supply, moved to Tijuana, and, almost overnight, became one of Mexico's leading traffickers.

At the meeting concluded earlier that day, Sicilia and his lieutenants had recapped the month's activities. By the end of May, they would have distributed to wholesalers across the United States—or warehoused in California for delivery—57 tons of marijuana. That meant nearly $7 million in profits to be absorbed, plus further earnings from cocaine and heroin.

In the past, Sicilia had invested the money in real estate: additional villas in Acapulco, Guadalajara, and Mexico City, and in La Jolla, Calif. The walk-in bank vault in his Tijuana mansion rarely held less than $500,000 in cash. He had accounts (most under an alias) with at least seven Mexican banks, and one with Barclays Bank in Nassau, the Bahamas. Yet the trick was not just to hide the money but to invest it for maximum return.

And so, taking his cue from U.S. organized-crime figures, Sicilia now decided to open a series of Swiss accounts. In Switzerland, bankers are forbidden by law to disclose identities of depositors. Besides secrecy, Swiss banks offer some of the world's finest investment services.

Stacks of $50 Bills

By the end of May, 19 tanker trucks—ostensibly returning empty to the United States to reload with asphalt—had delivered the 57 tons of marijuana to California. The last truck contained three tons of marijuana, compacted into bricks, sealed behind baffles in the front and rear of the tank. It crossed the border at San Ysidro at 3 PM on May 31, and that evening pulled in to a small ranch outside Corona. By dawn, the bricks of marijuana had been stacked in a tin-roofed warehouse. Three customers had been lined up to purchase it, at $120,000 a ton, cash in advance.

On the evening of June 10, the money—in $20, $50 and $100 bills—was delivered in several suitcases to a small apartment in San Diego. Working through the night, two women carefully sorted the bills into stacks, by denomination. Then the $360,000 was placed into two footlockers and sealed.

Early the following morning, a courier collected the trunks and placed them in the rear of his automobile. Since U.S. Customs has limited search authority over outgoing travelers, cars are rarely inspected when they cross *into* Mexico. Thus, by early afternoon June 11, the money had been safely smuggled across the border and was logged in by Sicilia's accountant.

There were, of course, expenses to be paid: $1000 to the driver of the tanker truck; $3000 to the owner of the ranch where the drugs were warehoused. There were commissions to Sicilia's principal partner, an American named Roger Fry. Sicilia's own share was $230,000.

Money Moves

The money remained in the walk-in vault for several days, where it was joined by hundreds of thousands of other dollars. Sicilia was now ready to begin the first step in disguising—or "laundering"—these profits. The telltale bills would be exchanged for other notes, to erase any possibility that marked bills had been used by U.S. narcotics agents to trace the sales. Since he had bribed local bank employes, this step presented no problem. As soon as the money was deposited in Sicilia's account at Banco Longoria in Tijuana, mingling with the deposits of hundreds of other customers, it could no longer be traced.

Sicilia now made plans to fly to Switzerland at the end of June—accompanied by his sister, Mercedes, and by Roger Fry and Fry's wife, Paulette. All four would open accounts.

Meanwhile, on June 19, an armored car called at the Banco Longoria on its regularly scheduled pickup of cash and checks being shipped to institutions in the United States. On board was Sicilia's $230,000. Later that day, this money was deposited in a U.S. bank with which the Banco Longoria had a correspondent relationship. From there the funds were immediately transferred—at the touch of a teletype key—to the Barclays Bank in Nassau.

There is a U.S. banking law that requires all banks in the United States to record the international movement of funds. Called the Bank Secrecy Act of 1970, it is aimed at syndicate figures attempting to hide their profits in secret foreign bank accounts. The law also requires travelers or couriers transporting more than $5000 in currency across U.S. borders to file a report with Customs. However, international transfers through normal banking channels are not subject to this requirement. So this transfer did not appear on any U.S. Customs reporting form. Completed, the transaction brought Sicilia's Nassau account to well over $1 million—all of it safe, unreported, undetected.

Wizards of Zurich

On June 28, Sicilia flew to Zurich. He chose to deal with the prestigious *Schweizerischer Bankverein*—the Swiss

Bank Corporation—one of Switzerland's legendary "Big Three" institutions, a bank respected throughout the world for more than a century. As with all Swiss financial institutions, only a limited number of high-ranking employees and the bank officer who dealt with a depositor directly need know his identity.

Sicilia introduced himself as a "businessman" with wide real-estate interests, living in Miami, Florida. He produced a Cuban passport ostensibly issued in Havana in September 1972. The bank officer had no way of knowing it was false— one of several acquired by Sicilia in different names for various illicit purposes.

Besides anonymity, Sicilia explained, he must have total liquidity so he could obtain funds on a moment's notice. The bank officer suggested "certificates of deposit" paying 9 percent interest, and "Eurobonds" of various companies, purchased through such stock markets as those of Zurich, Frankfurt, and Amsterdam, which can be sold at any time. These would all carry only the name of the Swiss Bank Corporation, making the investment on behalf of an unnamed client.

Sicilia beamed. "You can expect the first deposit on July 3," he said. "You will receive $800,000 from Barclays Bank in Nassau. Then, in about 10 days, you will receive $1.5 million in cashier's checks from my bank in Mexico."

On June 30, Sicilia flew back to Mexico. Thereafter he was in constant touch with the Swiss bank officer. In two years, he moved $60 *million* between the United States, Mexico, and Switzerland. Meanwhile, he set up other accounts, including escape accounts in Spain, France, and Panama to which he could transfer his assets in a day if he felt endangered.

Chink in the Armor

So vast were the Sicilia organization's operations within the United States that they could not indefinitely escape notice. In fact, a group known as CENTAC 12—a unique task force of DEA agents, based in San Diego—had for some time been painstakingly assembling evidence. They now had enough to link Sicilia and his key lieutenants not only to the tanker-truck shipments of marijuana but to several large cocaine transactions as well. In July 1975, a federal grand jury handed down a secret indictment against Sicilia, Roger

Fry, and 42 other codefendants in both Mexico and the United States.

Indicting Sicilia was one thing; penetrating his protection in Mexico to make an arrest was another. For weeks, CENTAC 12 agents sought a way. They found it in a newly signed agreement with Mexico providing for the joint arrest and prosecution of international drug traffickers.

DEA agents asked Mexican authorities to make the arrest. The opportunity came when Sicilia was at his villa in Mexico City, where Tijuana officials could not protect him. And so at 10 PM on July 2, 1975, heavily armed federal police broke into Sicilia's villa and arrested him. He had a fully loaded .45-caliber automatic hidden in his bed, but did not resist.

From the villa, police seized a thick stack of bank documents, checks, and balance sheets. Confronted with this evidence—and after four days of intensive interrogation—Sicilia confessed.*

The sums appearing on the bank statements were staggering. Sicilia and his top four lieutenants were pulling in $3.5 million from U.S. drug sales *each week.* His bribe payroll amounted to no less than $16 million per year. He had some 20 foreign accounts.

After examination of the documents, DEA agents and analysts were able—for the first time—to obtain a clear picture of how a major drug network disposed of its profits and financed activities. This was a vital breakthrough.

Death Blow

But even with the Mexican documents, large gaps remained. the CENTAC 12 analysts' "paper chase" had led them through the front door; what of the back door, the one no one saw? Answers to many questions could be unearthed only in Switzerland. But would Swiss officials cooperate?

On April 25, 1976, U.S. Justice Department lawyers sent an official request for assistance to Swiss authorities. They included excerpts from pertinent U.S. narcotics statutes, copies of the indictments against Sicilia and Fry, and evidence that their profits derived from narcotics. Officials

---

*He has been in a Mexico City federal prison for three years now, but is still appealing his consignment.

in Bern quickly established that the two men had violated Article 19 of the Swiss code—which stipulates that those who traffic in narcotics, even outside Switzerland, have committed a felony—and so were not protected by the strict laws governing bank secrecy. In July, Swiss police forwarded the records of 13 different Swiss accounts held by Sicilia and associates.

Unfortunately, by the time a court order was handed down to seize the monies in the various accounts, authorities could find only $205,000 left. Funds had been transferred to other countries: Paulette Fry and Sicilia's relatives had used powers of attorney to close out accounts or withdraw large sums.

The Sicilia organization nevertheless was dealt a death blow. Roger Fry—who had pleaded innocent to all charges—paled and nearly collapsed when he learned that federal prosecutors were in possession of the Swiss bank records. Faced with a possible life sentence if found guilty, Fry immediately changed his plea—and was sentenced to ten years in a federal penitentiary.

Meanwhile, thanks to the Sicilia documents, law-enforcement agents now have intelligence on which to base current and future investigations into the profit-hiding techniques of narcotics traffickers. And choke points are being established along the routes these vast sums are funneled. No longer can criminals be assured that their illicit earnings will escape detection through the anonymity of a numbered Swiss bank account.

Postscript

On January 23, 1977—after five years of negotiation—a legal-assistance treaty between the U.S. and Swiss governments came into effect. From now on, as soon as U.S. narcotics traffickers (and other criminals) are exposed as having violated tough Swiss laws, no matter where the offense took place, monies in their Swiss accounts will be seized and the records sent back to the United States. Last year alone, Swiss police and justice officers made 19 bank-account investigations on request of the U.S. government.

Regrettably, there are other nations and territories whose banking laws offer the kind of total anonymity that shields criminals—among them the Bahamas, Panama, and the Cayman Islands, three important receivers of U.S.

drug profits. The Carter administration should exert strong diplomatic pressure on these financial havens to strip away the secrecy that surrounds the bank accounts of proved narcotics traffickers.

Finally, the Bank Secrecy Act does not require individuals to file a report with Customs on currency moving across our borders through normal banking channels. Congress should insist that *all* large international currency shipments be reported. And it should amend the law to give Customs agents authority to enforce such regulations, in order to stop the flow of drug money.

(Reprinted by permission from the September 1978 Reader's Digest. Copyright©1978 by the Reader's Digest Association, Inc.)

The ABC's of Foreign Reporting

If you itemize your deductions, you'll find the following question on the back page of Schedule B, to be included with your 1040: "Did you have at any time during the taxable year, a financial interest in or signature authority over a bank, securities, or other financial account in a foreign country?" If you answered "yes," you are required to fill out details on a separate form.

Prior to 1978, holders of foreign accounts had to file IRS Form 4683 along with their 1040. Now, however, they must file a new form, called Treasury Form 90-22.1 (reproduced in the appendix). This new form must be filed by June 30 if you had a foreign account during the previous tax year. It is sent directly to the Treasury Department in Washington, no longer to your regional IRS office. This innocent-looking change is, in reality, of dramatic importance. Previously, the names of foreign-account holders were scattered among a dozen regional IRS offices. Now, however, under the new reporting system, the names of these foreign-account holders can easily be placed in a central file, perhaps on computer, at the Treasury Department. In addition, the Treasury adds this warning: failure to file a report or filing a fraudulent report can, "under certain circumstances," result in a fine of up to $500,000 and imprisonment of up to five years, or both! In a letter reproduced in the appendix, the Treasury explains why the penalty is so high.

Once again, the announced purpose of these strong measures is to beef up the fight against "organized crime" and tax evaders, but there may be less lofty motives. These include foreign-exchange controls, as Congressman Steve Symms has argued convincingly in an earlier chapter.

The new Treasury form is asking for details. You're required to report the name under which the account is maintained, the account number, the bank branch and its address, the type of account, and the maximum value. If the account is worth $10,000 or less, you needn't report any of the above information. If you have over 25 foreign bank accounts, you aren't required to report anything about any single account.

The Treasury revised the 90-22.1 form for 1978 to exempt, for the first time, small foreign investors. You are no longer required to file a report if the total value of your accounts does not exceed $1,000. A spokesman for the Enforcement Division of the Treasury Department explained that the exemption was made to eliminate the paperwork of thousands of insignificant accounts, where illegal activity (tax evasion, drug smuggling, or organized crime) would be improbable. Needless to say, the exclusion is so small that few will be able to take advantage of it.

It's surprising how many Americans are simply not reporting any foreign bank account. As a matter of fact, the Treasury's Enforcement Division has come under Congressional attack for not enforcing these provisions of the Bank Secrecy Act. A recent study notes that the IRS started including the question about foreign bank accounts in 1970, but many taxpayers neglected to answer the question one way or the other (there are two boxes, one for "yes" and the other for "no"), especially when the question was not on the first page of the tax forms. In 1970, for example, there was only a 33 percent response rate to the question, while in 1973 the rate was just 37 percent, and in 1974 the rate was 36 percent. When nearly two-thirds of American taxpayers are ignoring the foreign-account question altogether—millions of citizens—the risks of not answering the question, of leaving it blank, appear extremely low. One hard-money advisor warns against this technique, however; ignoring the question makes your tax return *incomplete*, he maintains, and therefore eliminates the three-year statute of limitations on an IRS audit of your return.

Another suggestion quite frequently made is that you open two or more accounts and report only a nominal, idle account (less than $10,000 in value), while maintaining an *active* foreign account elsewhere. Technically, however, you are required to report *all* financial accounts if the total value exceeds $1,000.

Important Note: If your account value "did not exceed $10,000 at any time during the year," you don't have to report the account number, bank, or address—only the existence of the account. Many international investors have purposely limited their investment abroad to this amount in order to keep from divulging too much financial information. One method often suggested is to reduce your foreign holdings below $10,000 just before you file your Treasury form, afterward raising the amount back to previous levels. This does *not* appear to be a loophole, however. Note the phrase in the instructions, "did not exceed $10,000 *at any time during the year.*"

Does a taxpayer who fails to report a foreign bank account automatically subject himself to criminal penalties? What are the penalties if an investor simply refuses to check the box on whether he has a foreign account?

According to the Bank Secrecy Act (Public Law 91-508), failure to answer the yes/no question on Schedule B of Form 1040 carries a $1,000 fine and/or a one-year sentence. Also, anyone who answers "yes" to the question and fails to file the Treasury Form 90-22.1 is subject to the same fine. However, from a practical point of view, we have noted how millions of American taxpayers have previously failed to answer the yes/no question. Thus, it appears that Treasury would enforce this provision only in cases where some other illegal activity is involved. In a letter to a congressman, Assistant Secretary of the Treasury Gene E. Godley states: "A criminal violation is only a misdemeanor unless there are aggravating factors in the case. When the violation is in furtherance of some other violation of federal law or is committed as part of a pattern of illegal activity involving transactions exceeding $100,000 in any 12-month period, the violation becomes a felony. Anyone convicted under this provision is subject to imprisonment up to five years and a fine of not more than $500,000." Such federal crimes would include narcotics trafficking, securities violations, gambling operations, and tax evasion. This statement is corroborated by the Treasury letter reprinted in the appendix.

What about the person who refuses to answer the yes/no question, but dutifully pays taxes on profits earned on a foreign account? *Deaknews* editor Steve Beckner answers, "It seems reasonable to assume that the government could not prosecute a person for criminal violations of the reporting requirement *unless it was able to prove a deliberate failure to file in connection with some other illegal activity. . . .* This should not, however, be construed as a legal opinion. . . ." Beckner reports that several investors have added a note to their tax return stating that they are not involved in organized crime, narcotics, tax evasion, or other illegal activity, and therefore that the reporting requirement does not apply. To his knowledge, no one has thus far been prosecuted. (But what about maintaining a low profile?)

The issue becomes thorny, however, when an audit takes place. How do you prove to the satisfaction of a field auditor that your profit and loss statement from your foreign accounts is properly figured? The burden of proof is on the foreign investor to verify his profit-and-loss statements, which undoubtedly would mean that he must reveal details of his foreign transactions—and compromise his privacy.

What is Reportable?

Several financial and legal experts believe that there are at least five lawful ways to beat the reporting requirements of the U.S. Treasury. I will discuss these loopholes below. But remember, what follows is not meant to be the final word on the subject. Certainly, Treasury officials may take a different view (and could, of course, specifically amend the reporting requirements at any time). Treasury has not *officially* recognized any exceptions to the foreign-account reporting requirements except the $1,000 nominal exclusion. It is an untested, gray area of the law. Since this is a controversial area, you should check with your own legal advisor before taking any action.

1. *A foreign safe-deposit box.* Banks in Canada, Mexico, Switzerland, and most other countries around the world offer safe-deposit boxes, which do not constitute a foreign account. Safe-deposit boxes cannot be opened on signature authority and the bank has no claim on the contents of the box, which are legally yours. Unfortunately, though it may successfully avoid the reporting requirement, a safe-deposit box does require you to come in person to make deposits and withdrawals. Yet it may prove worthwhile if you travel frequently to Mexico, Canada, Switzerland, or to some other foreign country.

The *Investment Bulletin* of the American Institute Counselors states: "The safest and most direct method of investing in gold through a Swiss bank is simply to purchase bullion or coins in person at the bank's bullion department and then place the assets in a personal safety deposit box. This arrangement insures the complete privacy of the holdings and presumably need not be reported on the Department of the Treasury Form 90-22.1 as a foreign financial account. However, inasmuch as the investor must be present in Switzerland while all transactions are carried out, this arrangement may be inconvenient for some individuals."

2. *Deak's Gold Certificate Program.* Counsel to Deak and Company has informed me in a letter that the firm is "positive" that this gold certificate program avoids the reporting requirement, which may explain why American investors have poured over $40 million into the program since its inception. Essentially, you purchase gold bullion stored in Zurich, at 3 percent above the value of the gold at the time of purchase, plus 1 percent on the sale of the gold and a small storage fee billed to you annually. Originally, Deak intended to make these bearer certificates, but decided against the idea when the SEC said it would consider the certificates securities. So, for the time being, they are registered in your name and nontransferable. (So, under a court order, Deak could be forced to release the names and addresses of certificate holders to the government.) For full details on the Deak program, write Deak and Company, Washington, 1800 K Street, NW, Washington, DC 20006.

3. *Merrill Lynch's Gold Bullion Program.* This little-known investment plan is the cheapest way I know of to buy gold bullion. The gold bullion is stored in London, so in some ways it is similar to Deak's program. It avoids the reporting requirement. At present, the minimum investment is one kilo bar, worth over $16,000, at a purchase price,of three-fourths of one percent over the London gold price, with no storage fees, and selling at three-eighths of one percent commission! (No doubt their fees will increase if this program becomes popular.) Merrill Lynch, like other brokerage houses, operates under the "know your customer" rule, so privacy is invaded to some extent.

Bache has a similar gold bar program, except that your gold bullion is stored by Johnson Matthey Ltd. in Canada.

Citibank has also developed a gold purchase plan, where the gold is stored in London. There is no storage fee the first year.

4. *Swiss franc insurance policy.* Some insurance experts have told me that a foreign insurance policy does not con-

stitute a foreign account, but rather a "contract." The term *insurance policy* does not appear anywhere in the instructions for the Treasury form. Insurance policies are available in any foreign country, but perhaps the best plans are available in London and Switzerland.

There is another good reason for buying a foreign insurance policy besides avoiding the foreign reporting requirement. You may have someone you would like named as a beneficiary without the knowledge of your spouse, children, or parents. Foreign insurance companies are both reliable and discreet.

The London insurance market is full of interesting bargains. One particularly attractive feature of policies written by British companies is that they can be written in any of several currencies, including U.S. dollars or Swiss francs. In an inflationary climate, term life insurance is the best policy to obtain in most cases. For example, the Crusader policy issued by the C.T. Bowring Group offers a 10-year term, $20,000 face-value policy for a man 30 years old at only $36 a year—substantially lower than what any U.S. insurance company would charge.

You may wish to obtain an insurance policy in a hard currency such as the Swiss franc or German mark for financial rather than confidential reasons. British companies offer substantial savings in these markets as well. A man aged 31 buying a five-year term insurance policy with a face value of SFr 189,190 ($100,000) would pay an annual premium of around SFr 263, compared with a net premium of SFr 633.78 if he went through a Swiss insurance company! The only concern I would raise about these London-based insurance programs is the financial strength of the underwriters. The British insurance industry lacks reliable financial ratings, so your best bet is to deal with a reliable insurance broker in London who knows the better companies. One older brokerage firm is Glanvill Enthoven, 144 Leadenhall Street, London.

Some policies issued by Swiss insurance companies offer unique advantages as well. One excellent program is called the "single-premium endowment" policy. Essentially, it acts like a Swiss franc savings account without the disadvantages accompanying savings accounts at Swiss banks (such as the negative interest penalty, the 35 percent withholding tax, and the foreign-bank reporting required by the United States). Under the program offered by the Fortuna Life Insurance Company of Zurich, for example, you would deposit a minimum of SFr 10,000 (or about $6,000). You need not make any further deposits. You automatically receive life insurance of 155 percent of the value of your investment and no medical examination is required. Finally, you can postpone your decision to report the income until you actually receive it—perhaps many years hence.

When your policy matures, you receive the full amount of your original investment plus a guaranteed dividend based on your age and the term of the policy. The return, at present rates, results in almost double what a Swiss bank pays on a regular savings account! And you can get your money out at any time, although you'll have a small loss if you withdraw during the first two years of the policy. You can also borrow against your account, either in dollars or Swiss francs (because the dollar is a weak currency, you should borrow against dollars, not francs).

Swiss secrecy applies to insurance contracts as well as to banking, so you can be assured of confidentiality.

There are several programs available. For additional information, write to a company that welcomes American clients, such as Assurex SA, P.O. Box 209-16, 8033 Zurich, Switzerland, or International Insurance Specialists, P.O. Box 949, 1211 Geneva 3, Switzerland. I have also written a book on the subject, called *New Profit From Your Insurance Policy* (Mark Skousen, P.O. Box 611, Merrifield VA 22116, $15).

5. *Custodial accounts.* These are accounts where bullion, coins, or banknotes are held in a bank vault for a customer. Many banks, including Mexican, Canadian, and Swiss banks offer custodial accounts, which are similar in nature to safe-deposit boxes. According to E. C. Harwood, "Neither coins nor gold in bulk storage abroad that is held for you by the storage entity constitutes a bank account reportable on your income tax return." Other investment advisors such as Harry Browne, Terry Coxon, and Walter Perschke have confirmed this view. However, a recent *Investment Bulletin* of the American Institute Counselors, an organization founded by Col. Harwood, contradicted this advice: "Assets held in the custody of a Swiss bank are reportable as a foreign financial account. . . ." Thus, the issues remain unresolved and highly controversial. Signature authority for withdrawals and deposits is possible with custodial accounts, so on the surface it would appear that such accounts do constitute a foreign bank account and are reportable. However, some

financial experts argue that it is not a bank *account* per se because the assets held by the bank are *yours*, not the bank's, and are under your name exclusively. Thus, if the bank went bankrupt, its creditors would have no recourse on the assets—whether coins, bullion, or securities—held for you under a custodial account. This is the most controversial technique, however.

There are other possibilities. For example, you can purchase foreign stocks simply by opening a securities account at your local brokerage firm, which does not constitute a reportable foreign account. Of course, secrecy is lost because your securities account is on record and can be made available to the government. But at least you don't automatically alert the government to its existence and you won't be on the computer list. The foreign stocks are held by a New York bank as ADRs (American Depository Receipts), but you can insist on delivery of the securities if you wish. Some investors have been concerned about the fact that their names are on record at New York banks as holders of ADRs. These individuals fear that the government could freeze accounts of customers holding South African gold shares and other politically unpopular ADR issues. The only alternative is to hold the shares outside the country.

Owners of foreign corporations may not have to report their foreign bank accounts. However, a U.S. shareholder who directly or indirectly owns more than 50 percent of the voting stock or more than 60 percent of the value of the shares of any foreign corporation has a duty to report such ownership to the Treasury (Form 2952 and Form 3646). Also, a U.S. shareholder who owns more than 5 percent of a foreign company is required to fill out a separate information return. Keep the percentages below this amount to avoid the reporting requirements.

It's also possible to purchase "products" overseas—such as wine, commodities, and real estate—without any reporting requirements.

One final note. Be circumspect in your foreign dealings. Don't do anything imprudent simply to avoid the foreign reporting requirement. Consider the investments you're making—are the foreign banks or companies reputable? Is the investment wise on its own merit? What are your financial goals besides privacy? One investor who apparently wanted to avoid the foreign reporting requirement at all costs established an extremely complicated scheme of loans, corporations and trust arrangements through a little-known private foreign firm operating out of several tax havens. Only after pouring $50,000 into the company's grandiose scheme did he find out that the company was far from reputable and there was a good chance that its methods were illegal. He is trying to get his money back, but who knows if he ever will? *Lesson:* Hucksters pry on people's naivete and their yearning for privacy.

5
The Private Investor

Today's investor may engage a multitude of middlemen to handle his money—brokerage houses, account executives, insurance companies, banks, mutual funds, fund managers, foreign bank managers, among others. His investments may be scattered around the country and throughout the world. Some accounts are open to government scrutiny and are reported annually to the Internal Revenue Service. Others are entirely private, where knowledge of your investment portfolio is the carefully guarded secret of one or two individuals. In this chapter, we will examine the different kinds of investments that can be made, how confidential they are, and where you should place your money for maximum safety and minimum disclosure. We will also investigate the proper uses of assumed or fictitious company names in carrying out your investment decisions, as well as the importance of maintaining confidentiality when dealing with account managers and investment counselors.

Reported vs. Unreported Investments

The following list of investment vehicles is broken down into three categories: investments reported to the government, investments not automatically reported but available for disclosure, and investments that are neither reported nor available for public disclosure.

REPORTED
- Interest from bank savings accounts
- Dividends from registered stocks and bonds
- Most foreign bank accounts
- Foreign brokerage accounts

NOT REPORTED *(But Available for Disclosure)*

- Commodity futures contracts
- Non-income-paying securities
- Call and put options

NOT REPORTED

- Omnibus accounts
- Foreign bearer bonds and securities
- Some Treasury notes
- Municipal bonds
- Coins
- Foreign currency, foreign travelers checks
- Diamonds
- Art and other collectibles

Privacy and Your Brokerage Accounts

Many investments handled through a brokerage account are either reported to government officials or available for their inspection. Dividends, like interest on a bank savings account, are reported annually by your brokerage firm—so the government is made aware of your account and the amount of dividend earnings you received for the year. Trading, in options, commodity futures, nondividend securities, and municipal bonds is not reported, but your trading activities are recorded and are open for inspection by anyone the brokerage firm sees fit to reveal them to. All brokerage houses consider your account confidential and access is typically limited to the account executive, the bookkeeper, and the office manager. If your account is unusual, it may occasionally be discussed between broker-dealers, but this is frowned upon.

Government officials, particularly IRS agents, can gain access to records without much difficulty. In *The April Game*, the author, who calls himself Diogenes, tells us, "Anytime I like, I can walk into a brokerage office and ask to see a taxpayer's account records. The records will tell me what he has bought and sold over the years and what prices, and if he has been cheating, I've got him by the tail." Diogenes says that this is not routine by any means, but the power is there, nevertheless. The IRS is well aware, we are told, of the gambit of opening up two or more brokerage accounts and reporting only one of them. In one case, a disgruntled mailman secretly (and illegally) monitored a suspected tax evader's mail and "somehow" delivered to an

IRS agent copies of hidden brokerage accounts. As Diogenes comments, "This procedure is, of course, illegal. Not even the Revenue Service, which recognizes few restrictions on its prying license, is supposed to open a citizen's first-class mail. (Revenue agents sometimes do, but, technically, that is against the rules.)" Technically?

An office manager for one of the largest brokerage firms in America told me that occasionally an IRS agent has requested to see an individual's account. He said that he willingly acquiesced only if the agent showed a subpoena. However, he was unaware of the difference between a court subpoena and an administrative summons, mentioned in Chapter 2.

When you open an account, brokerage firms will require you to fill out a form, giving your name, your spouse's name, your address (most insist on a street address, not a post office box, although you can have a separate mailing address), your bank account, your social security number, and your occupation. Some firms want to know your salary and tax bracket, while others request a salary level in general terms (between $20,000 and $30,000, for example). Some request a net-worth figure, depending on the kind of transactions you plan to make. In many cases, you can refuse to divulge this information, though to do so could prevent you from engaging in some kinds of transactions. The more risky the investment, the more financial information a brokerage house will require. Merrill Lynch, for instance, requires a complete net-worth statement if you plan to open a managed commodity account. References must be provided to verify the information.

Brokerage firms receive requests for account information from banks, creditors, and credit bureaus more often than from government agencies. At times you may want to list your brokerage firm as a reference on a loan from a bank or other lending institution. But many firms will not reveal information to a third party without your permission, and it's best to insist by contract that they will not do so.

Brokerage firms accept corporate accounts. Corporate accounts are used not only by large corporations, but by individual dentists, doctors, and other professionals. A professional corporation can trade under its own name, and if titled properly, will retain the anonymity of the real owner. Movie stars and other celebrities frequently use corporate names to open up accounts. Unfortunately, many times the corporate name will suggest the identity of the celebrity, disclosing the person's financial activities. Brokerage accounts will accept the use of an assumed company name, whether incorporated or a single proprietorship. However, the chief company agent responsible for making investments, meeting margin calls, and so forth, must be listed when opening the account. Privacy is maintained only at the trading level. Outsiders can still gain access if the brokerage firm chooses to reveal the true owner. Individual assumed names or pen names may be permitted, but the office manager will probably insist on knowing the reason. Movie stars have been known to trade under numbered accounts, but now they generally use corporate names.

Of course, you don't have to go through a brokerage firm at all to invest in the stock market if you don't want to. How? Through no-load mutual funds! Today there are over 270 no-load mutual funds which invest in virtually any kind of stock market activity—gold share, sunbelt stocks, technology, energy, bonds, etc. Their association states, regarding privacy, "You deal directly with the no-load mutual fund of your choice. You do not have to go through bank trust departments, securities salemen or other middlemen. In other words, your investments are strictly your own business." Of course, any interest or dividends earned from the funds are automatically reported to the Federal government.

For a list of all 270 or so no-load funds, write for your free copy of the 1980 Membership Directory, No-Load Mutual Fund Association, Valley Forge, PA 19481. Be sure to use your company name and post office box—your name will be rented out to various mutual fund companies!

Omnibus Accounts: Anonymity Preserved

Omnibus accounts are accounts held by a brokerage firm on behalf of a bank (foreign or domestic). For example, the trust department of a bank may have a securities account at a local brokerage firm. All securities transactions, dividends, margin loans, and so forth, will be in the name of the bank's trust department rather than of the individual settlors or beneficiaries of trusts being managed by the bank. The brokerage firm has absolutely no information on individuals behind the trusts.

Foreign banks operate under the same principle. They maintain omnibus account with major brokerage firms in

New York and other major financial centers in the United States. If you traded on the New York Stock Exchange through a Swiss bank, the Swiss bank would execute your trades and receive dividend payments for you under its own account—your name would never appear as the one making the trades. Secrecy is completely assured, much to the consternation of the U.S. Treasury Department. Just before World War II, U.S. Treasury agents entered Swiss bank branches in New York, demanding to see bank records, stock certificates, and individual accounts. The Treasury officials hoped to find proof of German investments in the United States through Swiss banks. But the Treasury was completely frustrated. As T.R. Fehrenbach relates, "Every Swiss dollar held in American branches or affiliates and every Swiss stock certificate or bar of gold, was not held in the name of individuals but for the account of banks in Basel, Bern, Zurich, or Geneva. Swiss banks always operate this way. Every Swiss stock purchase in Wall Street, for example, was made in the name of one of the three largest Swiss banks, never in the name of the actual customer for whom the bank was buying." The Swiss refused to reveal such information—because the Swiss banking code of 1934 made disclosure illegal—The Treasury froze all Swiss assets in the United States in June 1941—six months before the U.S. actually entered the war! Only after the war were accounts allowed to operate normally.

Recently, increased efforts have been made by U.S. securities and commodity authorities—the Securities & Exchange Commission and the Commodity Futures Trading Commission—to get brokerage houses to reveal individual foreign speculators. This issue is currently being litigated in the Federal courts, but I suspect that the regulatory authorities will soon be asking Congress for authority to ban trading by "secret" parties.

Bearer Shares and Bonds

Bearer shares are common outside the United States. These securities belong solely to the person having possession of them. Like cash, they cannot be replaced if you lose them. They can be transferred to anyone, freely and without notice to the company. They are as private as paper money. Obviously, companies cannot record the names of shareholders who possess bearer shares.

Bearer shares and bonds generally come with numbered

coupons, which can be clipped and sent to the company for dividend or interest payments. Bearer securities are neither liked nor permitted in the United States for two reasons. First, shareholders don't automatically receive notice of company events. Often the holder of bearer shares must rely on the newspapers for information on company meetings and actions. Second, and more important, the Treasury Department can't keep track of the names of shareholders receiving dividend or interest payments. In other words, bearer shares and bonds can be ideal for tax evasion. Virtually all U.S. securities must be registered, and any dividends declared are reported each year to the IRS under the name of the shareholder. (Capital gains and losses, however, go unreported. If you declare dividends on your income tax forms but not capital gains or losses—gains, especially—you may be in for an audit!)

Outside the United States, bearer shares are permitted in many of the tax and money havens: Switzerland, Panama, the Netherlands Antilles, Liechtenstein, Costa Rica, Liberia, and a few others.

Austrian banks offer a unique bearer instrument for Austrian citizens only: bearer passbook savings accounts. The holder of the passbook is the owner. The passbook is identified by number only, not by name. Austrians can present the passbook to the issuing bank and receive cash—no questions asked, no identification required.

Many foreign stocks traded on Wall Street can be held in bearer form in Europe, but not in the United States. That is why the Guaranty Trust Company of New York (now Morgan Guaranty Trust Company) began issuing "American Depository Receipts" (ADRs) for international securities held in safekeeping abroad. Under this arrangement, an American bank, on orders from a brokerage house, orders common stock in Europe, places the bearer certificates in safekeeping, and issues registered certificates called ADRs to American investors. The ADRs are registered and the dividends are reported, while the bearer shares remain overseas.

Although bearer shares are relatively uncommon in the States, they are apparently not illegal. Capital Preservation Fund, a money-market fund based in California once attempted to introduce bearer certificates. The Securities and Exchange Commission and the Internal Revenue Service pressured Capital Preservation Fund to give up the idea.

Of course, registered certificates offered by most money-market funds can be almost as versatile as bearer certificates. You can trade the registered certificates or sign them over to another party without revealing anything to the fund or the government. In fact, you can endorse most non-dividend-paying securities over to a new purchaser in complete privacy. In some cases, you can even leave the securities blank as long as you sign over to the bearer the power to transfer the securities.

Honor Bonds

During the mid-1970s, several Eastern and Midwestern banks and savings institutions began offering "honor bonds"—long-term certificates of deposit identified by serial number only. The certificates were payable to the bearer, so the interest wasn't reported to the IRS as it is with the standard savings account or bank CD. Minimums were as low as $25 with no upper limit. Plus the bearer certificates were freely transferable—offsetting the illiquidity of long-term bank CDs. (Federal regulations impose penalties for early withdrawal.) Because the market for these honor bonds was widespread and because they were of tremendous interest to numerous small investors, the reaction of federal and state officials was both swift and negative. A major fear was that thousands of small investors would use the honor bonds for tax evasion. The IRS ruled that the banks would now be required to record the name of the purchaser and the redeemer of the bond. However, there is no limit to the number of times an honor bond can change hands between the time it is bought and resold at the bank.

Too bad. Here was an opportunity for the small investor to gain liquidity, high return, and privacy through these bearer certificates of deposit. The banks were partly to be blamed. Some of them advertised boldly: "The bank will not issue an IRS 1099 form. Since no name appears on the bond and no customer identification number is required, the honor bond you buy is completely anonymous."

Of course, tax evasion was not the only reason for purchasing the bond. We have already referred to the need for investor liquidity. Moreover, customers may seek privacy in buying the certificates for a number of reasons. One lady purchased an honor bond to hide her money from her husband, who was abusing her. Here was the first and possibly the only vehicle available in the United States that provided the small investor with privacy, liquidity, and high yield.

Treasury Securities

Amazingly enough, while one part of the Treasury Department (the IRS) tries to eliminate bearer or honor bonds, another part of the Treasury Department (Securities Division) issues its own bearer certificates. Treasury bills issued to mature in less than a year are no longer sold in bearer form; they are simply entered or registered on computer. Long-term Treasury bonds, including Series E and H savings bonds, are also registered in the name of the holder. But Treasury notes with a maturity of two to 10 years are still available in bearer form (although they can also be purchased in registered form). Bearer Treasury notes carry coupons that are clipped and redeemed as interest. Minimum investment is $5,000. These notes bear no name and are the property of the possessor. If they are stolen, they cannot be replaced.

The IRS wants to tighten up on the reporting of interest payments. Even though Treasury bonds are registered by name, the names of those receiving interest payments are not automatically reported to the IRS unless the interest paid reaches $600 or more. (Note, however, that any Treasury securities held for you by a brokerage house are reported to the IRS.)

Certificates of Deposit ($100,000 or More)

Bank certificates of deposit for $100,000 or more, maturing within a year, are traded as bearer certificates with no record of buyer or seller. No 1099 form is reported to the IRS for these certificates, which trade daily in New York security markets. They are held in the vaults of banks, brokerage houses, corporations, and other individual holders.

Commercial Paper and Bankers Acceptance

Unsecured promissory notes of major corporations, commonly known as commercial paper, come in bearer form. They mature in nine months or less and carry ratings by Moody's and Standard and Poor (like bonds).

Bankers Acceptances—imprint credit instrument backed by a New York bank—are traded freely in bearer form.

Municipal Bonds

Municipal and some corporate bonds are issued by serial number only. Brokerage firms keep records of the names of buyers and sellers, but all intermediate purchasers are unknown. Brokerage firms will check to see if the bonds are stolen when you liquidate them, but nothing is reported to the government. Banks also buy and sell municipal bonds.

For reporting purposed, brokerage houses separate the tax-exempt municipal bonds from registered dividend-earning securities in your account. Only taxable dividends are reported.

Like interest from some Treasury notes, interest from municipal bonds is not reported, primarily because you are placing money with the government, in this case city or state governments, and the tax break is an added incentive to invest your funds with them.

Coins

Bullion and rare coins are an excellent investment vehicle for the private investor. Coins do not have any markings or serial numbers attaching them to any particular person, so they are as confidential as cash. Until 1975, Americans could not legally own bullion gold coins—coins selling for a slight premium over gold-bullion value, like the South African Krugerrand, Mexican 50 Pesos, and Austrian 100 Coronas. Because there is always the possibility that the federal government could again outlaw private ownership of gold bullion and gold bullion coins, it will pay to keep transactions in gold bullion coins as confidential as possible. Purchase them anonymously with cash or money orders and make sure that coin dealers do not keep records on you as a customer. Rumors abound that government agents have on ocassion demanded the records of coin dealers without notice, perhaps to check for tax evasion. But such records could also be used in compiling lists of "hoarders."

Silver bullion and silver bullion coins such as the pre-1965 "junk" silver U.S. dimes, quarters, and half dollars, have not been subject to the same government restrictions in the past, and are not as likely to be in the future. A low profile is again advised to protect yourself against being a target for burglary.

Rare gold and silver coins—$20 gold pieces, silver dollars, and so forth—have never been confiscated in the United

States. The government has traditionally regarded them as numismatic, or collector, coins.

In sum, coins may fulfill your dream of a perfect investment: confidential transactions, little government intrusion, ease of storage, ease of transport, great potential for appreciation. To quote coin expert Walter Perschke: "If privacy is important to you, consider the fact that the coin market is one of the last truly free markets left. It is not subject to government regulation or recordkeeping requirements, except normal business practice and fraud statutes that cover all businesses. Because it is a cash market, it is relatively easy to consummate confidential transactions. Under the U.S. Gold Reserve Act of 1934, no one was required to turn in numismatic gold coins. No one was prosecuted under the provisions of this act for retaining numismatic gold coins." (Numisco, 175 W. Jackson Blvd., A-640, Chicago, IL 60606).

One of the best places to purchase your coins is at a coin show. Coin shows are held quite frequently in the major metropolitan areas. (Call a local coin shop for information). If you are asked to sign up when you arrive, be sure to use an anonymous address (such as your post office box). At a coin show, you can examine every coin you select and you do not generally pay sales tax (dealers assume that buyers are fellow dealers, not retail buyers), postage, or insurance—and the deal is completely confidential. You can buy rare or bullion coins, stamps, Franklin Mint series, and banknotes at these coin shows. There is a wealth of investment opportunity.

Some coin dealers are willing to accept a personal check for payment, but if you want privacy, use cash.

Warning: If you pay for your coins with cash or travelers checks, and the transaction exceeds $10,000, the coin dealer is required to file a Currency Transaction Report (Form 4789—see Appendix) with the Treasury Department. The form asks your name, address, occupation, and other information. To preserve financial privacy, keep each transaction to $10,000 or less. Or use a cashier's check or money orders (*not* made out to cash). A coin dealer tells me that if you try to purchase coins too frequently—on a daily basis, for example—each time using substantial amounts of cash ($10,000 or less), the coin dealer is supposed to report such unusual activity.

Diamonds

Diamonds are another investment that escapes detection but also has popular speculative appeal. Diamonds are the world's most concentrated form of wealth. Aside from ease of concealment, their principal virtue is as an inflation hedge. Diamonds won't show up on airport detectors. Unfortunately, the major defect of diamonds as an investment is an illiquid and uncertain selling market. They must be accompanied by a reliable certificate (such as one issued by the Gemological Institute of America), which appraises the stone's color, grade, and carat weight. Unlike bullion or rare coins, diamonds cannot be sold at a moment's notice at a decent price. You should plan on at least two or three weeks for the transaction to be completed.

Stamps

Stamps fall into the same category as diamonds and coins: they have great potential as an inflation hedge, are small and portable, and have a ready market (more so than diamonds, but probably less than coins). Most stamps are unmarked and can be bought and sold around the world without fanfare, or held in your safe-deposit box or other private storage compartment.

As Dawn Schultz, editor of *Exodus*, comments, "Stamps are safer than diamonds or gold coins because they are simply not detectable if you carry a few with you; customs men are not looking for them and their metal detectors cannot pick them up. In a letter sent abroad they are also not detectable on any letter examiner. Added to that, stamps have been increasing in value over the years to compare favorably with most other forms of investment."

Collectibles

The collectibles market, in general, is a good source of confidential investments—art, Oriental rugs, paintings, photographs, wines, books, jewelry, clocks, antiques. The key, where privacy is concerned, is to avoid one-of-a-kind investments. Stick with items produced *en masse* but in sufficiently limited numbers to have collector appeal. From a privacy point of view, you would not want to purchase an expensive Picasso that was well known in the art world and would bring you publicity if you sold it. Auctions are, by their very nature, public affairs. With this in mind, you should appoint a representative with no formal connection to do your bidding. The auction house can also arrange to handle the sale of your art work in complete confidence without revealing the true owner of the collectible. A foreign company or trust might also be useful to bid for you.

Once again, these recommendations are made with the clear understanding that privacy should be only one of the considerations when it comes to investing in collectibles. Privacy is not always the overriding force at work. In fact, you may wish to forgo financial anonymity in favor of other factors—profit or pleasure, for instance—in purchasing an art work.

Foreign Currency

Normally, the holding of cash, banknotes, or government promissory notes is not regarded as an investment. But since the world's currencies began floating in 1970, the holding of certain "hard" foreign currencies has proven to be both profitable and confidential. Countries that have maintained a conservative monetary policy have consistently appreciated over the past decade. Two such currencies are the Swiss franc and the German mark. If you had held these two currencies in banknotes in your safe over the past seven or eight years, your investment would have tripled in value. And there is no sign that these currencies will not continue their appreciation.

Swiss and German banknotes are like any other currency note—distinguished only by serial numbers. But since these numbers are not related in any way to the present bearer (unless marked bills were stolen from a bank), the banknotes go unrecognized among the millions of others.

You can take advantage of this situation by purchasing banknotes in various denominations, or coins, or foreign travelers checks. In the United States, they can be purchased at a foreign-exchange dealer, such as the Deak-Perera Group, with offices in major cities of the United States (New York, Washington, Chicago, San Francisco, Los Angeles), or at major banks. Swiss or German travelers checks can be purchased from American Express, Deak-

Perera Group, or Thomas Cook travel agencies. In each case, for maximum privacy I suggest you purchase them with cash or a money order, without revealing your identity. Travelers checks can be stored indefinitely. There is no time limit for redemption. In addition, you have built-in insurance in case they are stolen or lost, which you don't have with cash. And, in many cases, the travelers checks can be purchased free of commission (although you will pay a premium over the exchange rate for actual banknotes).

How to Invest in Real Estate Anonymously

One of the most frequent questions I've been asked in doing workshops on the subject of financial privacy is, "How can I invest in real estate confidentially?"

I once read in the *Wall Street Journal* how an investor purchased a large, expensive office building in Atlanta without revealing his name to the public. The bank handling the transaction honored his request for anonymity. It was rumored that the buyer was a group of foreigners.

Yes, you can purchase real estate privately, at least without the press or snooping individuals knowing about it. It may be more difficult to keep the government from knowing if they wanted to. Here are some ways: establish a company or corporation, naming your attorney or account as officers of the company, and purchase real estate through this new company name. Also, you can ask the mortgage company or title insurance company to keep the ownership of the property in their name, while arranging a separate private contract on the property between you and the bank or insurance company.

Your Investment Advisor

How private are your financial dealings with an investment advisor? If your counselor does business with the public, he is probably registered with the Securities and Exchange Commission as an investment advisor and is subject to the Investment Advisors Act of 1940. The SEC has tremendous powers to "protect the public" from "inappropriate" advice from an investment counselor. The local SEC officer may drop in for an occasional unexpected visit with your investment advisor. He may examine accounting

records and correspondence with clients. Financial newsletters are also registered with the SEC. The pretense for
examining correspondence is to make sure that the investment advisor is "properly" handling consumer complaints
and requests for advice.

At some point in the future, however, this excessive
SEC power could be abused, especially since the SEC doesn't
need a subpoena. The agency could, for example, obtain the
names of subscribers to a registered investment newsletter
and investigate them for allegedly illegal activities—foreign
exchange violations, secret bank accounts, confidential
investments, or food storage. This is not mere conjecture.
The SEC went after the subscriber list of a registered
Mexican investment newsletter soon after the 1976 Mexican peso devaluation. Rumor has it that the real intent was
to turn the list over to the IRS for investigation of tax evasion.
The only reason the list was not confiscated was that it
was located in Mexico City, where the law requires secrecy.
In its battle with Col. E.C. Harwood and the American
Institute for Economic Research, the SEC obtained the names
of all participants in the ill-fated Harwood gold program in
Switzerland, and for years prevented them from regaining
their assets.

There are various degrees of privacy that you can insist
upon with your investment advisor. If you seek complete
confidentiality, deal only with your counselor in person or
by telephone. Insist that all correspondence be confidential
or destroyed after a period of time. Insist that your name
and address not be recorded on a name file. Finally, require the investment advisor to notify you of any third-party
requests for information about your portfolio or your financial dealings with him. Unfortunately, American financial
dealings are not like those of Swiss banks, where secrecy
laws cover even conversations on the premises of the bank.

You might consider taking your name off any sensitive
statements you write to your advisor. Place the sensitive
material on plain paper, and mail with a cover letter.

Barter

The private investor and entreprenuer should not overlook
one other important way to transact business discreetly—
through *barter*. Barter is the alternative economy that escapes

written records, price controls, and credit crunches—and minimizes taxes in numerous cases.

The shrewd investor will seek out opportunities to exchange one kind of investment for another—real estate for gold and silver coins, cars for pool tables, furniture for dental work, the list and possibilities are endless. Many such barter transactions are legally tax-free. Several sections of the tax code deal with "like-kind" exchanges of goods and services. Personal property swaps are typically tax free because they are used goods. The mutual exchange of gifts is tax free.

Barter exchanges leave no trace, like cash transactions. The only exception to this rule is when the exchange takes place through an organized barter club, where the central organization assigns "credits" to these exchanges. These credits are placed on computer, and are available for inspection by government and private investigators. I would strongly recommend that you avoid such organized barter exchanges unless you deal in barter on a large scale. One organization which avoids such credits is Comstock Trading Co., 1926 Tice Valley Blvd., Walnut Creek, CA 94595 ($75 a year membership fee, which includes its monthly exchange letter).

Caveat Emptor

A note of caution for the "private investor": While your financial affairs should be kept as discreet as possible, that privacy should not be a two-way street. Brokers, advisors, and others vying for your investment dollars should be frank and willing to discuss all aspects of a business deal with you. They should encourage you to check them out before any transactions are made. Don't let your desire for privacy make you easy prey for moneysharks, hucksters, and con artists who insist that speed and confidentiality will make you a bundle. Too often these characters disappear once they have your money, knowing that the last thing you want is a big court suit and publicity. Be suspicious of a business that operates out of a post office box without listing an actual street address, or that does not have a telephone number. And be particularly wary of strangers offering the opportunity of a lifetime—if it sounds too good to be true, it probably is.

I can't overemphasize this point. The private investments I have discussed up to this point, including coins, diamonds, collectibles, and foreign currencies, are areas open to anyone who wishes to go into business. With little government regulation in the field and few industry standards or ombudsmen, there have already been numerous cases of people defrauded by counterfeit or inferior coins, diamonds, and bearer certificates. Deal only with reliable, aboveboard, well-established companies.

Your Private Secretary

An often overlooked aspect of financial and personal privacy is your personal secretary. Legally, she is not immune from testifying against you. You should make it very clear that she is to keep confidential all financial dealings she might gain knowledge of. It is quite common for corporate executives, for instance, to have secretaries type correspondence and perform other functions related to personal business. You should determine beforehand how much of this activity your secretary should engage in. Your privacy is at stake. Secretaries have been known to reveal all to federal officials, private investigators, or other uninvited guests—information crucial to a civil or criminal proceeding—all quite innocently because the secretary was unaware of her legal and moral responsibilities to her boss. Security-minded executives hire secretaries with great care.

6
Protecting Your Correspondence

On each landing, opposite the lift shaft, the poster with the enormous face gazed from the wall. It was one of those pictures which are so contrived that the eyes follow you about when you move. BIG BROTHER IS WATCHING YOU, the caption beneath it ran. . . .

In the far distance a helicopter skimmed down between the roofs, hovered for an instant like a bluebottle, and darted away again with a curving flight. It was the Police Patrol, snooping into people's windows. The patrols did not matter, however. Only the Thought Police mattered. . . .

There was of course no way of knowing whether you were being watched at any given moment. How often, or on what system, the Thought Police plugged in on any individual wire was guesswork. It was even conceivable that they watched everybody all the time. But at any rate, they could plug in your wire whenever they wanted to. You had to live—did live, from habit that became instinct—on the assumption that every sound you made was overheard, and, except in darkness, every movement scrutinized."

—George Orwell
1984

The "Big Brother" environment portrayed so vividly by George Orwell may still be fiction today, but our society is undeniably moving in that direction. The right to correspond privately with your friends, relatives, and business acquaintances is being seriously eroded today. We read of illegal wiretapes by the FBI, the opening of mail from abroad by the CIA, and the bugging of telephone conversations by similar bureaucracies. Privacy is not compromised solely by government, either. Private investigators and large corporations have been known to listen in on conversations.

How widespread is this unwarranted intrusion into our daily lives? Are there any safeguards against telephone bugging, wiretapping, or mail surveillance? These are essential questions if we are to find true personal and financial privacy. The fact is that financial security is closely allied to written and verbal correspondence. And it's difficult, sometimes even impossible, to transact financial business with a foreign or domestic bank or brokerage house, or to make a host of routine purchases (magazines, books, catalog items) without using the telephone or the mails.

Will Your Conversation Be Overheard?

Unless you go out of your way to keep it private, your telephone number is public information. It's probably listed in the White Pages. George O'Toole, in his fascinating new book, *The Private Sector,* calls the telephone "the greatest threat to the client's privacy."

The telephone company itself can compromise your privacy. Under the federal wiretapping law of 1968, the telephone company has virtual carte blanche to eavesdrop on your conversations. The alleged purpose of this privilege is to catch people who use a blue or black box to make free long-distance telephone calls. During a recent five-year period, the telephone company listened in on 1.8 million telephone conversations and didn't file or obtain a single warrant! The company discovered that only 2 percent of these conversations represented illegal or fraudulent use of the telephone. The potential for eavesdropping abuse is obvious. Since the White Pages, which lists both the telephone number and address of nearly all telephone subscribers, is public information, it is frequently used for commercial solicitations. I'm sure you have experienced the irritation of having dinner interrupted by a "junk phone call" from some persistent salesman who picked your name out of the telephone directory.

Every year, one major private company, Reuben H. Donnelly Company, compiles the names and addresses of everyone in the country who has a published telephone number. A spokesman says: "We start with the compilation of a national list of approximately 52 million residence telephone subscribers. We buy all published telephone directories as input to this compilation. We compile name and

address, telephone number . . . sex or title, if available . . . and,
because of the technique of compilation, are able to include . . . length of residence for each name." When information from the White Pages is combined with information gleaned from such public records as motor-vehicle
registration files, census data, and credit bureau records,
the Donnelly company can break down its lists according
to income, age, special interests, political affiliations, and
many other categories. The resulting well-defined commercial mailing and phoning lists are rented out to thousands of
mail-order companies, real estate and insurance agents,
and so forth.

Getting an Unlisted Phone Number

An unlisted phone number provides some protection from
this commercial exploitation. Despite an additional monthly
fee for *not* listing (the telephone companies try to discourage
unlisted numbers), it is probably worth getting one. Already
over 10 percent of Bell System customers have unlisted
numbers. There are, admittedly, many conveniences in a
listed phone number. Legitimate friends and business associates may need to contact you, but have lost or forgotten
your number. An old acquaintance passing through town
may stop at a phone booth to look up your address. It's a
shame that this information is being abused by unscrupulous
business and government pests.

If you do decide to continue listing your telephone number
publicly, don't list your *street* address in the telephone
book. Some telephone employees may deny it, but in many
states you can give your post office box as an address, or
even give no address at all. (*Privacy Journal*, a newsletter
edited by Robert Ellis Smith dealing with privacy issues,
lists only its telephone number in the White Pages.). Also,
you might consider listing only your initials, particularly
if you are a woman living alone. Another ploy is to list your
middle name, instead of your first name, to detect salesmen
immediately when they call. For instance, if your full name
is Gerald Thomas Dickson and your friends and associates
call you Jerry, list your name in the White Pages as G. Thomas
Dickson. If anyone calls asking for Tom, you can safely ig-
nore the call.

Many people are unaware of the fact that their billing
name can be different from their listing name. The tele-

phone company is not concerned about how your name is
listed as long as the *billing* name and address are real. So,
it's quite possible for you to make up a name to be listed
in the telephone directory. Some people resort to making up
odd, hard-to-pronounce names to ward off salemen working
through the White Pages.

But for some, the need for privacy will demand an unlisted number. An unlisted telephone number does not mean
your number will remain a secret. There are lists of unlisted
numbers and far too many employees have access to these
files. In fact, by requesting an unlisted number, you may
identify yourself as a customer to be watched. A recent
study showed that many Bell System companies routinely
hand over lists of unlisted numbers to a gaggle of federal
and state agencies, including the FBI, the CIA, the IRS, the
police, and the Army. In California, the Public Utilities
Commission recently ruled that unlisted telephone numbers,
credit information about telephone customers, and records
of long-distance calls can be turned over to government
agencies. Agency requests must be made in writing, except
during "emergencies," and within legal processes (subpoenas, search warrants, and court orders). The telephone
subscriber must be informed of the agency request within
30 days "unless the requesting agency certifies under
penalty of perjury that such notification would jeopardize
an ongoing criminal investigation." Yet you don't have to be
a criminal to be under criminal investigation. This is hardly
protection of one's privacy.

Your telephone records, particularly long-distance phone
calls, are another area of concern. As George O'Toole
observes, "The detailed list of the numbers you call, the
date and time you called them, and how long you talked,
forms a revealing index of who you know and what you're
up to." Fortunately, since 1974 it has been the Bell System's
policy to require a subpoena before giving up these records.

A few ordinary steps can be taken to avert revelation
of your long-distance telephone conversations. Collect calls
are not recorded on *your* bill. Nor are calls made on someone else's line or from a pay phone. Obviously, I would not
recommend using your telephone credit card, which logs a
complete list of your long-distance calls. Using a business
phone can muddy the waters, especially if numerous employees make calls over the business lines. But a pay phone
is the best way to conduct a confidential phone conversation.

Telephone Wiretapping

Before we leave the subject of telephone surveillance, we need to examine two methods sometimes used to reduce the risk of wiretapping. First, rumor has it that you can dial a certain telephone number in your area to determine if your phone is bugged. Supposedly, if you get a busy signal, your phone is being tapped. If you get a wavering, whistling sound, your phone is not being bugged. But in reality, this phone number will not tell you if your line is being wiretapped. Telephone operators use it to check whether a line is in working order. Moreover, when two people call at once, one will automatically get a busy signal, so it's not a foolproof system.

Second, a few private companies, such as MCI Corporation and Southern Pacific Communications, offer a special local number in most major cities that you can call to make long-distance calls. You actually hook up with their microwave lines and because you go through the private company's system, the number you dial and the length of the call are not recorded by the Bell System company. You do receive a billing statement, but it is from the private concern—which is not subject to Ma Bell's decision to open records to any agency that asks for it.

Both government agencies and private companies have been involved to varying degrees in telephone wiretapping.

Legal wiretaps by federal agencies are on the wane now that strict requirements must be met before a federal judge will permit the FBI or any other law-enforcement agency to bug a room or tap a telephone. That is not to say that illegal telephone bugging has ceased. George O'Toole states: "The Criminal Intelligence Division (of the Houston police department) had compiled thousands of dossiers on citizens having no criminal records or associates. Most of the individuals spied upon were political activists of one coloration or another. The spy files were full of personal information, often including sexual gossip, and much of the data could only have been acquired through wiretapping." And it could happen anywhere.

In a survey of 115 private detective agencies randomly selected in seven major cities, the National Wiretap Commission found that many of these private companies will install illegal taps for a price ranging from $30 to $5,000. The agencies sensed a strong demand for illegal bugging—from businessmen spying on their competitors, to suspicious wives checking on their wayward husbands, to worried parents eavesdropping on their children.

Jim Hougan, in his revealing book, *Spooks: The Haunting of America—the Private Use of Secret Agents*, tells us the state of the eavesdropping art:

> In the banks, supermarkets, department stores, and airports, *we're watched*—sometimes by kindly eyes, always by hidden ones—and have become accustomed to it. . . . Should we apply for credit or a job, the Metropolitan Bureau of Investigation, Inc., Uffinger's, or Mitchell Reports may well be hired to conduct a covert "background investigation" in addition to the usual checks we've come to accept from credit-reporting services. Meanwhile, at home our telephones are "monitored" at the absolute discretion of the Service Observance Bureau (SOB), a section of the Bell System. . . . the psychiatric invasion of our privacy can be accomplished almost anywhere by means of the Psychological Stress Evaluator (PSE), a lie-detecting device available from Dector Counterintelligence, Inc. . . . And if an individual has cable television, an *optical wiretap* can be installed to observe his actions in the home. . . . The state of the eavesdropper's art, moreover, is such that private conversations and movements in the home can be recorded aurally and optically *without breaking the law*: all one needs is the wherewithal to rent the services of spooks to operate sophisticated equipment, lasers, and other devices, unforeseen by antiquated legislation.

Not all private wiretaps are illegal. You can tape your own telephone conversations without anyone else's approval (including that of the person you're speaking to). The same applies in face-to-face conversations. Federal law simply requires that at least one party be aware of the recording. The U.S. Fifth Circuit Court of Appeals has upheld this law, so there is nothing keeping you from taping your own phone with a tape recorder, and many business executives do it as a matter of course. This works both ways, however—you can be the subject of a legal but unknown bug as well as the instigator of one. Also, the courts have ruled that an employer can eavesdrop on his employees without their knowledge.

How do you know if you're being bugged? In many cases, it's not obvious. If you have a party line or an extension phone, you can easily notice a difference—a click or a loss in volume—if someone has picked up the other line. But when professionals do it, the telephone line is tapped electronically and may be impossible to detect audibly. The most common device used by private detectives is called an "in-line transmitter," a tiny, low-power FM station that broadcasts both sides of a telephone conversation. Since the receiver must be placed within a couple of hundred feet, it is often set up in a parked automobile close to the telephone.

Another ploy to bug your conversations, both on and *off* the telephone, is by placing a live transmitter in the telephone itself.

A telephone wiretap hooked up directly to your line is almost impossible to discover, even by professional "countermeasures" detectives, and this is the method most commonly used by the police, FBI, and other law-enforcement agencies. The hookup is placed at a "junction box," where your line converges with others in the same area, or directly at the telephone exchange.

Listening in on long-distance calls can be a bit more tricky because about 70 percent of these calls are on microwaves, not wire or cables. The Soviet Union supposedly bugged long-distance calls of Americans by picking up microwaves with special receiving equipment—and private spies could do the same with the proper equipment. Again, there is no way such bugging devices can be detected.

As George O'Toole says, "Checking your phone for bugs is no guarantee that some high-powered industrial spy outfit hasn't tapped your line on a telephone pole six blocks away or that the Feds aren't doing the same thing down at your local telephone exchange. You don't know that the telephone company, itself, isn't eavesdropping on you for business or pleasure. And you have no assurance that the KGB, the Mafia, or some other organization isn't listening in on your long-distance calls as they bounce across the continent on microwave beams."

What about voice scramblers? Federal agencies and corporate executives often use them to conceal top-secret conversations. Only the more expensive scramblers really work, since a good electronics technician can decode the cheap ones fairly easily. Another drawback is that the scrambler requires both a sender and a receiver to make the conversation understandable by both parties, and unless you have frequent conversations with the same person, this is highly impractical. Moreover, having a scrambler on your telephone will raise suspicions from the very beginning—what's this person up to? Finally, a scrambler often makes it very difficult to hear at the other end.

Fortunately, electronic inventors in the private market are coming up with better and cheaper ways to search out eavesdropping devices. The Associated Press recently reported that "an inexpensive device designed to protect private conversations from eavesdropping is being kept off the market by the government because the nation's most secret intelligence agency (the National Security Agency) claims the unit threatens national security." According to the inventors, the anti-eavesdropping device would cost less than $100 and work with currently available radios. It could be adapted to scramble telephone conversations. The inventors maintain that they designed the device specifically for individuals seeking privacy. They had no intention of jeopardizing national security. It will be difficult to keep these devices off the market for long.

Room bugs are a related eavesdropping device, and a common one at that. Today, technology has reached the point where ultrasensitive microphones can be the size of a match head; and even when attached to a battery, they can be as small as an aspirin tablet. A room bug of this size can be obtained for about $2,000. The countermeasures man will try to debug a room by tuning in on FM signals until he encounters the same frequency as the bug. This will lead him to the location of the room bug. But the task is becoming more and more difficult with increased technological capability. An even more sophisticated device transmits only when an outside "subcarrier" bug turns it on—the debugger may completely miss the "sleeping" bug.

Protecting Your Mail

Letters, telegrams, and packages can reveal a great deal about your activities, motives, and thoughts. Government agents and private investigators have long seen the value of snooping through people's mail to interpret people's private affairs. For years, the post office turned foreign mail over to the CIA, which opened and read letters to and from politically active Americans. Compliant postal employees have monitored the mail of suspected tax evaders, photocopying secret brokerage accounts each month, noting the addresses of foreign financial correspondents, and reading personal correspondence.

Unofficial snooping was and still is illegal, and if suspected, can bring an investigation by postal inspectors in a hurry. But official snooping, as practiced by the CIA, was not necessarily illegal. Postal regulations state that first-class mail is confidential, and opening first-class mail *while it is in the hands of the post office* is a criminal offense. The Postal Manual actually states: "Sealed first-class mail *while in the custody* of the Post Office Department, is accorded absolute secrecy. No persons in the postal service, except those employed for that purpose in the dead-mail offices, may break or permit the breaking of the seal of any matter mailed as first-class mail without a legal warrant, even though it may contain criminal or otherwise unmailable matter, or furnish evidence of the commission of a crime." (Emphasis added.) If the post office merely turns over certain first-class mail to the CIA, which then opens that first-class mail, it may not be considered an illegal act, however. The CIA has publicly acknowledged this practice and has promised to discontinue it. Nevertheless, the regulations continue unchanged.

The Mail Watch

In the late 1960s, the post office routinely photocopied the outside front and back of letters coming from Swiss banks in an effort to catch tax dodgers and unreported income. Even though Swiss banks never list a return address, postal meter readers were able to pinpoint where the letters came from. The IRS linked the postal meters to a particular Swiss bank, and then checked to see if the addressees had declared income on a Swiss bank account there. In many cases, the IRS discovered unreported income and prosecuted. The defendants argued that the photocopying of the outside of envelopes was an invasion of privacy, but ultimately the courts ruled in favor of the government. So today, the post office, at the request of any government agency, can monitor your mail without your knowledge, and you would be surprised how frequently this is still done! This is just one of the casualties of a government-imposed monopoly on first-class mail service in this country. Undoubtedly, the post office would take greater care to preserve customers' privacy if private carriers were permitted to deliver first-class mail. No wonder the government fights so hard to keep this unwarranted monopoly power.

To maintain financial and personal privacy in you correspondence, you should consider renting a post office box. This, together with an assumed name, can almost assure

confidentiality in your dealings by mail. Don Stephens has
written a very interesting article on this topic:

POST OFFICE BOXES: ONE KEY STEP
TOWARD PERSONAL PRIVACY

By Don Stephens

Not too long ago, I saw an article in the evening paper
that reported another burglary at the home of John Q. Citizen,
555 South Something Street, the sixth such break-in in the
past twelve months. The write-up described what steps Mr.
Citizen has taken to foil such burglaries and just how these
intruders had overcome those measures. The piece concluded by quoting John Q. on the extent of his losses, "They
got my cash, a camera and some ammunition, but they didn't
get my guns!" A month later another article reported Mr.
Citizen had once again been robbed, and this time it was his
firearms collection.

I would never say a person deserves to fall victim to
thieves, but Mr. Citizen and that newspaper certainly simpli-
fied that seventh break-in by their combined poor judgment.
Those last burglars were able to glean not only John Q's
name, security strengths and weaknesses and what he had
which was worth stealing from the article, but also the key
piece of information—*his address.* Laying it all out that way
was an open invitation to the criminally inclined.

Unfortunately, given the skyrocketing crime rate today,
this is far from an isolated incident. Burglaries growing out
of imprudently released newspaper reports are becoming
commonplace. Obituaries are so often followed by break-ins
of the deceased's home during funeral and graveside services that private guards are being retained to house-sit at
these times in many parts of the country. The night a friend
of mine was reported hospitalized with neck injuries, his
house was relieved of $1,500 of stereo equipment. Travelers
who announce their plans in the society pages all too often
find their homes ransacked upon returning home. Prudent
individuals don't give their addresses to reporters and responsible papers should refuse to print them.

But newspaper coverage isn't the only way the criminally
inclined obtain unguarded addresses. Several news magazines recently have reported that thieves are purchasing
copies of selected mailing lists, which help them single out

homes most likely to offer premium booty. Such lists include subscribers to publications directed at the affluent or those in typically high-paying professions.

Telephone books provide another source of addresses to a variety of social misfits. Again, doctors, lawyers, businessmen, bankers, and others easily identifiable with wealth often unnecessarily list their home addresses. And the readily available "reverse directory," where addresses are organized numerically by street, is a great boon to a variety of lawbreakers. They can locate a likely house, look it up, and call to see if anyone is really at home or if those lights were just left on as a ruse.

What To Do About It

If you are among the many who haven't been aware of these hazards, the best first step is the acquisition of a post office box. For only a few dollars a year you can remain accessible to those wishing to contact you by mail without compromising the privacy and security of your place of residence.

There are several factors to consider in selecting a post office box. The first is availability; in some areas, you may have to join a long waiting list just to get one. However, in an adjoining zip zone, boxes may be in plentiful supply. If you are in an urban area with several post offices, you might want to give consideration to which would most conveniently suit your needs. Some people like to pick up mail near their homes, others choose a box near work. If you desire the greatest time flexibility, consider a box with 24-hour access in an area of town you would feel safe visiting in the wee hours. If off-street parking is available, that too is worth considering in making your selection. And, once you have settled on a particular post office, if there is a choice of boxes available, choose one that is at a convenient height, with an easy-to-remember number.

In applying for your box, you will usually be required to provide identification. I've found a social security card sufficient for this purpose. They also often require a home address. In order to accomplish your goal of maintaining residential privacy, you may want to try telling them you've just moved to this part of the country and are living in your camper on the street. If you are forced to divulge your home address, indicate in writing that it is for their information only and that any breach of its confidentiality without court order will result in legal action against them. Incidentally, this same tactic should be used whenever you must release your address to schools, banks, service companies, etc.

Also, request that all mail addressed to the box be placed in it. This will assure that you will receive items sent to you with the wrong name or name spelling. It will also allow authorized friends to receive mail at your box and permit you to request material under a pseudonym, should you ever wish to do so. To make certain that this order is being carried out, try mailing yourself envelopes under a variety of names and spellings and see if they get through.

Once you have the post office box, send changes of address to magazines and anyone else from whom you receive mail. Also, call the telephone company and see if they can list you by box number; if not, and this varies with public utility commission tariffs in the various states, at least have them list you without an address. If in doubt about your rights in this regard, contact your local office of the PUC. Often the people at the phone office are surprisingly unfamiliar with regulations on this topic. Also indicate, preferably in writing, that you want your residential address deleted from all other directories including the temporary one used by information operators and the reverse directory. It's a good idea to check this by calling information and requesting your own phone number and address; in Los Angeles it took over three months before they got ours right!

Finally, use judgment in deciding who can be trusted to know your home address. Never give it to the newspapers. Ask your friends to guard the confidentiality of your address and explain why they may also want to take similar steps. Then be a friend and don't give out others' addresses and phone numbers unless they have specifically authorized you to do so or unless they already have made such information public. The time has come to be more considerate of each others' privacy and more protective of your own.

(©1977 Inflation Journal Letter)

You can use your post office box to receive sensitive mail, especially mail-order books and products, under an assumed name. You could send a money order through the mail without revealing your true identity. For example, I once sent away for a booklet on a gambling scheme because I was doing an article for my newsletter on gambling as a speculation. Unfortunately, I gave my real name and my home address.

Suddenly my name was on a mailing list of gamblers that has been rented out a thousand times to promote some strange products. I was bombarded with this kind of trash. I wonder what kind of impression people might get if they saw that kind of advertising coming to my home all the time—perhaps that I was a compulsive gambler? And what might the IRS think when I never report any wins—would the auditor believe it's because I never gamble? But if I had used an assumed name and a post office box, I would have received the information I needed and I wouldn't have had to worry about my reputation.

There are other safeguards that you may take to protect your correspondence. Avoid using a return address with your name on it and suggest that your correspondents do the same. Swiss banks and other financial companies concerned about privacy do not put a return address on their envelopes (let's hope your address and postage are correct!).

Seal the envelope with Scotch tape and cover the apertures on the sides. This will prevent easy access to your correspondence—by steaming open the letter, for instance (which often leaves telltale signs of crinkling), or by using a piano wire to wind up and extract the letter from inside. Informing the postal inspectors will also deter snoopers.

Mail-Forwarding Services

Another method frequently used for maintaining privacy in correspondence is mail forwarding services. These are private firms that allow you to use their address to receive mail. They will hold mail for you or forward it to an address you give them.

These services are extremely helpful to people who travel or move a great deal and don't want the hassles of having to send address updates to everyone they know. And they can also be a valuable asset to the person who doesn't move but desires total privacy.

Fees for this service vary from $5 to $50 per month, plus the cost of postage. It's often possible to use code names and have your mail forwarded to a post office box, even outside the country.

The Directory of Mail Drops in the United States and Canada, available from Loompanics, P.O. Box 264, Mason, MI 48854 ($4), lists mail-drop services in both countries. Unfortunately, the reliability of these services differs widely and, therefore, you may need to experiment with several services before making a full commitment. Also check the classifieds in various magazines for mail drop services.

Keeping Foreign Correspondence Private

If you have dealings with foreign banks, brokerage firms, and investment counselors, you may wish to take certain precautions. There are several alternatives.

First, you can have your Swiss bank or other financial correspondent hold all mail. This is a frequent request, and account forms at several banks ask you whether you would like correspondence held or forwarded to your address.

Second, you can have foreign mail sent to your friends or to accommodation bureaus, such as the mail-forwarding services mentioned above. Thus, no mail will be sent directly to you from abroad.

Third, you can use a correspondence-and-document file service. One such service in Bermuda is called the SOS Secretarial Service, P.O. Box 1721, Hamilton, Bermuda. According to a letter from the director, "You may send us any papers you wish, which will be placed in a file in your name in a locked cabinet in this office and would be made available only to you or a properly authorized person. The post office box number of this office could be used by you and your mail would either be forwarded or retained on your specific instructions. You may have mail sent to us from anywhere in the world using our post office box number and we would forward it on to you or retain it in your file, per your instructions. For this service, our fee is $25 per annum, payable in advance and, of course, in addition, any outlays for postage. We would appreciate a $5 deposit towards postage and when that has been exhausted, we would bill you accordingly."

Mailing Lists and "Junk" Mail

Mailing lists can compromise your privacy by categorizing your lifestyle in terms of income, tastes, occupation, and interests. Previously, I mentioned the Donnelly company and its compilation of some 60 million names and addresses based on listed telephone numbers—which reveal your sex, occupational title, name, address, and length of residency. In addition, the R.L. Polk Company compiles from official records in 40 states a list of 43 million car owners in America, 11 million truck owners, and nearly three million motorcycle owners. Other companies compile lists of hunting and fishing licensees, property owners, and registered voters. The mailing-list compiler can come up with a surprising amount of information on you, your car, your home, your children, and so on. Finally, the list owner can make a good guess at your living and spending habits; census information will tell him the median income level of your neighborhood.

Have you ever wondered how your name got on a piece of mail you received today? Often, your name is selected because you made a similar purchase by mail. But with these independent list collectors scouring the country for names, you need not do anything to get on the list.

What are the lists used for? One industry spokesman stated: "Our commercial clients and their purposes in renting out lists include magazine publishers to secure new subscribers; automobile companies to distribute new car catalogs and promotional pieces and to secure new credit accounts, make discount offers, and secure new members in travel clubs; . . . insurance companies to sell insurance directly or to develop leads; retail stores to announce new stores, advertise sales, and secure credit accounts; charitable organizations to raise funds; research firms to determine consumer likes and dislikes about such things as automobile design, dealers, and service; and packaged goods firms to distribute free samples or . . . discount coupons."

Because these many lists are compiled from sources you cannot generally control, it's almost impossible to keep your name off them all. Much junk mail comes addressed to "occupant." (This tends to be innocuous literature.) The Privacy Commission believes that it's possible for a person to keep his name off these lists only "by paying cash for all his purchases, not owning a car, giving to charity anonymously, always buying magazines at newsstands, never responding to a door-to-door survey, never signing a petition or guest book, never registering to vote, and never attending a meeting, conference, or newsworthy social event." Even then you will get some "occupant" mail.

To minimize your presence on mailing lists, use only your post office box for ordering merchandise by mail or requesting information. Use an assumed name, if you prefer. List your post office box on any request for an address that does not specifically require a street address.

How to Get Your Name Off a Mailing List

When you purchase a product by mail, you can ask that

your name not be placed on a mailing list. It is more difficult to get your name off a mailing list once it's already
there, but it is possible. It usually does no good to write the
company that rents the list. That firm is not the owner of
the mailing list, but is simply renting the names for one-time
use. You must write directly to the owner of the list. This is
how I had my name removed from the gambling lists. Admittedly, tracking down the original source of a mailing list
can be difficult.

Several companies have an official policy of taking your
name off their mailing list if you request it. It makes good
business sense—why should they spend money for materials
and postage if you never intend to buy? American Express
Company has a policy of letting a customer choose whether
he wants to receive any advertising from American Express.
Interestingly, just over one percent ask to be removed from
the lists. Another company, Computerworld, reports that
over 10 percent prefer not to receive advertisements.

You can ask the post office to stop delivering mail to your
home by filing Form 2150, which eliminates "pandering"
mail. (But, ironically, people filing this form are listed publicly by the U.S. Government Printing Office!) The Postal
Service also offers a form to block the delivery of pornographic literature, but the postal authorities, not you, decide
what is pornographic.

You can also write to the Direct Mail Marketing Association, 6 East 43rd Street, New York, NY 10017, requesting
its Mail Preference Service Form. By filling it out, you can
have your name removed from lists used by 400 mailers
(who account for 70 percent of third-class mail). The same
organization also offers a form to *add* your name to mailing
lists. Don't confuse the two!

Congress is considering legislation that would force a company to remove your name from its mailing list at your
request, but, according to the Privacy Commission, "some
were willing to admit that unsolicited mail could be a
nuisance, an annoyance, or even an abomination—but not a
trespass on personal property."

Finally, you can always use the time-honored method of
failing to give the post office your forwarding address
when you move. This will keep you off most mailing lists, for
a while anyway. Recently, several commercial enterprises
and publishing houses have developed new ways to track
down missing subscribers. *TV Guide*, for example, has a

sophisticated system to find people who have moved without leaving a forwarding address (a system, by the way, that has interested the federal government).

7
Traveling Incognito

The state's attack today is focused on the individual's enjoyment of his right to privacy, in an effort to further encroach upon liberty and property heretofore beyond the state's reach. In the statist view, privacy is a black market in liberty and a barrier to establishing a 1984-style omniscient state.

Jerome F. Smith

The right to travel freely to and from our country is an essential right of every American. Nothing is more like imprisonment than being restricted from moving from one place to another. Ask any Soviet dissident seeking asylum outside the Iron Curtain—if you can get in to talk to him.

The freedom to travel is closely connected with your financial situation. Obviously, your freedom to travel is severely restricted if you aren't permitted to spend the necessary funds to reach your destination, or if you are restricted in how much you can take to spend once you get there. Over the years, numerous governments have placed artificial restrictions, some harsher than others, on citizens' rights to travel: immigration and emigration laws, visa and passport limitations, laws requiring permits to move from one city to another, and limitations on the amount of domestic or foreign currency citizens are allowed to take when crossing the border.

Traveling Americans and the Bank Secrecy Act

Americans have experienced relatively few restrictions over the years on their ability to travel, compared with the citizens of other nations. A national crisis could change that, however. A major international incident involving the United States could precipitate special regulations on travel and the amount of money you could take out of the country.

The 1970 Bank Secrecy Act, a law I have discussed at length in previous chapters, has already established the mechanisms needed to impose travel restrictions and restrictions on the flight of capital. Specifically, the Act requires the reporting of international movements of currency and certain monetary instruments valued at more than $5,000. A traveler carrying over $5,000 in cash, travelers checks, or certain bearer instruments is required to file a report with the U.S. Customs Service when he leaves or enters the country. The same rules apply if you mail cash or a check made payable to cash outside the country. Conversely, a U.S. resident who receives more than $5,000 in cash, travelers checks, or certain bearer instruments, through the mail or hand delivered, must file the form (called Form 4790, "Report of International Transportation of Currency or Monetary Instruments," which is sent on to the Treasury Department). See the Appendix for a copy of this form. If you fail to report, the currency or monetary instruments may be seized and confiscated. In more serious cases—involving illicit drugs or organized crime—heavy fines and imprisonment can be imposed.

How to Avoid
the Currency Reporting Requirement

The private investor may wish to place large sums of cash in a foreign account in the most discreet manner. He could legitimately carry $5,000 cash with him to avoid reporting, but if he had a considerable sum over $5,000, it would be too cumbersome and expensive to make multiple trips, each time carrying only $5,000 or less.

In addition to the currency reporting requirements of the U.S. Treasury, you may have to worry about currency restrictions by foreign countries. Many countries impose strict requirements on how much currency—foreign or domestic—you can carry into or out of the country. Recently, for example, Switzerland imposed a 20,000 franc limitation on the amount of money you could bring into Switzerland, chiefly in an effort to curtail contraband cash coming across the Italian border. Other countries have even more severe limitations.

There are simpler ways to avoid the currency reporting requirement. First, consider carrying rare U.S. gold and silver coins, which are still legal tender in the United States, *at their face value.* In other words, if you took your U.S. silver dollars, dimes, quarters or half dollars (dated before 1965), or double-eagle gold coins, to a Federal Reserve bank, the bank would exchange them for you into current dollars at face value—admittedly with some question about your sanity. Currently, you don't have to report legal-tender U.S. coins when entering or leaving the country as long as the *face value* is $5,000 or less. So even though the market value of a hundred $20 gold coins is over $30,000, their face value is only $2,000—far below the $5,000 reporting level. Sometimes even a single extremely rare gold or silver coin can have a market value exceeding $5,000—and such coins are easily concealed. I know of several coin dealers who move rare coins in and out of the country without having to report or fill in any forms. Once you reach your destination, you should have no problem converting the coin into the type of monetary investment you wish to make, whether you plan to open a bank account in Switzerland or buy life insurance. The large international coin market is quite familiar with major U.S. rare coins, so you can be sure to receive a fair price. Or you may simply wish to store the coins in a foreign safe-deposit box.

Another ploy is to carry bullion gold and silver coins, diamonds, gems, and other commodities. Commodities do *not* fall under the currency reporting requirements. Therefore, you can carry any amount of coins, diamonds, or gems out of the country without reporting them to U.S. customs.

Bullion gold coins—the Krugerrand, Mexican 50 Pesos, Austrian 100 Coronas, British Sovereign, and others—are quite small in size for their value. A roll of 10 South African Krugerrands can easily fit into your pocket unnoticed, yet they have a value of over $2,000. You should carry them with you, not inside baggage that you check on board (lost baggage is becoming a major problem these days and the insurance per bag is extremely low). Leave coins in your carry-on luggage or bag, not on your person. That way, the coins will appear on the x-ray machines, arousing no interest, and will not cause a buzzer sound when you travel through the detectors. Even though the coins are legal, you don't want to call attention to the fact that you are carrying them. Pickpockets love airports.

Some travelers have questioned whether it is possible to avoid customs reporting by carrying Krugerrands. Since the South African government considers the Krugerrand legal tender, some customs officials began requiring a customs declaration for the coins if their *market* value exceeded $5,000. The latest word from the Treasury Department is that the Krugerrand is still exempt from customs declaration, but how long that will last is uncertain.

The problem of the Krugerrand raises a real concern. The Treasury Department has wide latitude in establishing the regulations for customs declaration of monetary instruments; it could, at any time, amend the regulations. If Krugerrands or other gold or silver coins became a common means of escaping the customs reporting requirements, the Treasury could, overnight, issue new regulations requiring the reporting of *all* valuables crossing the border. You would therefore be wise to check current regulations before attempting any of the methods described in this chapter to avoid customs declarations.

Diamonds and Other Gems

Diamonds are probably the best-known vehicle for international smuggling.

The story is told of a Jewish diamond dealer in Amsterdam who made financial preparations as the Nazi army advanced on Holland during World War II. When Hitler's troops marched on Amsterdam, the diamond dealer left in a hurry with only a palmful of quality diamonds worth about $100,000 at the time. He traveled through Spain, South America, Mexico, and Canada, and finally arrived in the United States. His travels lasted for several years, and by the time he arrived in New York City—a diamond center—he had only a quarter of his handful remaining. But he had survived, and is today a millionaire living in Manhattan.

Coins cannot compare to diamonds in their ability to be transported inconspicuously. A million dollars worth of diamonds can be carried abroad without notice. And diamonds, unlike gold, do not show up on x-ray. Diamonds are also acceptable in trade throughout the world, particularly in the major capitals of Western Europe. You should have little problem cashing in your diamonds once you reach your destination.

As Ian Fleming, the creator of James Bond, observed, "You can carry enough diamonds on your naked body to set you up for life."

Large assets can also be hidden in the form of jewelry when carried abroad. An interesting story is told about a Mafia drug dealer who had arranged a meeting with underworld executives to sell heroin. An informer tipped off the Narcotics Bureau, which invited the IRS in on the case (to prove unreported income on the Mafioso's income tax form). Government agents closely watched the penthouse suite where the meeting was to take place. After the meeting, during which agents were sure the heroin and money had changed hands, the agents watched the Mafia leader leave the hotel with three suitcases, an attache case, and his girlfriend. They headed for the airport, where they booked a flight to Paris. The government agents arranged to have the flight delayed so that they could check the suitcases. All they found was clothing; no cash, no payoff.

The attache case? Perhaps, so they wired to Paris to have special French customs officers check the case thoroughly. When the plane arrived, the case was checked—but no evidence of a payoff showed up. The U.S. agents were completely baffled. Where did the money go?

It was weeks after the Mafia man and his girlfriend escaped that it finally dawned on them what had happened. His girlfriend was loaded with fine jewelry. Sure enough, when the agents checked, they discovered that an expert jeweler had been present at the heroin exchange. Diamonds and other expensive gems had been the payoff and were placed in inconspicuous jewelry to escape detection by the Feds.

Dealing with Immigration and Customs

When you enter the United States, you first encounter the Immigration and Naturalization Administration—an immigration official. His main purpose is to make sure you have a valid passport. INA cannot refuse you entry into the United States as long as you hold a valid passport. But if you appear on its "lookout book," it can detain you for questioning. The INA lookout book contains the names of known deportees, smugglers, convicted tax evaders, and fugitives wanted by the FBI. INA compiles the book from lists received from government agencies that are searching for people convicted of illegal activities.

According to immigration officials, INA does not keep a file on all Americans, nor does it have a list of current passport holders. In major cities, it does check airline passenger lists from time to time—so beware.

What about the customs declaration form you're required to make when entering a country? To be sure, U.S. Customs doesn't automatically distribute declaration forms when people leave the country, so it's easy to take bullion coins, diamonds, and other commodities abroad. But what about customs declarations once you reach your destination? The fact is that you may have to report these commodities upon entering a foreign country, even if there is no import duty imposed on bullion coins, diamonds, or other gems. As I suggested before, Krugerrands may avoid this problem altogether. I once traveled throughout Europe carrying a couple of gold coins I had purchased abroad, and I was never questioned about them—even upon returning to the States. If I had been asked, I was prepared to make an oral declaration, not a written one (customs keeps written declarations on file). By the way, there is no import duty currently on gold or silver though there is on diamonds and gems.

Another area of concern in dealing with customs is the customs computer network now in operation at airport and border terminals across the country. Could this giant "big brother" machine be used to spy on the traveling habits of American citizens? Could this giant computer be used to monitor travelers who make frequent trips to the Bahamas, Mexico or Switzerland?

The computer system is officially called the Treasury Enforcement Communications System, or TECS for short. There are TECS computer terminals at approximately 1,000 ports of entry in the United States. The system has the following kinds of individuals on computer tape:

- Individuals listed by the National Crime Information Center (for stolen cars and other goods)
- Individuals suspected or convicted of smuggling
- Suspected illicit drug dealers
- Businesses involved in import fraud
- Persons wanted for stolen property, guns or securities
- Individuals wanted for jumping bail and trial
- Convicted tax evaders

The TECS system has been in operation since 1970. When your name or social security number is entered in the TECS system, it responds either "yes" or "no." If TECS answers "no," there's no problem. If it answers "yes," you will be interrogated and possibly detained. A customs official maintains that no one has been falsely identified by TECS. The official also states that it's possible to purge your name from the system. But TECS records are not accessible under the Freedom of Information Act.

Customs denies that it keeps records on how many times you come and go through ports of entry. Customs regulations state that you can take advantage of the $300 duty-free exemption only once every 30 days, but officials say that the rule is enforced only by word of mouth ("How long have you been outside the country?"), not by checking their files. The customs declaration cards could be used for monitoring entrances and exits through U.S. borders, but for now these cards are held at the point of entry only for three years and then destroyed. No central file is kept.

It is curious, though, that the customs declaration form asks for your name and address and sometimes your occupation—information that could be used for surveillance in the future.

According to *U.S. News and World Report*, some customs agents have suggested that "the computer may be asked in the future to pull out the names of travelers who merely cross the border an unusual number of times or who use different border crossings in what may look like a suspicious pattern, although it may be innocent."

In any case, there are only a few ways to lower your profile with the customs computer. One is to take indirect routes to sensitive financial centers. For example, if you plan on traveling to Switzerland to transact business with your Swiss bank, consider a flight to London first, where you can then purchase your ticket to Switzerland. (It's surprising how frequently this is done. London is known as a careless customs area.) Other possible routes include Montreal and Toronto.

Courier Services

Another way to maintain a low profile in carrying out international transactions is through a courier service. As stated earlier, these include foreign exchange dealers, foreign banks, and underground operators. Stick only with reputable firms, however. The courier will be required to file the Treasury Form 4790 if the amount of cash is over $5,000, but the customs form makes exceptions for foreign banks and foreign-exchange dealers.

Privacy and Your Passport

An essential aspect of your freedom to travel and to carry on financial transactions abroad is the passport. The passport application asks numerous personal questions beyond the usual name and address. It asks for physical characteristics, including visible distinguishing marks, occupation, marital status, children's names, birthplaces, and birthdates—it almost reads like a criminal record.

There are several questions that it is not mandatory to answer. You should avoid these questions if possible—purpose and length of trip, number of previous trips abroad, means of transportation, and countries to be visited. You are not required to state your social security number and you could be vague about your occupation.

Despite this invasion of privacy, a passport for you and your family members is critical. Surprisingly, only 17 percent of Americans have a passport. Even if you have no immediate plans for traveling abroad, you should have a valid passport hidden away in case, for some unknown reason, you need to travel abroad suddenly. If you wait until the moment of crisis, it may be too late—it takes several weeks to get a passport under normal circumstances, and if the situation concerns millions of fellow Americans, you could have a long wait ahead of you. In addition to the passport, you should have in your possession a legal certificate of citizenship, such as a birth certificate (which is often the only requirement to enter certain countries, such as the Bahamas—and it's far more confidential than a passport).

Since World War I, governments throughout the world have imposed all kinds of restrictions on passports and travel. As Douglas R. Casey observes in his book, *The International Man* (available from Kephart Communications, 901 North Washington St., Alexandria VA 22314, $14.95):

> Today there is a very high correlation between the ease with which a passport is available to a citizen and the amount of freedom in the country generally. Obviously, police states are slow to issue travel documents since they might quickly find themselves without a citizenry. Nazi Germany, the Sino-Soviet Bloc, and most of the Third World are all distinguished by a low volume of outbound (or inbound, for that matter) tourists, largely because of state controls. One hallmark of India's status as one of the world's totalitarian nations can be found in its 1967 Passport Act. The Act states that—

among other reasons—the state may deny issuance of a passport to any citizen 'whose travel, in the opinion of the central government . . . would not be in the public interest.' The law further specifies that the government cannot be forced to disclose its reason for denial, nor can its denial be appealed.

Casey has an excellent section in his book on the topic of passports, which I highly recommend. He notes the advantages of having a diplomatic passport, a black passport with gold lettering issued to diplomats and their families. The State Department also issues them to nondiplomats for a variety of reasons. What are the advantages of the diplomatic passport? There is no expiration date, so you don't need to reapply every five years (with up-to-date personal information). Also, Casey states, "They are marvelous for intimidating customs inspectors, police, and any other officials you may come in contact with. A bit of a brassy attitude combined with possession of this document can result in special privileges, immunities, and favors."

Recently, there was a furor over Bert Lance, former budget director under President Jimmy Carter, and his diplomatic passport. Finally, he surrendered the special document. The *Washington Post* reported: "Bearers of diplomatic passports are afforded special treatment—for example, freedom from customs searches—not available to regular international travelers. In Lance's case, critics argued that the special passport might facilitate his contacts with Saudi investors and other international businessmen with whom he has been dealing."

Timothy Green says the diplomatic passport is a common means for avoiding customs searches. "A diplomatic passport is another perfect front for smuggling because a member of a diplomatic corps is usually immune to casual customs searches. Because of this, many diplomats, especially from small South American and African countries, have become globe-trotting smugglers carrying everything from diamonds to heroin in their diplomatic bags. So many diplomats are mules that the joke in smuggling circles is that the letters, C.D., which stand for *Corps Diplomatique*, should really mean *Contrabandier Distingue*, or distinguished smuggler."

Douglas Casey lists three ways to obtain a diplomatic passport: at the discretion of the State Department; through an honorary consul of a small, poverty-stricken country that needs representation in Washington; and by direct purchase of a "lettre de chancellerie," a document indicating that a foreign country has retained your services and thus you are eligible for a diplomatic passport.

Should You Obtain Another Passport?

Frequently, international investors ask, "Do I need a second passport, and if so, how do I legally obtain one?" Several experts on financial survival, including Harry D. Schultz, have argued that you may wish to obtain an additional passport or two to give you more freedom and ability to move in and out of countries as the need arises. No one can predict the future with accuracy, and there may come a time when, as Schultz says, "passport control is tightened, and no trips can be made abroad without state permission, full tax clearance, and a deposit made in case you don't come back (Brazil does this now). Passport renewals may be restricted or even curtailed except in special cases."

You might need to leave the United States for any number of reasons, and a passport issued by the country of your destination could provide immediate relief and acceptance that a U.S. passport would deny. Many persecuted individuals have sought and received asylum and citizenship in a friendly country.

How do you obtain a second passport? Some methods—forgery, theft, or use of an alias—are illegal. Obtaining a legal second passport seems to be a gray area. First of all, the State Department estimates that several million Americans legally hold two passports because they are naturalized immigrants from other countries. Thus, they remain citizens of both countries and legally have access to two passports.

For American citizens born in this country the task is more difficult. The problem arises because the U.S. government reserves the right to revoke your citizenship, as well as your passport, on several grounds: if the applicant is no longer a U.S. citizen, for example, or has taken an oath of allegiance to a foreign state. In other words, if you legally obtain another country's passport by taking an affirmation of allegiance, your U.S. citizenship could be revoked. Becoming a citizen of another country is in no way a criminal act subject to fines or imprisonment; but you may forfeit the privileges of U.S. citizenship, such as the right to vote, to obtain a U.S. passport, and so on. This is a price I would consider too dear. But the U.S. State Department might not act even if it discovered that you had obtained a second passport. Furthermore, it's very unlikely that the State Department would ever find out about the passport, especially if you used it discreetly, in foreign countries only. You should be aware of the risks involved, particularly if your reason for desiring a second passport is also a reason for the State Department to be interested in you.

Some countries, such as Canada, South Africa, and Switzerland, require that you renounce your U.S. citizenship before they will confer their citizenship on you. Obviously, those countries should be avoided unless you were born there and are already a citizen. Others will notify your mother country that you have applied for citizenship, and these too should be avoided. Finally, some countries make no such requirements, including Taiwan, Israel, and Ireland.

The basic technique is to establish residency in a foreign land (usually up to five years), after which citizenship can be obtained and a passport can be issued. There are many ways to speed up the process, including marriage to a foreign national, descent from emigrants of that country, and proof of persecution or refugee status. A world-reknowned figure with a good reputation can often change citizenship quickly. And peculiar aspects of foreign laws may hasten the process in some cases. Obtaining a second passport in certain countries requires extensive (and expensive) use of a lawyer.

Can you legally use an assumed name to obtain a U.S. or foreign passport? Generally, you cannot, although it depends on the circumstances. Passports with assumed names are put together for government agents on secret missions, but are not generally available to the private citizen. It's possible if you are adopted into a family to acquire another name, or you may be able to use a pseudonym if it can be proven that you are easily and generally identified by that name. In either of these cases, using an assumed name would not provide much secrecy—especially since the State Department is likely to print *both* names on your passport!

One method for obtaining a passport with a fictitious name is to search out the name of someone who was born about the same time you were, but died as a child. Since birth and death records are not generally kept together, you could submit your picture with the child's birth certificate when applying for a passport. This technique is illegal—it is a criminal act to receive a passport on the pretense that you are someone else, even if that person is dead. But it is not an uncommon practice.

A final comment about passports. If you are abroad at the time you need to renew your passport, you will receive IRS Form 3966, which requests extensive confidential information, answers to which must be affirmed under oath, subject to criminal penalties. You are *not* required to fill in this form, however. It is simply a request. The purpose of the form, according to the IRS, is to inform Americans of their tax obligations, but there could be ulterior motives. At the very least, it is an invasion of privacy.

Keep Your Passport Confidential

One final recommendation about your passport. Avoid using it for identification if at all possible. Some foreign banks, especially in Switzerland, request that you identify yourself when opening an account in person. This is a perfectly normal request because the Swiss want to know whom they are dealing with. If you refuse to provide such identification, the Swiss banker may refuse your application. You might consider using another form of identification, but play it by ear.

Another tip: Many countries do not automatically stamp your passport unless you ask them to. While this may be a fun way of saying, "I was there," it also is a very official accounting of when and where you have traveled outside the country. Buy postcards instead.

Become an Expatriate?

A few financial advisors have suggested the idea of leaving the country as a means of achieving personal and financial independence. This method has its advantages. You remove yourself *physically* from the long arm of the tax collector. The field audit becomes a bit more expensive for the IRS! There are special tax breaks for Americans living abroad. And moving to another country may be more suitable in terms of personal privacy and financial freedom.

But with the advantages come the drawbacks. Although you may be physically out of the U.S. government's reach, you may still be dunned for federal income taxes. The Internal Revenue Code says that if avoidance of U.S. taxes was one of the principal reasons for renunciation of your citizenship, the government reserves the right to impose these taxes for the next 10 years—even though you are now a nonresident alien. Government agents feel that they need only show that loss of citizenship resulted in a substantial reduction in U.S. taxes, which is almost always the case. The burden of proof is on you to prove otherwise.

Moreover, despite its lower tax base, the country you may move to may not enjoy the same degree of freedom as Americans do under the Bill of Rights. As a matter of fact, most Western nations are not as conscientious in providing for these constitutional rights—many countries do not, for instance, require a search warrant to enter your home. American expatriates have been disappointed with the lack of constitutional rights in such countries as Canada, Mexico, Germany, and other Western countries, and find themselves moving from country to country rather than returning to the United States, because they have burned their bridges.

8
The Confidential Loan

The makers of the Constitution . . . sought to protect Americans in their beliefs, their thoughts, their emotions, and their sensations. They conferred, as against the Government, the right to be let alone—the most comprehensive of rights and the right most valued by all civilized men.

Justice Louis D. Brandeis

Several years ago, James Millstone, assistant managing editor of the *St. Louis Post-Dispatch,* was startled to learn that his insurance company was planning to cancel his car insurance. Outraged, Millstone demanded to know the reason. The insurance company directed him to a consumer-credit investigating firm, O'Hanlon Reports, Inc. His file, which the credit-reporting firm was required to reveal under the Fair Credit Reporting Act, contained damaging allegations about Millstone's lifestyle. In part, it stated:

> The file shows that you are very much disliked by your neighbors at that location (Millstone's previous Washington residence) and were considered to be a "hippie type." The file indicates that you participated in many demonstrations in Washington, D.C. and that you also housed out-of-town demonstrators during demonstrations. The file indicates that these demonstrators slept on floors, in the basement, and wherever else there was room on your property. The file shows that you were strongly suspected of being a drug user by neighbors, but they could not positively substantiate these suspicions. You are shown to have had shoulder-length hair and a beard on one occasion while living in Washington, D.C. The file indicates that there were rumors in the neighborhood from three previous residences in Washington, D.C. prior to living at the 48th Street, N.W. location.

Other derogatory comments were made about his wife in the file, but were not revealed to Millstone. Ultimately, the report was found to be a slipshod production, based on hearsay and a quick interview with disenchanted neighbors. Little, if any, of the file was found to be accurate.

Millstone sued the firm. After a four-year, $4,000 ordeal, the courts ruled in Millstone's favor.

The Millstone case may be an extreme example of the damage an unconfirmed credit report by a private investigating firm may do. But it can happen to you—it happens to thousands of individuals each year, many of whom are unable to go to court to clear their reputation.

It would be difficult, though not impossible, to avoid credit completely. We live in a credit-conscious society: "buy now, pay later. . . . Take out an instant loan. . . . A hundred dollars down and the car is yours—monthly payments are just $150 with four years to repay."

If you're smart, you won't take the bait. But even if you do stay out of debt, you will still be the subject of credit reports! If you rent an apartment, the landlord may first check on your credit worthiness. If you open a checking account or a brokerage account, the bank or broker may check on your financial standing with the local credit bureau. Merchants you're dealing with on a long-term basis want to know your *ability to pay.*

Your Right of Access to Credit Records

There are about 2,000 credit bureaus in the country today. The largest are TRW Credit Data, TransUnion, and Credit Bureau, Inc. These information gatherers carry data on individuals such as:
- Social security number
- Address
- Telephone number
- Full name
- Spouse's name
- Annual income
- Employment
- Credit history
- Existing credit obligations (often on a monthly payment basis)
- Arrest and conviction records
- Bankruptcies
- Tax liens
- Lawsuits
- Bureau subscribers asking for your credit report

Almost anything goes into the credit file and is accessible to practically any paying subscriber. This includes police and the federal government if they have a court order. And, except when the IRS asks for the records, the credit reporter isn't required to notify the customer that his report has been given to a government agency.

Under the Fair Credit Reporting Act, you can demand to know what is in your credit file. If you disagree with any information in the file, you can insist that another investigation be done, and if that doesn't resolve the matter, you can enter your own statement as a permanent part of the credit file.

Robert Ellis Smith, editor of *Privacy Journal*, has had some experience with his credit bureau in Washington, D.C. over this question of access. Smith visited the credit bureau and asked for a copy of his record. He was charged $4 (a copy is free if you have suffered adversely from the file). His report showed the following: present and past addresses, employment, age, estimated monthly income, each department store account (when opened, its terms, and recent balance), a rating index (from 1—"pays on time"—to 9—"bad debt"), checking accounts, bank loans, and whether the checking account balance is "hi," "low," or "med." The report also listed a department store account that he did *not* have. He asked that it be deleted. Later, when he saw his report again, the department store account had been deleted, but a national credit card he had never applied for was listed. So you can see how easy it is for a credit report to contain erroneous information and unsubstantiated claims.

I would strongly recommend that you check with your local credit bureau to see what kind of data they have on you. You may not be allowed to see the file itself—but you are entitled to know the "nature and substance" of the information in your file. The only exception is medical information; that's off limits. Information must be given to you in your own language, not in "computer language."

Unfavorable Credit Data

Generally, a credit bureau must eliminate unfavorable information in your file after seven years. This includes lawsuits, tax liens, arrest records, and unpaid accounts. The seven-year statute of limitations does not apply to the following important categories:

1. Bankruptcies will remain in your file up to 14 years.

2. If your report is used as background for a transaction involving $50,000 or more (including an application for life insurance), unfavorable information may remain in your report after seven years.
3. If the report is used to screen you for employment at a salary of $20,000 or more, unfavorable information may be included beyond seven years. Inflation is likely to increase these figures over time.

Some states have specific laws about credit reporting. For example, California, New Mexico, and Kentucky disallow reporting of arrests and indictments that do not ultimately result in conviction. Virginia and Florida prohibit the reporting of an outstanding debt as unpaid or delinquent if the individual is disputing the debt.

How to Apply for a Confidential Loan

Much of the information in the credit bureau's files comes originally from the individual customer, who provides it to obtain a credit card, a bank loan, insurance, or other consumer service. The key to maintaining financial privacy, then, is to minimize the amount of information you give creditors, whether a bank, insurance company, credit card center, or brokerage house.

How can you get a loan without broadcasting your financial affairs? Let's examine some possibilities.

Collateralized Loans

A banker or general lender will require the most information about your background, the purpose of the loan, and your ability to repay when the loan is unsecured; that is, when you do not contract to give up certain property in the event that you do not repay the loan. You can reduce this invasion of your privacy by putting up collateral for the loan—your automobile, real estate, coins, stocks, bonds, or even furniture.

In the case of a passbook loan, where you place an amount equal to the loan in a savings account at the bank, the bank may not even be interested in the purpose of your loan, although this varies. (Passbook loans are not generally a good idea, however, since you will be paying the bank interest for the privilege of borrowing your own money.)

A collateralized loan will also reduce the interest rate you pay for the loan.

The Provident Loan Society, 346 Park Avenue South, New York, NY 10010, makes collateralized loans without investigation. The limit is $3,000. Acceptable collateral includes coins, jewelry, diamonds, stamps, silverware, and furs. Provident undertakes no investigation of the borrower and the money is loaned confidentially by mail. You send the collateral by registered mail for appraisal, and the loan is sent to you. Surprisingly, the borrower is under no obligation to repay on a monthly basis, and Provident will extend the loan beyond the typical one-year period upon request. But interest is steep: 18 percent a year. The Provident Loan Society is a quasi-philanthropic organization, founded in 1894, and has eleven offices in New York.

If you don't want to put up collateral for a loan, you may want to try unsecured personal executive loans by mail—a very discreet way to borrow money. The following article is taken from a recent edition of the *Washington Post:*

LOANS BY MAIL ARE DEAR, DANGEROUSLY EASY TO GET

By Jane Bryant Quinn

NEW YORK—What's it worth to you to get a fast loan, no collateral, no personal interview, confidentiality guaranteed? How about 14 to 23 percent? That's the going price range for hush-hush loans, made through the mails to people with better-than-average incomes.

If you're a teacher, civil servant, businessman, lawyer, doctor or other professional, you will probably qualify. All you need is a minimum income of $15,000 to $25,000 (depending on the lender), and a passable credit rating.

Some lenders are small, independent operators. Others are subsidiaries of major financial institutions, like Citibank, Bank of America, and the Commercial Credit Corp. They advertise discreetly in professional publications, or through the mails to lists of likely borrowers.

Who would borrow at those high rates, if he or she has enough income to get red-carpet treatment from a conventional lender?

• People who want to free up collateral for other uses. If They've pledged some stock to a bank, for example, they could take one of these loans, repay the bank and get the stock back. That makes it easy to sell the stock or use it as collateral for another loan.

• People who want unsecured loans for longer periods than banks will give. Mail-order loans may be stretched over five years or more, while more conventional lenders may want repayment in three years.

• People who don't want to discuss their personal finances with a bank officer. Confidential loans are handled by mail, with only a routine credit check. You just fill in a financial statement and mail it to the lender. These loans are often granted to people whose financial condition is too overloaded to be acceptable to banks.

• People who want to keep the loan, or the purpose of the loan, a secret. It's a fact that some borrowers use these loans to finance a gambling or woman habit, or make other expenditures they'd rather no one knew about. Confidential loan services don't ask the purpose of the loan. And they are happy to address borrowers at their offices rather than at home.

The loan probably won't even show up on your record at the credit bureau. Many of these lenders don't report to regular credit bureaus. If they do, it's apt to be one in their geographical area, which may be far from where you live.

The existence of the hush-hush loan business is proof that for some there is nothing easier than getting into debt over their heads. Confidential loans permit some people more credit than they can reasonably handle.

The loans are worth more in credit than just the amount of the loan itself. Not only does the borrower get instant money, but whatever collateral he has can be used for additional loans. Since the loan probably will not show up on a credit record, other lenders may not realize that a borrower is overextended.

If you ever get to the point where you have to seek a hush-hush loan, take it as a warning sign. You are pushing your income too far.

Columnist Jane Bryant Quinn is unduly harsh in criticizing executive loans by mail. As I have pointed out repeatedly in this book, there are significant reasons for financial privacy other than "a gambling or woman habit," or illegal activity. Obviously, these mail-order loan companies are offering a unique service. You pay a higher interest rate for the privilege of getting a confidential, unsecured loan.

The following firms offer executive loans by mail:

Nationwide Finance Corp.
Suite 927
1660 South Albion Street
Denver, CO 80222
800-525-2131 (toll-free)

Dial Financial Corp.
2007 South Main Street
P.O. Box 2321
Santa Ana, CA 92707
714-556-0810 (call collect)

Beneficial Executive Loan Services
2858 Stevens Creek Boulevard
San Jose, CA 95128
800-538-6811 (toll-free)

Postal Thrift Loans
703 Douglas Street
Sioux City, IA 51102

These finance companies generally charge a flat rate of 18 percent interest, no matter what the size of the loan. Unsecured loans are available up to $15,000 with up to 60 months to repay. Everything is handled confidentially by mail. There are no interviews and no co-signers or witnesses necessary. The loan can be processed in about two weeks. Your income should be around $20,000 to qualify. The purpose of the loan need not be revealed.

Nationwide Financial Corp. has an interesting program that provides even greater financial privacy. It establishes a line of credit that you can take advantage of at any time, whenever you need it. As Nationwide's literature states: "Apply once, then never again. Once approved, you have a personal line of credit to use whenever the need for funds arises. Without having to reapply each time. Use payment orders that look and work just like checks to borrow up to $15,000 . . . on your signature alone . . . anytime, any place. Only you will know you have made a loan. Cost free until used. Lower monthly payments than bank credit cards, most installment loans, and store financing. Available credit renews as you pay back. No obligation to use."

The main advantage is that as time goes along, your financial situation changes, sometimes dramatically, for better or for worse. And yet, under this credit arrangement, you're not required to fill in *new* forms stating your present salary and financial situation. Rather, the loan is based on your salary and financial situation when you originally applied, which could change drastically. A tremendous advantage. Of course, the interest rate isn't really less than with bank credit cards, as the ad implies. It's the same—18 percent.

Overdraft Checking Accounts

Nationwide's instant loan is similar to a bank checking account with overdraft protection.

The overdraft checking account is essentially a line of credit through your regular checking account. (In some cases, the credit line operates through a separate checking account or your credit card.) When you write a check for more than what you have in your account, the bank pays the "overdrawn" check, instead of sending it back, and automatically lends you the money at a stipulated daily interest charge. Interest rates vary, but many banks are now offering overdraft protection at 12 percent interest (others go as high as 18 percent). Lately, banks have become considerably more liberal in their overdraft programs, especially in the major cities. Maximum lines of credit now reach $25,000 in some cities, but most have a limit of $5,000.

Overdraft checking is, in many ways, the "perfect loan," as I call it in my book, *The Insider's Banking & Credit Almanac* (available from Kephart Communications, Inc., 901 N. Washington St., Alexandria, VA 22314, $14.95). Not only is overdraft checking a convenient and extremely flexible way to borrow, but it minimizes public exposure of your financial affairs.

First of all, you apply for the overdraft account only once, at the beginning, and never again—even though your financial situation may change drastically. If you run into financial trouble, the bank will probably not learn about it and you can still use your overdraft account for emergency expenditures. And, if you pay off your overdraft account promptly, the bank is likely to increase your credit limit as time goes along, even without your reapplying.

Second, you need not reveal the purpose of the loan. This is a tremendous advantage. You can use the overdraft privilege to purchase a color TV, finance your new car, pay for your child's education, purchase gold or silver, start up a new business, or even finance a campaign for public office. Your banker will have no idea what the money is being used for, nor will he care, as long as you pay it back. The overdraft check clears just like any other check, as long as you don't exceed your credit limit. Traditional sources of personal loans have always been wary of what the money was to be used for. If the bank didn't think the money would be put to good use or would be used for a "speculative" or "capricious" venture, it would be refused. Not any more.

Third, you can open an overdraft account by mail, in most cases. Simply call up your bank, ask the bank to mail you an application, fill it out and return it, and presto, you have borrowing power without ever having sat down with a loan officer. You haven't even stepped inside the bank. They don't even know what you look like. That's privacy.

Fourth, you can take out a loan at any time, without the bank's permission. With most traditional loans, it's next to impossible to borrow money overnight for an emergency or for a secret reason unless you are willing to pay exorbitant interest rates to a finance company, loan shark, or pawnbroker. Banks do not generally want to rush into anything, especially in an emergency. As the old joke goes, you have to prove to the bank that you don't need a loan before you can get one. Well, that embarrassment is over with overdraft checking.

There are numerous other advantages of this "perfect loan" that are unrelated to the issue of privacy (such as tax deferral and the ability to borrow indefinitely). In sum, overdraft checking is quite flexible and more private than most traditional loans.

Privacy and Your Business

Financial privacy is extremely important in your business affairs. Credit reporting is not limited to consumer or personal situations—they keep records on your business as well. And financing is essential to keep your business going.

The two largest commercial reporting services are Dun and Bradstreet and Equifax Services. Both firms investigate and collect information about business firms from past and present creditors and sell this information to other interested companies and subscribers. These reports list all kinds of data about businesses, including capital, assets, liabilities, current income, financial status, and basic information on major figures in the business.

Commercial reporting companies are not regulated under the Fair Credit Reporting Act, which imposes safeguards on the dissemination of information about individuals. Congress is, however, considering rules that would cover these companies.

Although Dun and Bradstreet investigators supposedly do not gather information on "an individual's personal health, lifestyle, or . . . his personal financial dealings," they do report on criminal convictions of owners or managers, and on impending bankruptcy.

Here's an example of how a false credit report can destroy a man and his business. In the early 1960s, an owner of a conglomerate of companies including clothing stores and supermarkets left the country for a short period. On his return he found that a bankruptcy petition had been filed against one of his companies. He was ready to fight the bankruptcy proceeding, but a major commercial reporting firm had already reported to credit grantors that the owner's company was bankrupt. The report also made derogatory statements about the owner himself. As a result, the company did in fact go under. The owner filed suit against the commercial reporting firm and a New York court ruled in his favor.

Although this was a rare case, it is important that you, as an executive officer in a company, make sure that commercial reports on your company and yourself are accurate and kept current.

9
The Private Company

Although this guidebook is primarily devoted to the privacy of personal valuables and investments, businesses also hold a great deal of wealth, so this chapter will focus on privacy in business. It's impossible to estimate the total amount of wealth controlled by major corporations and independent businesses, but the figure is immense, somewhere in the trillions. If you own a business yourself, what steps can you take to ensure financial privacy? How can you minimize the disclosure of sensitive financial information to government agencies such as the Federal Trade Commission, the Internal Revenue Service, and the Securities and Exchange Commission? What advantages does a private corporation have over a publicly held corporation? Are there any disadvantages to a closely held company? How can your company keep unpatented information and techniques confidential and unavailable to competitors? These are just some of the questions a man of means seeking privacy may wish to have answered.

Your Own Business

We have mentioned throughout this book some of the advantages of starting your own company, including the benefits of what is called, in law, the registered trade name. This is often an *unincorporated* business having a name with no special significance. The fictitious name is designed to preserve your financial privacy. Once you establish this company name, you may make investments, buy and sell property, or do anything you please without revealing your true identity. You must register the company and obtain a taxpayer identification number from the IRS—but you reveal little on the actual application forms.

Unfortunately, your registration is usually public information at the local county or state offices, where solicitors, particularly insurance companies, compile lists of new businesses.

Should You Incorporate?

You may lose some privacy in your financial situation by incorporating. Most states require far more detailed information about you and your company when you incorporate than they do when you form a single proprietorship. They ask for details on the nature of business, names and addresses of offices and directors, and reports on annual meetings and accounting procedures.

Ted Nicholas comments:

> Corporations are governed by state laws and there are differences from one state to another, although there are remarkable similarities too. A prevalent similarity is the requirement for filing annual reports. A corporation whose stock is traded on the market must invariably report all its financial details, including the compensation of its officers. This is, in fact, a requirement of the Securities and Exchange Commission of the federal government. But even a close corporation, one whose stock is closely held by one or a few persons and not publicly offered for sale, must file an annual report to the state in which it is chartered. The report usually has to contain the names and addresses of directors and officers, along with other information, and generally takes only a few minutes to complete. It is available for any legitimate examination by outsiders. This makes semipublic the kind of confidential information you might prefer to keep confidential, even at the cost of foregoing substantial benefits from incorporation.

In his bestselling book, *How to Form Your Own Corporation for under $50*, Nicholas says that since Delaware does not require a corporation to reveal who its stockholders are, owners of a Delaware corporation can remain anonymous. Forming a Delaware corporation is fairly simple, especially if you use the services of Nicholas' Company Corporation. In fact, over one-third of all new corporations in the United States are formed in Delaware because of the relative ease of establishing them.

It's also conceivable to establish a corporation using your attorney or accountant as director and officers of the company. If the state does not require the names of the shareholders, your financial privacy is practically assured.

Another possibility for enhancing corporate privacy is to form a company or corporation in a foreign country, especially in such tax havens as the Bahamas, Panama, the Cayman Islands, the Channel Islands, or Liechtenstein. All of these have been covered in the previous chapter on tax havens. While details of business transactions remain private, disadvantages include the travel distance, plus the fact that you are required to report the existence of a foreign corporation to the U.S. Treasury Department.

Public vs. Private Corporations

Not all corporations are created equal from a privacy point of view. New companies eventually face the major decision whether to go public—to enter the equity jungle, to issue public securities in order to raise much-needed capital for expansion.

In the 1960s, going public seemed to be the wave of the future, especially for high-growth industries. It was a way to guarantee rapid expansion of plant and market; and for the owners of many closely held corporations, it was a way to avoid heavy inheritance taxes.

But going public also meant a loss of privacy. It meant revealing much privileged information to the SEC, as well as answering to public stockholders. As a recent article in *Dun's Review* stated, "Traditionally close-mouthed corporations found themselves uncomfortably conforming to something called full and complete disclosure. For the first time, they were obliged to reveal their innermost financial secrets on 10K forms, publish quarterly as well as annual reports, and solicit proxies for annual stockholders' meetings that once took place in a small room but now required the grand ballroom of the biggest hotel in town." And stocks no longer were in a bull market in the 1970s, so that going public was no longer the way to raise capital. In fact, it made the company vulnerable to a sudden takeover. The president of one company that recently went public complained: "By the time you get finished, you might as well let your competitors walk through your plant."

Consequently, many strong independent corporations have remained private, including such large companies as Continental Grain, Koch Industries, Reader's Digest, Mars,

Summa Corporation, Hallmark Cards and Allen-Bradley. Taken together, they comprise a $300 billion industry.

Stock in private companies cannot be traded publicly. Therefore the private company doesn't have to worry about many of the problems facing public corporations. The SEC seldom gets involved. "We don't have the SEC on our backs," says one company president. Private directors can chart the company's long-term destiny themselves or can make quick decisions by calling a meeting of individual stockholders. While a public company thinks in terms of the short-term and quarterly reports (which have a grave bearing on stock prices), private companies can take a long-term approach to business planning. Emphasis is on cash flow, not artificial short-term profits. This is possible because shares of a private corporation "are closely controlled by a small coterie of founders, heirs, officers, and insiders and are virtually unattainable by the investing public," says *Dun's Review*.

Disadvantages of Private Companies

As usual, there are drawbacks. Although loans from banks and other financial institutions are not necessarily more difficult for private companies, family members often must give their personal guarantees to secure a company note. Moreover, closely held corporations bear the brunt of special scrutiny by the IRS, and are audited more often than public companies. This is because private concerns keep financial information as confidential as possible, including executive salaries and fringe benefits. One way or another, the IRS wants to get that information.

The Freedom of Information Act

In 1966, Congress passed the Freedom of Information Act in an effort to open the records of federal government agencies to public inspection. The Act has since been amended. The Privacy Act of 1974 required an inventory of all federal agency files. You can understand the need for an open-door policy with the American public. Files seem to be kept on everyone and everything. There are even files on people who have requested information or their own file under the Freedom of Information Act!

Naturally, there are significant exceptions to this freedom of information—and many agencies, particularly the CIA,

FBI, and Treasury Department, regularly use these exceptions to block investigations by citizens. These exceptions pertain to national defense and foreign policy, law enforcement, internal agency deliberations, trade secrets, and information specifically regarded as confidential.

Trade secrets are becoming a major issue. Businesses of all sizes are required to file numerous details about their operations, and they have a reasonable expectation that such information will be kept confidential—away from the eyes of competitors.

Major corporations file, on average, 177 different reports containing "private data" with the federal government annually. Once these reports are sent in, individuals may be able to inspect them under the Freedom of Information Act. More than 100 cases are pending in court over whether the FOIA permits this kind of disclosure. In short, the FOIA has been turned upside down. From being a citizens' tool for keeping track of the government, it has become a pipeline of private data on businesses. A closely held company can keep this intrusion to a minimum but cannot escape it altogether.

Corporate Spying

Millions of dollars are spent each year protecting secret corporate information—whether it's a new cookie recipe, computer software programs, chemical analyses, or unpatented inventions. The Patent Office has rigid standards on patent applications, so that many valuable trade secrets —formulas, inventions and technical devices—cannot be patented. Consequently, corporations must continually be on their guard against illegal entry, counterintelligence operations, or new employees working as spies for the competition.

One of the major concerns of a small company is information stored on computers—financial statements, lists of clients and contacts, mailing lists, and so on. It would pay to ask your computer company specifically about unwarranted intrusion into sensitive information stored on the computer. New, "unbreakable" codes are being developed right now that could safeguard these corporate secrets, but present technology is such that decoding is still cumbersome and time consuming.

Consider the confidential nature of correspondence, corporate records, and financial instruments held at the office. Are they strictly controlled and secure when officers have left the building at night? Have you established a burglar alarm system or hired a night watchman to protect your business when you're gone? These are concerns you should be aware of in any business—where a great deal of your wealth may be at stake.

Settle Financial Disputes Privately

Disputes are common between authors and publishers, workers and employees, customers and brokers, husbands and wives, and among heirs. How can you settle such disputes without letting the whole affair become a public circus?

One of the ways that is growing in popularity is *arbitration.* Private arbitration has an ancient history and is used frequently in business and financial disputes. There is no public record of the arguments and differences, even though courts will uphold, in nearly all cases, the final decision of a private arbitrator. This privacy can be extremely valuable to a business that wants to protect information, or to a family that does not wish to bring out its differences in public or in the daily newspapers.

Adam Starchild has written in *Inflation Survival Letter:*

> Because the circus atmosphere is eliminated, and there is no jury for lawyers to stand up and grandstand to, a fair decision can usually be reached much more easily. Sitting around a table, submitting the relevant facts is much more peaceful. And arbitration can be handled much faster than a court case. The stalling and preliminary maneuvers are eliminated—so losses need not mount up for years while a dispute is settled. The costs are generally much lower than in a court proceeding. And the evidence need not be limited by the formal rules of the court—which can be very valuable in getting all the facts into the issue, without restrictions which can sometimes cause an injustice in the courts.

The American Arbitration Association (AAA) is the oldest and largest private arbitrator in the United States. Disputes recently resolved by the AAA fall into the following categories: 14,000 involved automobile accidents; 13,000, labor-management disputes; and 4,000, contract disputes between businessmen. Other cases involved consumer complaints, medical malpractice claims, and family disagreements.

Another advantage of private arbitration is that the

parties can select an arbitrator who is an expert in the disputed area. The AAA provides a list of arbitrators from which the parties select suitable candidates. You may appear without a lawyer, which makes arbitration more affordable for small corporations.

For settling the arbitration, which is binding on the parties, the AAA charges an administrative fee of 3 percent or less, depending on the amount of the claim. No stenographic records are kept of the proceedings unless the parties request a transcript. Usually the arbitrator renders a signed, written decision within 30 days. The decision is final and not subject to appeal.

In sum, you may wish to add to the contracts you sign with business partners: "It is agreed that any disputes arising under this agreement will be submitted to the American Arbitration Association, whose resolution of the dispute will be final and binding on both parties. Fees for such arbitration will be determined by the arbitrator and paid by the party whose interests are decided against."

10
Safekeeping Your Valuables

The private investor knows that the best way to preserve his financial anonymity is to have real wealth in his possession. Owning a bank account or brokerage account, or a tract of real estate, invariably compromises financial secrecy to some degree, while buying and selling anonymously and storing wealth in hidden caches provides absolute security, the ultimate in financial privacy. Highly recommended "bearer" goods include gold and silver coins, stamps, diamonds and other gems, foreign currency, certain collectibles, bearer stocks and bonds, and cash.

Pitfalls to Avoid

Storing these anonymous instruments of wealth in large quantities is not always easy. Storage costs can be expensive, even if you do the storage yourself. You may have to go to some length to keep relatives, friends and neighbors, and government agents from knowing about these assets. You must be willing to remain discreet and quiet about your hidden wealth at social gatherings. It does no good to hide your money if you like to brag about the rare gold coins stored in the safe in your bedroom. Gossip gets around quickly.

The IRS doesn't take kindly to large amounts of cash and bearer instruments. It always suspects the worst—that you failed to report the cash as income. If you hold cash, be prepared to prove its origin. This is especially pertinent if the state tax authorities find cash in your safe-deposit box when they inventory the box upon death. The IRS simply assumes that cash is unreported income unless your heirs can prove otherwise.

Moreover, the possibility of theft is a fact of life. You should go over the basic steps for maintaining a low profile and secure your valuables properly. As I have stated throughout this book, the most important thing to keep in mind is to *maintain a low profile*. You may find that social prestige is something you dearly desire, but remember, you may be sacrificing privacy as a result. You may love to drive around in a big, expensive car (Cadillac, Continental, Mercedes Benz, Rolls-Royce), but it automatically marks you as a person of wealth and, consequently, a potential target for theft or worse. Recently, an Italian millionaire paid a king's ranson for the return of his kidnapped daughter. Unfortunately, she never made it back alive. The italian millionaire belatedly recognized that one of the primary reasons the kidnapping took place was that he had recently acquired a Rolls-Royce. "I wish I had never bought that Rolls," he confessed. "Maybe my daughter would be alive today." The climate for kidnapping is not as ripe here as it is in Italy, but that could change.

The same principle applies to the home you live in. In one large suburban area, burglars drove through upper-middle-class neighborhoods just before three-day weekends, taking down the addresses of homes with expensive travel vehicles in the driveway. The next night they burglarized houses where the campers no longer were parked.

Maintaining a low profile can even have tax advantages. Two millionaires were partners in a commodity investment firm in Chicago. One lived in a huge estate on the South Shore, drove a Rolls-Royce and had a summer cottage in California. He was audited every year. The other millionaire lived in a nice middle-class neighborhood, drove a mid-sized Chevrolet, and put his money in "out-of-the-way" investments. He has yet to be audited.

Perhaps it would pay, at least from a privacy point of view, to live less extravagantly, to drive less expensive cars, and to live in a less luxurious home. You could buy a home in a nice, but not ostentatious, neighborhood, a home with a modest *external* appearance whose interior contains the most expensive, refined merchandise you wish. A late-model Chevrolet will raise no eyebrows, but it could be loaded with heavy-duty suspension, a four-speaker AM/FM radio/cassette tape deck, air conditioning, and other gadgets and luxuries.

There's one final matter of grave importance: while your "bearer" assets have the advantage of complete privacy, that same characteristic makes them vulnerable to professional thieves. Burglars always prize the vault filled with bullion gold and silver coins, which have a ready *full value* market, just like cash. Jewelry, though somewhat unique, can also be sold for good value to fences. The "Silver Gang" took $5 million worth of silver and jewelry from upper-middle-class homes in the Washington, D.C. area and nothing else. Why? Because silver and jewels have no serial numbers and are hard to trace. So, in a word, you must be more than discreet in maintaining the secrecy of your assets, and you must be creative in deciding where and how to hide your wealth.

The most important question: Where are the best places to hide your physical assets? Let's examine several alternatives.

Safe-Deposit Box

Perhaps the most common means of hiding wealth is the safe-deposit box at your local bank or savings and loan institution.

Is your safe-deposit box really safe? Safe-deposit boxes in banks or savings and loan associations cost very little—only $5 to $75 a year depending on size. Some banks even offer "free" safe-deposit boxes for their top customers who keep savings accounts of, say, $2,000 or more. And rentals are tax deductible if stocks, bonds, or other investment materials are kept there.

I would not recommend that you take the deduction on your federal income tax for a safe-deposit box for one simple reason: This small item may run up a red flag, exposing your entire return to an audit. According to an IRS auditor, a deduction for rental of a safe-deposit box can lead to an audit if your return does not also show dividend and interest income, or capital gain or loss transactions. Taxpayers can deduct the cost of the box rental only if they use the box to store stocks, bonds, or other investments. If you held stocks or bonds in the box, it might mean you earned interest or dividends that year. Thus, the IRS may ask you to prove where the contents of the box came from. The minuscule rental deduction doesn't seem worth the potential fishing expedition on your tax return.

Privacy

But your safe-deposit box may be neither safe nor private. Most banks now require identification when opening an account, and will not *knowingly* permit you to open a box under an assumed name (though "professional" or corporate names are acceptable). Still, some people insist on trying to use an alias in opening a safe-deposit box. This can cause real trouble. Not trusting banks, a man once took out a box using a phony name and deposited a large amount of cash. When he died, his widow came to the bank and produced the key. Yet she was unable to obtain the money because she could not produce two witnesses to testify that her late husband regularly called himself by the alias. The money eventually went to the state. The Continental Bank of Chicago recently began taking photos of every entrant in an effort to eliminate unauthorized entry. These actions may help reduce the chances of theft or fraud, but only at the expense of individual privacy.

Bank Liability and Insurance

Banks do not generally assume full responsibility for articles and valuables left in safe-deposit boxes. Chances are that your box is not fully covered for loss due to theft, fire, earthquake, or other natural disaster. Thefts are rare, but not unheard of, as recently publicized cases in France and elsewhere have testified. Bank liability for thefts is still an unsettled legal question—most banks argue that their liability, like that of landlords, is limited only to the "exercise of ordinary care" or, at most, to some multiple of the annual rental fee, usually 300 to 1,000 times the rental. Check the fine print when you sign the contract. A California court recently ruled that banks there act as warehouses and are fully liable for box contents. But California is an exception to the rule.

You can insure the contents of your safe-deposit box through your homeowner's insurance policy. Aetna Life and Casualty Company charges 50 cents per $1,000 of protection, which applies to all valuables *except* cash (it does cover coin collections). This is by far the cheapest price we have seen on the market. You must keep an accurate inventory of the contents separate from the box.

By the way, safe-deposit boxes held by savings and loan associations may be safer than those in commercial banks.

Savings and loans keep little cash in their vaults, presenting less of an attraction to bank robbers.

What if the bank fails? During the 1933 bank holiday, customers still had access to their safe-deposit boxes, though office hours and other banking transactions were severely limited. Fortunately, banks do not legally own the contents of a box. Theoretically, then, you should have legal access to your box even during times of financial crisis or bankruptcy. But, remember, the bank *controls* access to the box by the hours it sets and its safe-deposit policies. Who knows when a bank may choose to close its doors to "protect the public" during an economic crisis.

Also, as David Krotz, author of *How to Hide Almost Anything,* suggests: "As part of a pattern of total economic collapse, banks would be the first target of uncontrollable pillage. Or you could find yourself accompanied to your box by a federal agent bent on taxation or confiscation. It should also be pointed out that as the economy worsens and random crime increases, so also will the organized criminal become more ambitious. Safe-deposit boxes offer a plum at least as attractive as the main vault itself."

Franz Pick has warned of the inherent defects of a safe-deposit box: "Experience teaches that bank vaults are not accessible to owners of safe-deposit boxes from Friday at 3 P.M. to Monday at 9 A.M. Dramatic monetary changes usually take place during this period. On one 'historic' Monday morning it could happen that seals will be placed on boxes and access granted only after government agents have verified their contents."

Problems at Time of Death

There are no strict rules governing safe-deposit boxes at the time of death. Each state has different laws on the subject. Many banks will simply seal the box upon notification of a death (they check the obituaries daily), and wait for the court or probate officials before the box is opened. Over half the states require an examination by the state tax authorities. Occasionally, joint renters have obtained entrance before the box is sealed, but this sometimes has unfortunate repercussions. Some contracts restrict entrance if one of the parties dies. Others require you to sign an agreement each time you enter the box that no joint owner has passed on. In addition, tax auditors routinely check to see whether an entrance after death has occurred.

The laws also vary on when relatives, attorneys, or executors can obtain access after death. Some states permit immediate access while others may require up to three weeks. Maine is perhaps the best state in terms of privacy: for a joint box only, the survivor has complete and immediate control, and contents are not subject to a state tax audit. However, since most states don't allow the immediate opening of a box, wills, cemetery deeds, or burial instructions should be left at home or with your lawyer, executor, or accountant. One person made the mistake of placing his will, burial instructions, cemetery deed, and life insurance in his safe-deposit box. After his death, it took several weeks before his family gained access to the box with a court order. Meanwhile, his widow buried him in a different spot than he intended and had difficulty obtaining cash to carry her over until the insurance policy was found.

There are two ways to avoid the problem of a sealed box upon death. One is to open a safe-deposit box in the name of a trust. The trust entity lives on after your death, so the box need not be sealed. Moreover, if the trust's income is less than $600 a year, no tax return need be filed. A corporation offers similar benefits.

There's an important drawback to a safe-deposit box, particularly with U.S. banks. As a result of a recent court decision, the IRS has the legal right to open your safe-deposit box at any time, before or after death. The U.S. Court of Appeals in New York ruled that the IRS can break open a box to look for valuables without giving the box holder the right to object. Citibank, the bank involved, says it will not appeal the decision. (Source: *New York Times*, March 29, 1977.)

Private Vaults

With so many disadvantages to a U.S. bank safe-deposit box, let's consider the most useful alternatives: non-bank private vaults, home-storage containers and safes, and foreign safe-deposit boxes.

Non-bank private vault companies exist in many cities across the United States. The Safe Deposit Company of New York is the oldest such company in America, and has never been compromised, according to a spokesman. Individual vaults, which cost $9 a year and up, are insured only against negligence, however. No joint boxes are permitted. Safe-deposit companies can be found in your own area in the Yellow Pages. Here are the addresses of a few such private deposit companies:

Safe Deposit Co. of
  New York
120 Broadway
New York, NY 10005

Day and Night Safe Deposit
  Vaults
507 Third Avenue
Seattle, WA 98104

Standard Safe Deposit Co.
25 Broad Street
New York, NY 10004

Wacker Drive Safe Deposit Co.
20 N. Wacker Drive
Chicago, IL 60606

Missouri Safe Deposit Co.
920 Walnut Street
Kansas City, MO 64106

Hawaiian Depository
  Company
2051 Young Street
Honolulu, HI 96826

Causey's Safe Rentals, Inc.
1806 Layton Avenue
Fort Worth, TX 76117

Deak & Co. Washington (1800 K Street, NW, Washington, DC 20006), offers a private, non-bank safekeeping depository for silver and gold customers. Coins and bullion can be stored with Brooks Armored Car Courier and Security Storage Company of Wilmington, Delaware. Brooks is an approved carrier for both the Comex and New York Mercantile exchanges, and a number of Eastern banks use its vaults. It has 25 years experience in the armored car service. Brooks' vaults are in no way connected or regulated by the banking system. Annual fees include storage and insurance.

Day and Night Safe Deposit Vaults describes its facilities as follows:

Our company was established in 1910 to serve as a safe place for people to store their valuables. This vault is a steel-reinforced concrete vault with a complete electronic alarm system, thus making it both fire and burglar proof. An added protection for this vault is its visibility from the street. We have been in business since 1910, providing protection to our customers without a break-in or fire loss. Of prime importance to many of our customers is the fact that this vault is completely independent of any bank. When banks were closed for President Roosevelt's "bank holiday" this vault was open as usual. This is one of the few vaults with booths inside the vault where the customers can have privacy without leaving the vault. Annual rental rates vary from $7 to $100 per year with various sizes and rates in between.

Other private vaults have not been as fortunate as Day
and Night Safe Deposit. Swiss Vaults, a private storage
company in Santa Ana, California, was robbed of about
$1.1 million of gold, silver, and currency on July 10, 1977.
The thieves apparently took nearly all valuables from the
vaults, including 100 safe deposit boxes, leaving only a
collection of stamps and numismatic coins. Insurance
covered only $1 million of the loss, however, leaving
Swiss Vaults with some liability. In addition, all cash on
deposit was uninsurable and not recoverable. Most depositors, though not all, had insurance on their coins and
bars.

This sad event points up one of the main disadvantages
of the private companies—many of them simply do not
have the security facilities of a bank. The advantage, on
the other hand, is that they are not required to seal your
box and notify tax authorities at the time of your death, a
requirement currently imposed on virtually all banks. The
tax authorities could, of course, force them to do so some-
time in the future, but so far it hasn't happened.

Foreign Safe Deposit Boxes

Consider opening up several safe-deposit boxes in foreign
lands. As we pointed out earlier, you don't have to report
the existence of a safe-deposit box abroad to the Treasury
Department, at least at this time. Boxes are available at
banks in Mexico, the Bahamas, Bermuda, Canada, and
other countries close to the U.S. border. If you travel frequently to Europe or some other part of the world, you
might consider stashing away some funds, commodities, or
bearer bonds in those locations as well. You may never
know when you may all of a sudden need to travel abroad,
and your foreign safe-deposit box may offer considerable
peace of mind and financial security. Be sure, of course, to
rely on large banks with secure vaults.

On the whole, I believe that your assets should be stored
in several locations—in a bank safe-deposit box, a private
vault, a Swiss bank, and at home. However, under no
circumstances should you hide large sums of cash in a
bank or a private company vault, since cash isn't insurable.

For businesses, one of the more interesting private vault
companies is Bekins Archival Service, 619 W. 51st Street,
New York, NY 10019. Bekins offers secret storage vaults for
filmed and taped records and other valuable commercial
articles. These vaults, which are located "somewhere" in

Los Angeles, New York, San Francisco, Oakland, and San Diego, are "impervious to the prying eyes of the IRS, the CIA, and spies of competitors," according to manager Art Lanman.

Another storage company catering to commercial clients is Underground Vaults and Storage, Inc., in Hutchinson, Kansas. About 15,000 firms and individuals have records and other material stored 650 feet below the ground in an old salt mine "somewhere." The company guarantees the confidentiality of the material stored in the mine. The mine is sold enough, and deep enough, to withstand an atomic attack.

Home Storage Containers and Safes

Valuables and documents can safely be stored at home in secret safes, buried containers, and hidden caches. Several articles in *Inflation Survival Letter* describe the latest information on this important topic. The first is "Alarms and Security Devices," by Roy Johnson. The second is "Ten Best Ways to Hide You Valuables," by David Krotz, author of the book, *How to Hide Almost Anything.*

ALARMS AND SECURITY DEVICES

By Roy Johnson

Theives do not select victims at random. Often they precisely identify what they are after and perhaps have already presold it. The primary source of information for the criminal is through associates who are in a position to observe assets and to evaluate the difficulty of getting to them: meter readers, mailmen, garagemen, bank employees, envious or disgruntled employees, and employees who pick up extra cash by tipping off full-time criminal associates. Probably the single most effective informant is the domestic employee; these people are poorly paid, exposed to expensive tastes they cannot hope to satisy, are usually held in low esteem, and usually live in social conditions that expose them to criminal exploitation, intimidation, extortion, and threats. Domestics are usually treated, at a superficial level, as if they were members of the family or firm and are privileged to your most intimate affairs. It is best not to discuss security plans in the company of the maid or gardener.

If everything you do reflects expensive tastes and a large cash flow—you are a target. Your mail, your garbage, and your habits tell much about you. Mail that reveals your assets should be sent to a post office box or to your office. Your garbage should not include wrappings from expensive purchases.

Deterrents to Crime

We enjoy using, displaying, and playing with our property. Works of art, jewels, coin collections, guns, and tools are not as much fun to own if you cannot readily inspect them and show them off. But this desire is not without drawbacks. The problem is that your assets are almost as readily available to a thief as they are to you.

The first step in solving this problem is to make your home unattractive to the thief. This means, from the outside, bright lights, fences or walls difficult to scale, lack of cover and hiding places from which to examine your home or to cover the actual break-in, lights and music from inside which indicate that you are home (perhaps controlled by a timer), the presence of formidable gates or doors, windows protected by burglar bars, and outside evidence of alarm systems. All are helpful in encrouraging a thief to look elsewhere for "easier pickings."

Inside your home simply storing personal valuables out of sight is a great deterrent. The conventional safe or storage vault is of questionable value because it is so very obvious. Most safes and vaults are light enough simply to roll on their casters to a waiting vehicle with the aid of a hoist. The conventional safe is also constructed of sheet steel with cement between the layers to add weight and is easily "peeled." If you have a conventional safe, it should be installed integrally into the foundation of the house, encased in massive concrete or camouflaged.

My personal preference is for completely hidden storage canisters, vaults, or chests buried in basement floors, built into walls or buried in the ground if long-term storage is desired. Such storage containers, when properly designed, are absolutely impervious to deterioration for more than a lifetime. If you do not own your home or if you live in a trailer home, put your valuables in a box so massive as to pre-clude movement without a forklift or even a crane. I recommend a large steel security vault constructed with hidden locks and hinges so you cannot get at them with bolt cutters or torches. No handles should be present to facilitate carrying and the fit of the lid should be so precise as to admit no prybar or hydraulic jack. If a vault is made of stainless steel, (which is expensive), it is impossible to cut with an ordinary torch. If the storage vault is filled with possessions and perhaps a ton of sand, brick or lead shot, it is nearly impossible to move.

Since I could not locate a commercial storage canister or vault that satisfied my personal requirements, I designed a permanent storage canister and a storage vault (which can be buried) and had them fabricated for several clients. Should you have a need for such storage containers, I have prepared a booklet, *Security and Equipment Storage Containers: Design, Construction, and Concealment,* which contains complete design and manufacturing specifications and instructions for concealing such containers to preclude detection with the most sophisticated metal-locating equipment. I will send you a copy of the booklet for $5 and you can have similar containers built locally—or if you prefer, I will have one constructed and shipped to you. Write Star Route 1-A, Box 32-A, Dripping Springs, TX 78620.

Detection

The wide variety of sensors and the flexibility of master control units make it possible to design a system capable of providing many levels of detection. One class of sensors detects the presence of an intruder near your property, another warns you of an actual break-in and entry into your home, another detects the presence of an intruder who has actually gained access and is inside your home, and another detects any tampering with a specific object within your property. These different classes of sensors can be interconnected in many ways or may be completely independent. Many of them are so powerful that they can detect the slightest movement or sound.

In addition, sensors are available to monitor many different situations such as smoke, gas, moisture, temperature, radiation and general industrial processes. If you cannot evaluate your alarm system requirements and install a system personally, you must deal with an "outsider." You will discover in seeking professional help that many of the better known security service organizations will not sell equipment for someone else to install; some security companies do not service private homes; many companies offer only a package deal—equipment, installation, and a maintenance contract. If you are persistent and reasonable, you may convince a company to make a home installation. The cost of a security system can range from $50 to several thousand. A minimum for a commercial installation would be from $500 to $1,000. The following selection criteria should help you evaluate professional help:

1. Deal only with reputable companies whose employees are bonded and whose equipment and work are guaranteed.

2. All equipment should be Underwriter Approved or Factory Mutual Approved.

3. Systems should operate on household current and have an independent power source (batteries).

4. Insist on system wiring diagrams, manufacturers specifications, and all operating-instruction booklets.

5. All wiring should conform to the National Electrical Code and local codes.

6. The system should be compatible with other UL approved systems.

7. Fire security must have multiple sensors.

8. All systems should be inaccessible to tampering and have antitampering circuitry.

9. Insist on company references.

10. Check with police or the Better Business Bureau before contracting security services.

11. There should be a test of the system and an alarm in case of system malfunction.

12. If a local license is required for alarm-system installation companies, ask to see it.

For additional information, I recommend you write the following companies requesting catalogs and addresses of local dealers:

Advanced Industrial
  Security
Division of ATO
2045 Peachtree Road
Atlanta, GA 30309
(Individual security
  systems)

Security Control Research, Inc.
Box 3660
Reading, PA 19605

Bullet Proof Equipment Co.
48 Cadman Plaza West
Brooklyn, NY 11201
(Security gates, doors, windows, etc.)

Pinkerton Electronic
  Security Co.
61 Sutton Road
Webster, MA 01570
(Security equipment)

Law Enforcement Associates, Inc.
86 Holmes Street
Belleville, NJ 07109
(Security systems and devices)

Simple Security Systems, Inc.
9 Frost Street
Collinsville, CT 06022
(Changeable pushbutton locks)

Impossible Electronic Technology, Inc.
121 Pennsylvania Avenue
Wayne, PA 19087
(Closed-circuit TV)

Simple Time Recorder Co.
35 S. Lincoln Court
Gardner, MA 01440
(Identification-badge entry locks and other equipment)

Law Enforcement Equipment, Criminal Research Products, Inc.
CRP Building, Hector Street
Conshohocken, PA 19428
(Security products)

Steelcraft Folding Gate Co.
44 Meserole
Brooklyn, NY 11206
(Security-controlled gates, doors, etc.)

Should you need to consider watchmen or security patrols, contact:

Burns International Security Services
320 Old Briarcliff Road
Briarcliff Manor, NY 10510

Pinkerton's Inc.
100 Church Street
New York, NY 10007

Holmes Protective Services, Inc.
370 7th Avenue
New York, NY 10001

In general, I recommend secret, invisible vaults rather than open safes. Thieves cannot tamper with that which they cannot see, and to search for hidden vaults takes time, a commodity most thieves value highly. Some experts have suggested an inexpensive decoy safe to keep small amounts of cash—in hopes of convincing a thief that there is no other storage vault.

A firm that specializes in concealed secret compartments is Survival Homes, 903 State Street, Hood River, OR 97031.

Survial Homes offers several books that feature detailed discussions of safes, concealed compartments and secret storage areas in your home. Write for a free brochure outlining their services.

TEN BEST WAYS TO HIDE YOUR VALUABLES
By David Krotz

A traditional approach to safeguarding wealth is the safe in the home. Certainly it is fine for securing documents from accidental fire, but safes can be cracked. Unless, that is, your safe is hidden. But hiding it behind a picture or a trapdoor under a rug wouldn't be worth the trouble. What you need is a secret compartment that will defy detection. I have constructed many such "caches" and can offer you some specific ideas.

Baseboards

One of the easiest-to-construct secret compartments is one behind a baseboard. This is the strip of wood, from four to 10 inches high, that runs along all of the walls next to the floor. It serves to cover the crack between the two perpendicular surfaces and is common to all houses and all rooms, including the closest. It is so ordinary that no one gives it a second glance and is a perfect place to hide valuables of modest size such as gold coins.

Choose a short section of baseboard (two to five feet long) which comes to an end at a corner or against a door jamb. Carefully pry it away from the wall with a crowbar or other prying tool, being careful not to damage the wall itself. If damage does result, you will simply have to repair it with spackling, wood putty, or paint. You might also consider putting in a completely new baseboard.

Once the designated section is removed, hollow out a hole in the wall behind it, the location for your items of value. One way to replace the baseboard is to shove its protruding nails back into their old holes. A few taps of the hammer will erase all cracks. But I prefer to mount a series of magnetic or friction snap cabinet fasteners to secure it to the wall. This facilitates access. In building secret compartments, it is always a good idea to use false nails (truncated nails pounded into the wood) to make the structure appear permanently affixed.

Walls

Hidden space is within every wall of every room in your house or apartment because walls are hollow. The ideal location for hiding valuables is not behind hanging items such as pictures but behind fixed, solid items. Most houses have secondary attachments such as coat racks, bulleting boards, spice racks or those boards along closet walls supporting the clothes hanging pole.

As discussed above, the first step is to remove the attachment from the wall. Next, hollow out a secret-compartment, which may require drilling and chiseling of plaster or cutting wood paneling, but the object is the same with any wall, to open a hole between the vertical wall studs. Once this is accomplished, you have the choice of hanging a sack containing your valuables down inside the wall or boxing it in with a lower shelf across the bottom of the hole. Finally, you must camouflage your handiwork. If you are dealing with something light like a bulletin board, cabinet fastener snaps will serve as connectors to the wall. But consider using the more sophisticated invisible hinge. These permit the "door" to swing open to reveal the compartment. Soss hinges are available at large hardware outlets in a variety of sizes, as are some lesser known brands of invisible hinges.

Paneling

Wall paneling offers another method of opening large areas of dead space between wall studs. Your best choice is not the four-by-eight sheets of cheap half-inch plywood, but actual boards nailed to the wall one by one. Very attractive, these have junction cracks between them, the inconspicuous being found with tongue and groove boards. Given an entire wall or room paneled in such fashion, excellent security can be obtained by making one or more of those individual boards movable. This can be accomplished in several ways. Choose an area behind furniture or in a corner out of normal traffic. You can have the "door" simply snap into place with cabinet fasteners. Or spring hinges could be attached to the back side so the panel holds itself tightly closed except when pushed or pulled open. Invisible hinges can be used in such a construct as well.

There is no reason why your access door can't consist of several panels (boards) connected together. One way to do this is to frame in a false corner protruding from a normal room corner. These are very common in apartments, of course, being support pillars or a route for plumbing. You can close in your false corner with paneling, making one side swing open as a door. Using the paneling approach, you could also make an entire false closet out ot sweet-smelling cedar boards, concealing a foot or more of space. Or, should you have inset wall space in one of your rooms, you could make it disapper behind a new wall of paneling. You might even apply this technique to hide a closet or a room.

Mirrors

A simple secret compartment offering little depth but a large area of space can be contructed right behind a full length mirror in your bedroom or in the closet door. Mirror tabs are small "L" shaped connectors that screw in at intervals around such a mirror to hold it in place. If you hollow out secret space behind the mirror, then mount it, all that is required to gain access to your valuables is to remove the top tabs and slide the mirror upward.

Beams

Ceiling and wall beams are very popular architectural features in homes these days. Besides those that are solid and functional, there are also false beams made from a "U" shape of boards, and manufacturers are even offering psuedo-beams made out of foam, which have the appearance of old hand-hewn wood. If you have beams or want to add them, they offer considerable secret storage area. All that is required is to make one of the beams movable with an opening hollowed out of its top or back side.

The methods discussed previously for "snapping" the movable portion shut can be adapted to this sort of secret compartment, but another method that can be used with a variety of plans is the large magnet. For small compartments you can employ a series of small magnets mounted to a stationary wall and metal plates affixed to the movable portion. But for something as large as a ceiling beam, you should use a large industrial or any surplus magnet and a single metal plate attached to the beam itself. When the movable portion is closed, the magnet attaches itself to the plate and holds the beam in place. When using magnets, the amount of effort required to pull the movable portion open can be adjusted by the size and number of magnets used in series.

Light Switch

Should you live in a rented house or apartment, you may not be able to undertake major construction. Here are some less involved hiding places.

An easy and highly deceptive secret compartment can be constructed behind an electric outlet plate or light switch plate. These are held in place by one or two screws and are easily removed providing fast and simple access.

Make certain the electricity is shut off. Choose an electric outlet behind furniture and remove the plate. Disconnect the electric lines and wrap with electricians's tape. This will free the electrical unit. Remove the plastic face to the plug-in unit and glue it to the wall plate itself. When replaced, all will appear normal. In the wall you will now have a small compartment suitable for jewelry or precious coins. This secret space can be enlarged by removing the metal electric box. As discussed above, this will provide you with access to the dead space down between the wall studs.

Furniture

Complicated secret compartments built into furniture have for centuries been favorites of those who could afford them. Since this requires uncommon craftsmanship and ingenuity in most cases, consider these simpler approaches. Moldings are similar in application to baseboards along walls. There is no reason why the edge molding of a table or desk can't be made removable. If you are working with an older piece of furniture, you may find it necessary to completely refinish the unit, but it is neither difficult nor too time consuming. As with the baseboards, the idea is to remove a side molding and drill or chisel a hole into the edge of the table or desk. This hold can be as large as a foot across, an inch or two high, and any depth. The attachment methods previously discussed can be used, but magnets and plates can be jarred out of place accidently in such a highly frequented location.

A little more ambition on your part could open a much larger storage area—an entire wood desk top can be made to hinge open. There are usually several inches of dead space between the top and the upper edge of the drawers. If this idea interests you, see the discussion of the nail lock below.

Bookcase

A very common source of easily overlooked hidden space can be found at the base of a bookcase. The lower shelf is usually raised above the floor level several inches and this unused space is enclosed with a base-molding, completely masking the area from sight. One way to gain access is through the molding itself, but a better method is to make the lower shelf movable. Obviously this is easier when constructing new bookshelves. The previously discussed closure methods all work here, or you could even rely on gravity to hold the shelf in place, covered as it will be with books and other objects.

Once the shelf is put in place, an added security may be obtained with a nail lock. It is common for bookshelves to be nailed into place through the vertical sides. Finishing nails, those with small heads, are employed, and are either set into the wood and covered with wood filler or left visible. The latter approach permits a locking device that will hold the movable shelf in place against all lifting pressure. Instead of driving nails into the edges of the board as with the other shelves, drill holes where nails would normally occur and insert the nails by hand. The nails will hold the shelf in place snugly but they can be removed with a magnet, freeing the board for removal.

This technique may be adapted to most secret compartments. Create a male protrusion of wood on the solid side which fits into a hollowed female hold in the back of the movable member. Take a closet support board under the clothes hanging pole, for example. Two nails may be inserted inconspicuously in the top edge of the board to intersect with a male protrusion attached to the wall behind it. This will hold the removable board in place until the nails are removed with a magnet.

Houseplants

Houseplants, when they appear in profusion, offer good possibilities for the concealment of valuables. If you choose one pot out of many plants along a window or wall and build a false bottom into it, the possibility of detection is minimal. The false bottom that is inserted inside the pot will have to have a hole drilled in it with an attached plastic tube to carry water drainage through the secret compartment itself.

If you have any big plants, such as trees, the large dirt bins provide you with a place to bury your treasure right in the house.

Buried Treasure

Probably the oldest hiding technique in history is to bury valuables in the ground. Some pirate treasure is no doubt still undiscovered. As long as you are careful to leave the ground as you found it, it is hard to fault this time-honored hiding place. Obviously an accurate map is a necessity. And you should also allow for accidental death, informing your family so they will be able to find the valuables. Since other people's land, even government land, is subject to building, bulldozing, and highway construction, the wisest approach here is to use your own land, preferably isolated in the country.   *(©1977 by Inflation Survival Letter)*

Final Comments

Once you realize that any structural-seeming object in a house or apartment could conceivably open to reveal hidden space behind it, your own ideas for secret compartments will proliferate. For maximum security, you should do the work yourself and pay close attention to craftsmanship. Cracks that appear around the movable member should be identical to those around similar fixed items. The force needed to pull "door" open should be considerable, to minimize accidental discovery. Fire is another danger worth anticipating. Fireproof metal boxes are highly advisable. My one last cautionary note really shouldn't be necessary. Do not reveal your hiding place to anyone. Your family must be sternly warned not to mention even the existence of such a place. Someday your survival may depend upon it.

Here are the names of two additional hideaway safes which you may wish to investigate:

First, for underground storage, Investment Rarities, One Appletree Square, Mineapolis, MN 55420, offers a free brochure on its "Midnight Gardener Coin Capsules," which are designed to hide gold, silver and other valuables.

The capsules come in three different sizes, costing anywhere from $12.95 to $39.

Second the J. Goodman Co., P.O. Box 88, Livingston, NJ 07039 is selling a "Hideaway" in-floor safe for storing valuables, personal documents, coins, and jewelry. The safe can be installed by anyone in a concrete block or concrete floors. The price is $109.95, which includes shipping.

11
Privacy and
the Taxman

Today, government has access to the most revealing personal records about an individual; yet the individual has no
ability to thwart or even contest such access.... Not to enter
into the relationships that generate individually identifiable
records would subject the vast majority of Americans to
severe economic and social burdens, disrupting the ordinary
course of their lives.

Privacy Protection Study Commission

One of the primary violators of financial privacy has
been the government, as I have shown over and over again
in this volume. My chief concern has been the government's
ability to abuse this power. Government agents profusely
deny that they want to go on "fishing expeditions" or to
attack someone because of his political or economic beliefs.
Yet the potential for abuse exists—and that is a real threat.
We need the proper safeguards to keep government from
using its power recklessly.

When the government went after Jimmy Hoffa, it wasn't
hard to get him on *something*. As Jim Hougan states,
"The slightest deviation in one's testimony before a never-
ending succession of grand juries becomes, in the absence
of governmental good faith, *perjury*. The slightest error in
computing one's income tax becomes *tax evasion*. An off-
hand remark to a friend is interpreted as a *conspiracy to
bribe*. The purchase of tape recorders for the purpose of
recording union meetings is evidence of *wiretapping*."

The Bill of Rights

The Bill of Rights was written two centuries ago to prohibit the government from trampling on the privacy of citizens.
The colonists were painfully aware of unwarranted intrusion
by the British on their lives, their private papers, and their
fortunes, and wanted to stamp out this evil once and for
all. The relevant amendments that concern the issue of
privacy are primarily the First, Fourth, and Fifth Amendments:

First Amendment: "Congress shall make no law . . . abridg-
ing the freedom of speech, or of the press; or the right of
the people peaceably to assemble, and to petition to the
Government for a redress of grievances."

Financial transactions and investments require free correspondence between investors and their brokers and advisors—by mail and telephone, and through financial inter-
mediaries. The First Amendment would seem to be violated
if the government sought to survey and read correspondence
of a financial nature, or restrict the dissemination of financial information or views contrary to government policy. The
SEC has restricted a certain amount of financial advice
through its enforcement of the Investment Advisors Act
of 1934. This act requires investment advisors and financial
newsletters to register with the SEC and to adopt certain
accounting procedures. The SEC also maintains that it has
the right to enter an advisor's or publisher's office without
prior warning and inspect accounts and correspondence
of subscribers and clients. SEC agents have also surveyed
publications of investment advisors for evidence of stock
manipulation and fraudulent stock recommendations. The
SEC insists that advisors warn their clients about an alleged
greater risk in purchasing foreign unregistered stocks. In
short, the SEC imposes limitations on the opinions of the investment advisors.

These questionable activities could become far more extensive in the future. Perhaps the government will deny
you the right to mail instructions to your foreign bank, or
forbid meetings that might be regarded as conspiracies
against the financial interests of the United States.

Fourth Amendment: "The right of the people to be secure
in their persons, houses, papers, and effects, against unreasonable searches and seizures, shall not be violated, and
no warrants shall issue, but upon probable cause, supported

by oath or affirmation, and particularly describing the place to be searched, and the persons or things to be seized."

This is clearly the most important amendment for our purposes. Yet it is amazing how the government has gotten around this specific provision. As the Privacy Protection Study Commission concludes, "No longer do there seem to be any personal documents inaccessible to government because they reveal 'intimate areas of personal affairs.'" The Commission finds this "troubling," to say the least, and offers some new legislation to combat this trend.

Government agents have been knocking at the door of personal financial privacy for years, but the courts have held the key. And consistently, the courts have opened the door to the government—particularly if financial records are held by third parties, such as insurance agents, brokers, banks or other financial institutions.

The upholding of the Bank Secrecy Act by the Supreme Court in *U.S. v. Miller* is a case in point. Clearly, the act violated the Fourth Amendment by permitting the government easy access to microfilmed checking account records, which should have been regarded as the depositor's private property. But the court ruled that the bank, not the customer, owns the checking and savings account records—despite the fact that banks have a long-standing tradition of returning canceled checks to the customer. Only since the Bank Secrecy Act in 1970 have banks been forced to maintain records of checks and deposits. Typically by microfilming.

Fifth Amendment: ". . . nor shall be compelled in any criminal case to be a witness against himself, nor be deprived of life, liberty, or property, without due process of law . . ."

Financial privacy is obviously an issue in the Fifth Amendment. No one should be required to incriminate himself. This is particularly evident in tax matters, but also pertains to cases of alleged fraud, stolen property, and other lawsuits.

The courts have narrowly defined private papers under the Fifth Amendment to include only those papers held by the customer himself, rather than third parties, with some exceptions (e.g., attorneys' records).

Taxpayer's Rights

The seeker of financial privacy will no doubt be tremendously concerned when it comes to the annual filing of his taxes and dealing with the all-powerful IRS.

Almost every conceivable financial transaction today has its own tax consequences. As Supreme Court Justice Potter Stewart has correctly noted, "Virtually all persons or objects in this country may . . . have federal tax problems. Every day the economy generates thousands of sales, loans, gifts, purchases, leases, deposits, mergers, wills, and the like, which suggests the possibility of tax problems for somebody. Our economy is tax relevant in almost every detail."

The point Justice Stewart was making is that because taxation can be the *raison d'etre* of every conceivable transaction today, the IRS can legitimately argue that it has the right to investigate every financial detail of your life. With the IRS bent on such an objective, there need to be heavy constitutional restraints on the powers of the taxing authority.

Unfortunately, the IRS has become a leviathan. An IRS administrative summons, which the agency itself prepares, can be used to reach nearly any conceivable record about an individual. Fortunately, the individual under investigation must now be notified of the summons, theoretically giving him the opportunity to object in court. But in all likelihood, it will do him no good. As the Privacy Commission notes, "To be sure, the individual may go into court, but when he gets there he has nothing to say, because he has no legal interest to defend or to balance against the government's desire for the record."

Without question, federal and state income tax forms are an invasion of privacy. Readers may be shocked to see how the federal government's lust for detailed information about its citizens has grown over the decades. Take a look at the original Form 1040 for 1913. Hardly any personal information was required. The tax rates themselves were startlingly low. The tax rate was only 1 percent on income over $20,000 and that was when the average income was less than $1,000.

Now take a look at the latest 1040 form. It asks such questions as: full name, home address, name of spouse, social security numbers, names and ages of your children (never let a future taxpayer go undetected), occupation, and other personal data (even whether you support the political establishment—the form asks whether you wish to contribute $1 of your tax money to the presidential campaign fund). If you itemize your deductions, which you undoubtedly must if you make any kind of middle-class income, you must also reveal the names of charitable organizations to which you contribute, how much gasoline you use, whether you

TO BE FILLED IN BY COLLECTOR.

Form 1040.

TO BE FILLED IN BY INTERNAL REVENUE BUREAU.

List No. ....

.... District of ....

Date received ....

INCOME TAX.

THE PENALTY
FOR FAILURE TO HAVE THIS RETURN IN
THE HANDS OF THE COLLECTOR OF
INTERNAL REVENUE ON OR BEFORE
MARCH 1 IS $20 TO $1,000.
(SEE INSTRUCTIONS ON PAGE 4.)

File No. ....

Assessment List ....

Page .... Line ....

UNITED STATES INTERNAL REVENUE.

RETURN OF ANNUAL NET INCOME OF INDIVIDUALS.
(As provided by Act of Congress, approved October 3, 1913.)

RETURN OF NET INCOME RECEIVED OR ACCRUED DURING THE YEAR ENDED DECEMBER 31, 191....
(FOR THE YEAR 1913, FROM MARCH 1, TO DECEMBER 31.)

Filed by (or for) .... of ....
(Full name of individual.) (Street and No.)

In the City, Town, or Post Office of .... State of ....
(Fill in pages 2 and 3 before making entries below.)

1. GROSS INCOME (see page 2, line 12)	$			
2. GENERAL DEDUCTIONS (see page 3, line 7)	$			
3. NET INCOME	$			

Deductions and exemptions allowed in computing income subject to the normal tax of 1 per cent.

4. Dividends and net earnings received or accrued, of corporations, etc., subject to like tax. (See page 2, line 11).........	$			
5. Amount of income on which the normal tax has been deducted and withheld at the source. (See page 2, line 9, column A)..				
6. Specific exemption of $3,000 or $4,000, as the case may be. (See Instructions 3 and 19)				
Total deductions and exemptions. (Items 4, 5, and 6)........	$			
7. TAXABLE INCOME on which the normal tax of 1 per cent is to be calculated. (See Instruction 3).	$			

8. When the net income shown above on line 3 exceeds $20,000, the additional tax thereon must be calculated as per schedule below:

	INCOME.		TAX.	
1 per cent on amount over $20,000 and not exceeding $50,000....	$		$	
2 " " 80,000 " " 75,000....				
3 " " 75,000 " " 100,000....				
4 " " 100,000 " " 250,000....				
5 " " 250,000 " " 800,000....				
6 " " 500,000....				
Total additional or super tax			$	
Total normal tax (1 per cent of amount entered on line 7).....			$	
Total tax liability...			$	

own or rent your home, what medical problems you have,
the educational classes you've taken—and the list goes on
and on. An IRS agent can get a pretty accurate profile of
your life from your religious, political, social, and financial
connections. As one in 220 million, you may not be too concerned, but perhaps the day is not far off when your profile will be on computer tape. . . .

Fortunately, some steps have already been taken to curb
the potentially abusive powers of the Treasury Department.
One, already mentioned, was an amendment to the Tax
Reform Act of 1976 that requires the IRS to notify an individual before requesting third-party records. Another
was a decision made in early 1978 to scuttle plans for a
nationwide IRS computer to monitor taxpayers. The White
House made the decision itself because it viewed the
computer network as "a threat to privacy and civil liberties." The program had called for a huge data-processing
system with 8,300 terminals stationed in IRS offices throughout the country, where over 48,000 IRS employees would
have had access to the detailed records of individual taxpayers and corporations. One congressman, Rep. Charles
Vanik of Ohio, charged that the computer "could become a
system of harassment, surveillance and political manipulation."

The IRS, however, continues to promote the use of computer terminals at regional IRS offices to monitor taxpayers.
The increased threat of an audit will encourage taxpayer
compliance, the IRS argues. All federal income tax forms go
through a huge computer to check the accuracy of the
taxpayer's arithmetic—a logical and practical use of technology. But the computer is also programmed to discover
any unusual deductions or activities and automatically to
kick out such returns for audit.

The IRS is generally circumspect about individual and
corporate tax returns, maintaining their confidentiality.
The tax code specifically states that "no collector, deputy
collector, assessor, or assistant assessor shall permit to
be published in any manner such income returns or any part
thereof, except such general statistics not specifying names
of individuals as may be made public under rules and
regulations that the Commissioner of the Internal Revenue
shall prescribe."

Although the confidentiality of tax returns has largely
been preserved against *public* disclosure, the IRS has not
resisted inspection of returns by other government agencies.

Since 1957, over 70 executive orders have instructed the IRS to turn over tax returns to various government agencies, including Congressional committees. Federal tax returns are also frequently inspected by state tax authorities. The Tax Reform Act of 1976 severely limited this dissemination. Unauthorized disclosure could result in a $5,000 fine and five years imprisonment.

How to Avoid an Audit

If just filling out your tax forms betrays your privacy, an audit strips you naked. This is especially true of the Taxpayer Compliance Measurement Program, the worst kind of audit. Every year, the IRS selects a small sample of taxpayers who are required to prove every single source of income and deductions. This TCMP audit program is used to assist the IRS computer program in selecting the returns best suited for audit. ("Best suited" means "most likely to bring in a lot more revenue.") If you're audited as part of the TCMP program, make sure you get a good accountant or attorney to represent you.

To maintain your privacy and keep what money is left from the taxman, you should make every effort to cut your chances of an audit. Here are a few tips suggested by Vernon K. Jacobs, editor of *Tax Angles:*

1. The return should be neat, but not necessarily typed. Legible tax returns create an impression of attention to detail. Signatures should be entered where requested.

2. Your figures should be mathematically correct, and transfers of figures from one page or schedule to another should be double-checked. The IRS computer will automatically kick out every return with incorrect arithmetic.

3. The return should include some small amounts of income that wouldn't be caught if unreported. This suggests to the auditor that you are a stickler for detail, and it may convey an impression of honesty.

4. All required supporting forms and schedules requested by the instructions should be prepared and submitted with the tax return.

5. Though some would disagree, copies of documentation or other information might be included to explain any questionable or unusual deductions such as large casualty losses, extensive medical bills, or big charitable deductions. But don't add an extensive explanation for anything that doesn't appear extremely unusual.

6. While not necessary, the signature of a CPA or attorney as the tax preparer may also reduce the chance of an audit.

7. Breaking income into smaller segments often reduces the chances of an audit. Thus, two separate businesses operating as a corporation and a proprietorship should be less exposed to the risks of an audit than they would be as a single business.

"The power to tax is the power to destroy," said Chief Justice John Marshall. And the powers of the IRS in auditing taxpayers are awesome. I have a friend who is a field auditor for the IRS. When somebody gripes about the government at social get-togethers, he always asks, "Now what did you say your social security number was?" Although he insists he's being facetious and has no power to influence an audit, the very fact that he plays on this joke, time and time again, is a tacit admission that the *power to destroy*, however latent, is still there.

Guilty Until Proven Innocent?

There are other disturbing characteristics of IRS powers. One is that you must prove questionable deductions before the IRS allows them. The burden of proof lies with the taxpayer, not the IRS. It is up to you to prove every claim you make on your tax return. In a sense, you're guilty until proven innocent—exactly the opposite of your rights in a criminal case.

It's a *Catch 22* situation. Take this exchange of letters in *Personal Finance* recently:

Q. A few years ago I invested several thousand dollars in gold coins. Now suppose I sell these coins. Do I have to report to the IRS the gain on such a sale? If I do, how can I prove the cost, since I do not have any receipt? The purchase was made in cash.

E.G.
Sherman Oaks, CA

A. The gain on the sale is taxable as a long-term capital gain if held more than a year. Even though you have no receipt, you can list the price you paid for the coins and the selling price. In the case of bullion coins, you can estimate the price you paid originally by checking bullion coin prices around the date of purchase. But when you report this transaction, you may open up a can of worms. Not only may the IRS arbitrarily assign you a purchase cost far below your actual cost (and the burden of proof will be on you to prove otherwise), but they'll probably ask for the source of the cash you used to buy the coins, and try to ascertain if you paid tax on it.

When the IRS seizes a taxpayer's property under a "jeopardy assessment" (in which the IRS believes the taxpayer is about to leave the country, transfer his property, or conceal himself), the taxpayer must petition the tax court to question the tax deficiency, or sue for a refund in a federal court. And the IRS can sell his property *before* he sues for a refund. In the words of Jeff A. Schnepper, in his book, *Inside IRS*, "Not only may the taxpayer be deprived of the use of his property 'without due process of the law,' but in certain cases, it may be disposed of as well. . . . The procedure amounts to a violation of the citizen's right to due process of law."

Consider these excerpts from *The April Game*, by an IRS agent who calls himself Diogenes. You'll see why he calls the IRS the "American Gestapo."

An agent of the Internal Revenue Service is a combination of policeman and spy, and an outrageously powerful one, at that. He may be, in fact, the most powerful in the country. There is no important piece of information concerning you that I am effectively forbidden to seek . . . we aren't that much concerned about search warrants or rules of evidence or other items of police etiquette. . . .

The Internal Revenue Service obviously has a lot of power to push the defenseless people around. It probably has, in the aggregate, more such power over more people than any other government agency in the United States. Such power can be abused . . . unavoidably, there are agents who enjoy their power too much. . . . The Senate Judiciary Subcommittee on Administrative Practice and Procedure held hearings on the topic and listened to so many horror stories about IRS agents, snooping and bullying tactics that the subcommittee chairman was moved to compare the IRS to 'a Gestapo preying upon defenseless citizens.' . . . The senators on the subcommittee heard taxpayers testify that IRS special agents casually open personal mail, tap telephones, pick locks, search homes and offices, all without warrants or other legal authority. . . .

One special agent told me with evident pride of a technique he had used to get the goods on a businessman he suspected of tax evasion. He approached the man's secretary and asked her to send him photocopies of the businessman's private mail. When she balked, he told her she could be subject to a long jail term for 'refusal to cooperate with a

federal officer.' This was sheer fiction, but it was enough
to worry the girl. She did what he asked. . . .

Yet my power scares me sometimes. If I can get at privileged information such as a doctor's private files, if I can
find out almost anything about any citizen without getting
permission from a judge or seeing the inside of a court-
room, what am I? I am a small-sized version of George Orwell's Big Brother—the eye to which all walls are glass.

Beware of the Special Agent

The IRS also has some flexibility in giving you your
"rights" when the agency suspects you of criminal tax
fraud. The Miranda-type statement (the right to remain
silent and consult an attorney, the warning that anything
your say may be used against you, etc.) need not be read
to you unless the person who interviews you is a special
agent.

Special agents work for the Intelligence Division of the
IRS and concentrate on cases of tax fraud. If you receive a
letter or call from a special agent, you can assume that you're
under investigation. You should not discuss anything with
him. Contact a tax attorney immediately.

A field auditor who is checking your return may think
he has discovered tax fraud. According to Diogenes, "An
IRS agent is supposed to advise a taxpayer of his rights
whenever a case appears to be turning into a criminal
investigation, but in practice, the agent generally waits to
utter the required warning until after he has gathered the
data he wants." In fact, a recent Supreme Court decision
permitted this incredible travesty of justice to continue.

One of the first signs that your return may be under
investigation for tax fraud is that the IRS summonses your
bank records. If you find that your checking account has
been or is being examined, you should seek experienced
tax counsel immediately.

Get a Tax Attorney

The tax laws are so complex now that many people find it
nearly impossible to fill out their yearly return by themselves. If you have someone else prepare your tax return
for you, what kind of specialist is the best? An accountant,
a tax specialist, a general tax service (such as H & R Block),
a tax attorney, or a combination of these?

If strict confidentiality is your major concern, only an attorney or lawyer-CPA is privileged not to reveal your conversations or records in court. Conversations and financial records you maintain with accountants, tax advisors, or tax preparers who are *not* attorneys are *not* confidential. Several court decisions have made this clear. To keep sensitive information private, deal only with a tax attorney. Although a tax attorney may cost more than an accountant or other tax advisor, the advantages of the attorney-client privilege are invaluable if you earn a high income and are an aggressive taxpayer (i.e., use every loophole available and pay as little tax as possible).

The courts have muddied the water a bit in this area, however. Recently, federal judges have distinguished between the *accounting* services and the *legal* services of a tax attorney. Under current rulings, accounting services provided by a tax attorney do *not* fall under attorney-client privilege. This may be hairsplitting, but it's another indication of the decline of financial privacy in the legal system.

YOUR RIGHTS IN A CRIMINAL AUDIT

By Charles W. Schoeneman

Tax practitioners are asked time and again, unfortunately almost always in the past tense, "What should I have done when the special agent visited me the first time?" Usually the taxpayer adds, "He warned me of my constitutional rights, told me I had a right to a lawyer, and said he just had a few questions." In too many cases, that is the end of the taxpayer's rights—he has already waived them because he talked.

Two Kinds of Audits

An IRS audit is simply the process of verifying the information reported on a taxpayer's return. Since an audit requires records and sometimes witnesses, both the taxpayer and persons with knowledge of the taxpayer's finances may be compelled to turn over books and records deemed "relevant or material."

A criminal audit or investigation differs from a civil audit in one important particular. It can lead to much more severe penalties—in some cases, to a $10,000 fine, or five years in prison, or *both*. There is a compensation, however:

the taxpayer enjoys much more extensive constitutional rights in an extraordinary criminal audit than he does in an ordinary civil audit.

The IRS has carefully trained a battalion of special agents to handle criminal investigations. These "specials" act quite differently from civil auditors. Hallmarks of the "special" are disarming politeness, apparent sympathy, and a willingness to be helpful and minimize any embarrassment caused by the agent's visit or questions. The cardinal rule for the taxpayer in both civil and criminal IRS investigations is the same: if you say anything, make sure you tell the truth. If there is one thing worse than full disclosure to a special agent, it is intentional misrepresentation of material (or even minor) facts. Almost as many taxpayers—some innocent of tax evasion—are prosecuted and convicted of "false statements" under Title 18 of the U.S. Code (the criminal sections) as are convicted of actual tax crimes under Title 26 (the Internal Revenue Code).

Constitutional Rights

A taxpayer's constitutional rights against the IRS come into play the moment a criminal investigation begins—when the special agent appears, shows his badge, and perfunctorily warns the taxpayer of his rights. But remember, these rights under the Fourth (against unreasonable searches and seizures) and Fifth (against self-incrimination) amendments apply only in a criminal investigation and do not apply to corporations at all, though a corporate officer may claim his own constitutional rights. Most precious is the right to remain silent, at least until you have consulted with your attorney, and he and you have decided whether to cooperate fully or selectively with the special agent.

Burden of Proof

The burden is on the government to prove its criminal case "beyond a reasonable doubt." It must ordinarily prove that you willfully failed to file or that you evaded taxes. So remember, you always have the right under the Fifth Amendment, whether with or without your attorney, to say, "I respectfully decline to answer your question on the grounds that my answer might tend to incriminate me." Don't think for a moment that this answer will get the special agent to pack his bags and terminate the case. He'll hang in there either until he has made a case that permits him to recommend criminal prosecution or until he can recommend against prosecution because conviction is unlikely.

Furthermore, don't imagine that the special agent will call off his case if you simply pay whatever tax the government says you owe. In fact, paying voluntarily can be absolutely the worst thing to do. It may provide the very evidence of willfullness or cash on hand that the government needs to make its case.

Required Warnings

What does the special agent tell you about your rights? How do you know that a special agent is on the case? Is there anything you can do at the outset to prevent a criminal investigation? The special agent's manual requires him to show his badge indicating that he is an agent of the Intelligence Division of the Internal Revenue Service and to read the taxpayer his constitutional rights. ("Specials" almost always travel in twos so they can corroborate each other's testimony in court.) The statement, which some appeals courts have said isn't constitutionally required, runs as follows:

"In connection with my investigation of your tax liability, I would like to ask you some questions. However, first I advise you that under the Fifth Amendment to the Constitution of the United States I cannot compel you to answer any questions or to submit any information if such answers or information might tend to incriminate you in any way. I also advise you that anything which you say and any information which you submit may be used against you in any criminal proceeding which may be undertaken. I advise you further that you may, if you wish, seek the assistance of an attorney before responding."

When showing his identification, the special agent is also supposed to tell the taxpayer that "as a special agent, one of my functions is to investigate the possibility of criminal violations of the Internal Revenue laws and related offenses." While this is better than no warning at all, the "special" knows how to disarm the taxpayer psychologically. He speaks in a courteous, almost friendly tone of voice. He may approach the taxpayer at his place of business during normal working hours. The taxpayer, thrown off guard, will often cooperate completely.

Two aspects of these warnings bear scrutiny. First, the taxpayer is merely advised that he "may," if he "wishes," seek the assistance of an attorney before responding, the implication being that the taxpayer need not obtain legal advice before responding to some initial questions because legal advice later will be just as effective—which is not true. Also, it is misleading, to say the least, for a special agent of the IRS to state that "one" of his functions is to investigate the "possibility" of tax crimes when the principal and almost the *only* activity of an IRS "special" is to build cases of tax fraud (or tax evasion) against taxpayers who are already suspected of a crime. The most crucial "interview" of all is that first one. Unless the taxpayer immediately exercises his right to find a qualified tax defense lawyer and remains silent until he finds one, all can be lost.

Books and Records

The Fifth Amendment protects your books and records, as does the Fourth Amendment. But if you intend to decline to submit your records to the IRS special agent, try to refer to the Fifth Amendment specifically. A general refusal to produce might give the IRS evidence of "willful" tax evasion—the hardest element for the IRS to prove against you.

Just bring out your records and decline on constitutional grounds to turn them over for inspection. You have an absolute right not to turn over your records, so that the IRS cannot build its "net worth" fraud case against you by using your assets as a starting point.

The question recurs whether the taxpayer's bank or accountant must comply with an IRS summons. The answer is in almost every case unequivocally "yes." The only exceptions would be where (1) the case has already been recommended for criminal prosecution by the IRS, or (2) the agent (or special agent) is and can be shown to be merely harassing the taxpayer. Even a special agent conducting a criminal investigation can summons your records from your accountant (though perhaps not from your lawyer) and the summons will stick. Successful challenges to IRS summonses are few and far between and a recent Supreme Court case will make the chances of successful challenge to an IRS summons even slighter.

In closing, it cannot be emphasized too strongly that the individual taxpayer who faces criminal investigation has a constitutional right to withhold his (or his corporation's) books and records unless the IRS obtains a search warrant (Fourth Amendment). He has a right to counsel (Sixth Amendment), and a right to remain silent, which includes the right not to turn over records (Fifth Amendment). Never waive these rights. If a taxpayer permits a special agent to examine his books and records, it will be too late to object on constitutional grounds at trial. Similarly, a verbal statement given to a special agent can be used at trial against the voluble taxpayer even if he testifies to the contrary.   (©1977 by *Tax Angles*)

Your Rights in a Civil Audit
By Charles W. Schoeneman and
Vernon K. Jacobs

Taxpayers enjoy few "rights" in the course of a (noncriminal) audit of their tax returns.

Are Audits Constitutional?

The tax law is actually a collection of laws, brought together in the Internal Revenue Code. These laws are called statutory laws, as contrasted with constitutional law or with case law (often known as "common" law). When the courts find these statutes to be in conflict with the Constitution, the statutory law is invalid. Originally, in the 1890s, the U.S. Supreme Court held that an income tax was unconstitutional, because it conflicted with Article IV, Section 9 of the Constitution.

After much heated debate, the 16th Amendment was passed in 1913. It specifically granted the Congress the power to "lay and collect taxes on incomes." The Internal Revenue Code (IRC) spells out how incomes shall be taxed The Revenue Code also grants authority to the secretary of the Treasury (or his delegate) to "inquire after all persons...who may be liable to pay any Internal Revenue tax" and to "examine any books, papers, records, or other data which may be relevant or material to such inquiry" (IRC Secs. 7601 and 7602). Thereafter the Code goes on (and on, and on) to detail the powers of the secretary and his delegate—the commissioner of Internal Revenue.

Thus a normal audit of your tax return to "inquire after" whether you have paid all the taxes the Revenue Code says you owe is not considered a violation of your constitutional rights. This means that your "rights" during a tax audit (or civil proceedings stemming from a tax audit) are those specified in the Revenue Code or in administrative rulings of the secretary of the Treasury or his delegate.

Statutory Rights

About 99.9 percent of the Internal Revenue Code deals with your statutory duties or obligations and with the penalties that can be imposed if you do not choose to comply "voluntarily" with these 1,700-odd pages of Internal Revenue laws. The Congress assumes that every citizen is capable of reading and comprehending the law (which is something a very few of our congressmen and senators can do). It is therefore up to each taxpayer to discover and to make use of those few provisions of the tax law that may be helpful to him during an audit.

• *Right to retain counsel.* Even though a tax audit does not usually involve the criminal law, you are permitted to employ an attorney, a CPA, or a person who is enrolled to practice (as an advisor) before the Internal Revenue Service. Your advisor can act in your behalf if you provide him with a power of attorney (Form 2848). Of course, your advisor can also attend any meetings with you, to interpret the law for you. Certain information held by an attorney is immune from summons or subpoena (attorney-client privilege). By contrast, records in an accountant's possession are fair game for the IRS agent. Therefore, only your attorney should hold sensitive records that might have some relevance in the event of a criminal investigation.

• *Right to a reasonable time and place.* A portion of IRC Sec. 7605 (a) states that the IRS is to schedule audit examinations at a time and a place that are "reasonable under the circumstances" While this rule can't be used to avoid an audit, it can be brought to the attention of an agent who is demanding a meeting time or place that is or could be an unreasonable burden to the taxpayer. In many cases, a meeting may be wholly unnecessary if suitable documentation can be mailed to the agent. In addition, if you have moved from the district where your return was filed or if your records are kept in another IRS district,you may request that your case be transferred to the district where an examination can be completed more quickly and conveniently.

• *Right to provide only relevant and material data.* The IRS is authorized to "examine any books, papers, records, or other date," and to summon testimony from others, *"which may be relevant or material"* to the audit (IRC Sec 7602). While the courts tend to interpret this provision liberally in favor of the IRS, it can also be used to restrain the IRS from going on a "fishing expedition."

• *Right to limitations on frequency of audits.* Sec. 7605 (b) of the tax code says, "No taxpayer shall be subjected to unnecessary examination or investigations, and only one inspection of a taxpayer's (records) shall be made for each taxable year unless...the secretary (of the Treasury) notifies the taxpayer in writing that an additional inspection is necessary." The law was amended by the 1976 Tax Reform Act to eliminate the phrase "secretary of his delegate" (i.e., the IRS commissioner). However, the IRS has an administrative policy that goes even further. If you are notified of an audit involving an issue that was audited in either of the preceding two years' tax returns, and if there was no additional tax due the IRS as a result of the prior audit, then you should ask the agent's supervisor to call off the audit. This must be done before the audit begins.

• *Right to interpret the law to your advantage.* The tax code itself does not specify that each taxpayer has the right to construe the law to his advantage under ambiguous circumstances. Most lawyers take this for granted and simply assume that everyone knows about this obvious "right". However, there are a great many taxpayers who do not seem to realize that it is not a crime to interpret the law to your own advantage when there is some reasonable doubt about what the law really means.

• *Right to appeal tax assessments.* Every taxpayer has the right to appeal the decisions and interpretations of the examining agent. Generally, the appeal should deal with differences of interpretation on the facts of the case or the meaning of the law. The first and simplest course of appeal is to discuss the matter with the agent's supervisor. The agent may be new, or he might even be trying to make his record look good for a forthcoming promotion interview. Other avenues of appeal exist within the IRS and in the court system The February 1978 issue of *Tax Angles* discussed the informal Small Tax Case Division of the U.S. Tax Court, which gives taxpayers a less expensive way to contest an unreasonable tax assessment.

Use Common Sense

Many of the most effective weapons available to the taxpayer who is chosen for an audit are practical strategies and commonsense ways of dealing with the agent, rather than legalistic rights. The IRS agent has a job to do, and most agents simply want to do their job as quickly as possible, with the least amount of conflict. The agent's official duty is to verify whether you have paid what you owe, according to the IRS view of the intent of the law. Privately, the agent also wants to collect some additional taxes from most of the people he audits, because that is definitely a factor in his opportunities for pay raises or promotions. Thus, your strategy should be to create the unavoidable and obvious impression that you (1) keep good records, (2) pay all the taxes that you owe, and (3) are not inclined to underpay in doubtful situations. You want to avoid giving the agent even slight reason to suspect that you are a "juicy plum," ripe for some easy tax assessments. In the process, you want to be businesslike and clearly aware of your rights and your duties. Here are a few significant strategies to consider.

● *Don't waive your rights.* A practical question arises when an IRS agent asks you to waive (extend) the three-year statute of limitations to give him more time to conclude the audit. The practical answer is that such waivers should usually be denied if less than six months remains before the audit deadline on a taxable year would run out and the agent has not yet started his work examining your books for the year in question. If he has started his audit, his counterresponse is likely to be a "quickie" audit, resulting in a tax deficiency that is somewhat arbitrary. Then you may have to go to court to prove his assessment is incorrect.

● *Don't volunteer open years' returns.* Quite often an agent will come in to examine you return for a particular year and will also ask to see your tax return for later years. In many cases, the most recent return has not yet been processed to the point where the agent can obtain it easily and quickly. If the agent doesn't ask for the most recent tax return, don't volunteer it. If he does request it, you should ask him why he doesn't have his own copy.

● *Keep a log of requested records.* Where an agent is conducting an extended audit in your place of business or where you are spending extensive data (copies only) through the mail, keep a detailed log of the records you deliver to the agent and when the record is returned.

Dos and Don'ts

In closing, here are some suggested dos and don'ts when you are dealing with an agent. Every tax practitioner has his own list, but there are some basic guidelines we recommend:

1. Your attorney (or accountant) should be present only if there is a sizeable amount in question of if the disputed item will recur from year to year; or if the imposition of a criminal or civil penalty is indicated. You have a right to be represented. If an accountant or other return preparer is necessary to explain certain items on the return, he should be asked to attend. Otherwise, go alone.

2. Stick up for your rights. While constitutional (Fourth and Fifth Amendment) rights are technically limited to criminal cases (where an IRS special agent appears), make sure the agent doesn't start a criminal investigation and then turn his work over to a "Special." In such a situation, contract an attorney immediately. The IRS is upposed to warn you of your rights at the outset of any criminal examination.

3. You also have a right to call the agent's attention to items in your favor. One example would be deductions not claimed on the return. Here a tax attorney or accountant can be helpful before the audit by reviewing your return.

4. In the case of a field audit (an audit in your home or office), it is advisable to put the agent in a separate, neat, comfortable, but relatively bare or stark room or office, away from any employees. Instruct your employees to avoid any unnecessary contact with the agent. You or a designated employee should handle all discussions with the agent.

5. Courtesy is the best policy. It seldom helps to treat the agent rudely or to question his motives. But take care to avoid being too friendly or solicitous.

6. Candor is the next best policy. Withholding pertinent information can hurt. You want to avoid making the agent suspicious of your motives.

7. Don't answer questions that are not asked. And don't volunteer information that is not relevant to the issues raised.

8. Do not seek to cover up or intentionally confuse the agent by silence. The burden of proof is on you to substantiate your income and your deductions.   (©1979 by Tax Angles)

"Fifth Amendment Returns": Warning

As a tax protest, some hardliners, refusing to let the IRS invade their financial and personal privacy, have annually mailed a blank 1040 with the words, "Fifth Amendment" written across the form—the amendment says you can't be forced to self-incriminate. The Supreme Court as well as lower courts have ruled that filing a Fifth Amendment form is equivalent to not filing at all. And that is a criminal offense. However, the Supreme Court left open the question of whether you could plead the Fifth Amendment on specific questions asked on the 1040 form.

The question has not yet been tested in the courts, but once again we cannot recommend the method because it violates the first principle of privacy: *maintain a low profile*. This advice can not be repeated too often, I'm afraid. A Fifth Amendment filing, constitutional or not, is like waving a red flag to the IRS. It would be smarter to leave certain sections blank than to say "Fifth Amendment" in bold letters.

There are a few ways to avoid reporting private information on your 1040. One way, of course, is to make less than the amount required to file a tax form. The following incomes would exempt you from having to file a 1980 return:

If you are:	And your gross income is less than:
Single	$3,300
Single, 65 or older	4,300
Married	5,400
Married, one spouse is 65 or older	6,400

Married, both spouses are 65 or older	$7,400
Married, not eligible to file a joint return	1,000
Surviving spouse	4,400
Dependent of your parent who may claim you as an exemption and you have investment income of at least $750	1,000

You are required to file a return if your net earnings from self-employment are $400 or more.

These income levels move up gradually with inflation, but as you can see, very few people fall into this category. Another little-known exemption from filing is given if a person invests most or all of his money in tax-exempt securities like municipal bonds, which are free from federal and most state and local taxes. Such persons, usually millionaires, can avoid the filing requirement altogether! After all, why should the government care that you didn't file—they have borrowed *all* of your money anyway.

Taking the standard deduction (zero bracket amount) is another way of reducing invasion of privacy. If you don't itemize, you don't have to reveal a lot of personal information such as religious and political contributions, home ownership, educational opportunities, medical history, and so on. But if you make a considerable amount of money, you'll be paying more taxes than you need to just to maintain this financial secrecy in your life.

IRS Telephone Surveillance

One more important tip. If you must call the IRS office for forms, additional information about filing or deductions, or just to have a question answered, do not give your real name or home address. (Use your post office box to receive forms or instructions.)

Last year, IRS office supervisors made a habit of listening in on such conversations in an effort to ensure that taxpayers were getting "good" advice. The General Services Administration has been pressing the IRS to stop, but the IRS is fighting.

In addition, the IRS maintains a central file of individuals who have requested printed tax materials.

12
The Private Will

Bing Crosby knew about the "private will." When he passed away in late 1977, the world sorrowed, and the national press, fighting for a story, wanted to take a detailed look at his estate—how much Bing was worth, who got what, and all the intimate details of the death of the great entertainer.

But the reporters went away emptyhanded. There was no story—no accounting of Bing's assets and real estate, no revelation of who received what or whether any disputes had arisen. All that information was completely confidential. Yes, Bing had a will, but it wasn't available to the prying eyes of the public or the press. It was written for his heirs and close friends, his personal attorney, and a few tax officials who were prohibited from talking.

Bing had learned the hard way from the death and estate probate of his first wife, Dixie Lee Crosby. When she died of cancer in 1948, she left an estate of $1,300,000, but the probate courts made such an affair of her will that it cost Bing over $100,000 in legal and court fees to pay for probate.

The Cost of Probate

Bing's costs were not out of line with the probate costs of other important figures. The legal system took 11 percent of Franklin D. Roosevelt's $1,900,000 estate. Probate also took 11 percent of Gertrude Strong Achilles' $11 million estate. Arthur Vining Davis' will was so entangled that the courts took $6 million to pay court and legal fees. And this does not include the outrageous inheritance taxes that must be paid.

The legal fees can take an even higher percentage of smaller estates. The Research Institute reports that probate expenses, legal fees, and executor fees can run to some 5 to 6 percent of the gross of an average estate. The bill can run that high even for a nonlitigated, problem-free estate. And if you don't have a will, the court will write a will for you—that is to say, the court will appoint an administrator who will handle the estate proceedings and distribute your assets according to state intestacy laws.

The length of time it takes to probate a will can be devastating. Some time ago, the newspapers reported on a widow who was forced to go on welfare because five years had passed and she was still unable to take possession of the $765,000 estate left by her husband—all because of probate problems. The Research Institute concludes that probate is "not only a disconcerting and frustrating event, but generally a long-drawn-out and expensive operation."

Fear of Publicity

Publicity can be a major frustration in probate. Every newspaper assigns a reporter to the probate court. If you are a famous or notorious person in the community, or if you leave a substantial sum of money, or if there is anything peculiar about your estate, your will, or the circumstances of your death, you can be sure that it will be published in the newpapers. After reading about your will and estate in the newspaper, unscrupulous salesmen or confidence men may hound your heirs, trying to take advantage of their bereavement or lack of business acumen.

In summary, Norman Dacey, author of *How to Avoid Probate*, has stated, "Probate costs too much, takes too long, and involves undesirable publicity."

Introducing the Living Trust

The cost, delay, and publicity accompanying probate can be completely avoided through the use of the "living trust." Legally, it's called the *inter vivos* trust, and is quite different from the more common "testamentary" trust. The testamentary trust makes provision for the establishment of a trust *after* the will has gone through probate. Testamentary trusts are set up to keep inexperienced or imprudent heirs from squandering a large inheritance. With the assets in the hands of a responsible trustee, the inheritance can remain intact while beneficiaries grow in fiscal responsibility. Nevertheless, the testamentary trust does not avoid probate and is activated only *after* the probate process is completed.

The living trust, on the other hand, has no such defects and many advantages. A living trust is a legal entity to which you transfer all or part of your assets during your lifetime.

While you live, the assets are no longer in your name, but you retain complete control over the living trust. You can amend the terms of the trust completely. You can appoint a member of your family, a friend, a banker, or anyone you wish—even yourself—to act as trustee, and you can change the trustee at any time. You maintain absolute control of the living trust.

You can set up either a revocable or an irrevocable *inter vivos* trust. The revocable trust offers the greatest flexibility, permitting you to dissolve the trust if you wish. You *cannot* change an irrevocable trust.

The revocable living trust offers no tax advantages. By itself, the living trust does not save estate or income taxes. An estate-tax return must be filed. (Over a quarter of a million living-trust returns were filed last year.) You continue to treat all income, losses, and deductions as your own, and pay income taxes accordingly. Still, there are no tax disadvantages: all of the estate and income tax savings available through a testamentary trust are also available in a well-drawn living trust.

Advantages of a Living Trust

There are numerous advantages of a living trust. First, it completely avoids probate and administrative costs—which can run quite high. The living trust states simply that, for example, "I appoint John Smith as successor trustee and I direct that at my death the successor trustee shall dispose of the property as follows. . . ." There will be no executor's or appraiser's fees or probate court costs. It won't take two to five years or longer—generally, it will take two to five *days*. One's death immediately triggers the conversion of assets from the deceased's ownership to that of his family or heirs. The economic life of the family is not disrupted. Nor are the assets or estate tied up in probate while the lawyers finish transferring all assets, getting the estate taxes paid and audited, and so forth. This can mean a saving of thousands of dollars.

The living trust can also be used as a test of the trustee's ability to manage your money. If you don't like the way the trustee is handling your financial affairs, you can make a change. In fact, you can act as your own trustee if you wish (by establishing a "Declaration of Trust" wherein you declare that you are going to hold something in trust for someone).

The living trust is a great way to protect oneself against the inability to handle one's own affairs during later life. In effect, it can protect you against a time when you might become physically or mentally disabled. In probate court, disgruntled heirs may successfully contest a will by arguing that the deceased was incompetent at the time it was drawn. But in the case of a living trust, an unhappy heir will find that the transfer of property has already taken place, making it difficult or even impossible to contest the will.

Acme of Privacy

Perhaps the most significant reason for choosing a living trust is confidentiality. While the probated will invites publicity and protest, the living trust discourages it. As we stated earlier, probate opens to the public all kinds of previously private information—an inventory of what you own and owe, friends and relatives you did or did not like, and if a business is involved, information that may adversely affect efforts to liquidate it. Beneficiaries unaccustomed to their newfound wealth may also become easy marks for con artists. The living trust avoids all of these problems.

After your death, the management of the trust continues as before. The trustee performs the same duties as always, with no outside authority looking over his shoulder and asking personal and financial questions. The trust provisions can be carried out without publicity, unknown to anyone except the beneficiaries and, of course, the IRS. But the IRS must by law keep trust returns strictly confidential. In contrast to a regular will, the terms of the trust are not disclosed to a probate court, and both the assets and the identity of the persons to receive them remain closely guarded secrets.

A private will may accompany the living trust, giving instructions for the trustee to follow upon the death of the person establishing the trust. This private will explains who gets what, when, and other terms identical to what you would find in a conventional will—but probate is avoided.

Setting Up a Living Trust

Some attorneys may be unfamiliar with the living trust as a device for avoiding probate. But as the costs and delays of probate increase dramatically, more attorneys will become knowledgeable in this field. Certainly, the first place to turn for help would be an attorney specializing in estate planning, trusts, and taxes. Norman F. Dacey, author of the highly controversial book, *How to Avoid Probate*, states that an attorney is not necessary to establish a living trust. Dacey even includes sample forms in his book so that you can set up a one-party revocable living trust yourself without legal assistance. Yet I would offer a word of caution about this approach. You may feel more comfortable working directly with an attorney when you plan your estate. But be sure to find a legal counselor who is familiar with the local laws on trusts and estates.

Costs of setting up a living trust vary. Some fiduciaries don't want to set up an arrangement unless you start it with $250,000. Others will start one for you with as little as $1,000. Most suggest a minimum of $10,000. Fees range from a low of $190 to thousands of dollars per year. Many fiduciaries charge a set percentage of the trust's assets. If you do it yourself a'la Dacey's book, the cost will be only a few dollars plus any conveyance tax on real estate.

What do you put into your living trust? Theoretically, any asset you wish—savings accounts, checking accounts, real estate, coin collections, stocks and bonds, even your home. But for practical purposes, you may not wish to have all your assets held in trust. For example, many people wish to have neither their checking account nor their home held in trust. You can still avoid probate on these assets by maintaining joint ownership with right of survivorship. Thus, upon death of a spouse, the property will be assigned directly to the joint owner without the necessity of going through probate. But state laws differ on the probate consequences of joint ownership, so it would pay to consult with an attorney before switching any major assets into joint tenancy.

Incidentally, your safe-deposit box need not be sealed upon death—if it is owned by the living trust. This is an excellent way to spare your heirs the bothersome experience of having your box sealed by the bank until state tax agents take an inventory of its contents for tax purposes.

If you do hold assets outside the living trust, you will undoubtedly wish to maintain a regular will—if only for extra insurance against the possibility that you might overlook some assets. But in general, it would be best to keep all assets in a living trust or at least in joint ownership.

Multiple trusts are possible. You can set up as many living trusts as you like, naming either the same or different trustees for each beneficiary. You could, for example, set up a separate trust for each member of your family and name each individual as trustee to see how well he handles money. Thus, you can determine your children's financial ability while you're still living, and can change the trust if things don't work out.

13
Twenty-four Steps to Financial Privacy

The time to act is now. Throughout this book, I have made recommendations for minimizing intrusion on your financial and personal life. In this concluding chapter, I will list all of these recommendations briefly in an easy-to-follow form. By following these steps, you should be able to reach the level of privacy you desire. Keep in mind, of course, that you may not wish to follow *all* of the steps outlined. You may have other social and financial goals that conflict with these steps.

If you take all of these steps, it will be possible to become a private, independent individual in just a short time. Complete privacy will not be possible for at least five years (five years is how long it takes before banks will destroy records of checks and deposits).

Let's look at each recommendation:

1. Discontinue using your present bank account for sensitive purchases. If you need to, make up a list of such sensitive items, memorize them, and be sure not to use a checking account for such purposes. Use your present account for routine expenditures and deposits only.

2. Present a contract to your bank manager stipulating that you will be warned in advance of any third-party requests for your bank records. A sample contract is found in Chapter 2.

3. Make sensitive purchases with money orders, cashier's checks, cash, or other confidential media. Be sure to keep a receipt of all such purchases for tax purposes.

4. Establish another local checking or savings account for cashing checks and purchasing money orders, cashiers checks, or travelers checks.

215

5. Establish a registered company name, open a checking account, and use it to transact business of a sensitive nature.

6. Restrict your use of credit cards to routine expenditures only. Otherwise pay with cash, money orders, cashier's checks, or travelers checks.

7. Do *not* give your social security number for identification purposes unless required to do so by law.

8. Establish a level of cash or cash equivalent to be stored safely at home for emergencies and other uses. Keep proof or evidence of where the cash came from.

9. Open a safe-deposit box and place in it *some* portion of your wealth for safekeeping. The ownership of the box should be in the name of a company, corporation, or trust to preserve privacy of the contents and allow immediate access after death. Insure the contents and keep a record of contents separate from the box.

10. Place money abroad, either in person or by mail, in a discreet manner. Use this money for investment or emergency purposes. Select a country that maintains a strict policy of financial secrecy and has a fairly stable government.

11. Try to avoid providing financial details and personal information when making investments or opening brokerage accounts. Emphasize nonreportable investments, but keep strict private records of all transactions.

12. If you deal with an investment advisor, insist on a contract specifying that all correspondence and conversations are confidential. Even then, bear in mind that such a contract may not be enforceable in court. Keep your dealings discreet. Your contract should also insist that no information be given out to third parties.

13. Refuse to deal with any investment or business firm that will not reveal to you its address or salient financial information. Insist on references.

14. Consider obtaining an unlisted phone number to ward off unwanted telephone calls from high-pressure salesmen and other undesirable persons. At the very least, eliminate your street address from the telephone directory and list only your initials or middle name.

15. Rent a post office box to receive all or a portion of your mail. Always use a post office box for ordering information or merchandise by mail. Correspond under an assumed name or use your registered company name. Also consider the use of mail-drop services and file services outside the country.

16. Write to mail-order firms if you don't want your name on their mailing lists. Or write to the Direct Mail Marketing Association in New York City to have your name removed from most mailing lists.

17. Check on your credit records at your local credit bureau to make sure information is accurate. Correct any errors.

18. Borrow from sources that require the least amount of personal and financial information—executive loans by mail, overdraft accounts, or collateral loans.

19. Apply for a passport as soon as possible to give you flexibility in travel around the world. Consider the legal pros and cons of a second passport. Avoid using your passport for identification purposes.

20. If you incorporate, consider a Delaware corporation for anonymity, and avoid going public if at all possible.

21. Maintain a low profile. Take your name off the front of your house and your mailbox. Don't put your initials or any unusual words on your automobile (including license plates). Drive a nice but ordinary car. Buy a nice but ordinary house. Maintain a friendly but low profile with your neighbors.

22. Build concealed safes for your valuables, hidden from the naked eye. Maintain secret storage facilities.

23. Try to avoid audits of your tax returns while still being aggressive in keeping your taxes down. If you can afford it, hire a tax attorney to maximize the confidentiality of your return.

24. Set up an *inter vivos* or living trust through your lawyer to preserve personal and financial privacy—as well as avoiding the costs of probate—at the time of your death.

14
Update on Privacy

Maintaining financial privacy is a lot of work. Make sure you're not leaving out any important steps. Several books and newsletters will be extremely worthwhile in your efforts to remain a private individual. I highly recommend the following periodicals:

NEWSLETTERS

Privacy Journal, P.O. Box 8844, Washington DC 20003, 202-547-2865. Edited and published by Robert Ellis Smith. Monthly; $49 a year. A superb newsletter that keeps you up-to-date on personal and financial privacy in the computer age.

Exodus, Edited by Dawn Schultz with contributions from Harry D. Schultz. Monthly; $150 a year. Subtitled, "How to Keep Your Money and Freedom," with a heavy emphasis on foreign accounts, travel, passports, and financial freedom abroad. Full of interesting tips and techniques. Highly recommended.

Personal Finance, 901 N. Washington Street, Alexandria, VA 22314, 703-836-3313. I am a consulting editor. $65 a year for 24 issues. Published by Kephart Communications, Inc. My column. "Creative Finance," is published here, along with feature articles by top financial experts, a capsule advisory, and answers to your money questions. Topics include all areas of personal finance—investments, taxation, estate planning, gold and silver—from the point of view of "inflation survival strategies." Financial privacy issues are discussed frequently.

Tax Angles, 901 N. Washington Street, Alexandria, VA 22314, 703-836-3313. Edited by Vernon K. Jacobs. Monthly; $44 a year. This is another newsletter published by Kephart Communications, Inc. Editor Vernon Jacobs seems to be the only writer in the country today who knows how to explain in simple, yet *accurate*, terms the meaning of the tax laws and how to lesson the tax bit. One of the most important topics of *Tax Angles* is the question of privacy in your tax planning.

BOOKS

Personal Privacy in an Information Society, The Report of the Privacy Protection Study Commission, David F. Linowes, chairman, July 1977. Order from Government Printing Office, Washington, DC 20402. Contains a wealth of information on financial and personal privacy, plus recommendations to Congress to preserve privacy. $5.

Dirty Money by Thurston Clarke and John J. Tigue, Jr., Simon & Schuster, 630 Fifth Avenue, New York, NY 10020, $9.95. Swiss banks, the Mafia, money laundering, and white collar crime.

The Robert Kinsman Guide to Tax Havens, Dow Jones/Irwin, Homewood, IL, 60430, $17.50. The most up-to-date guide in establishing your foreign company in a tax haven. Kinsman has just updated his book on Swiss banks, *Your New Swiss Bank Book* (Dow Jones/Irwin), which is worth examining.

The April Game by Diogenes, Playboy Press, 919 North Michigan Avenue, Chicago, IL 60611, paperback, $1.50. An insider's view of IRS tactics. Highly entertaining, as long as you're not being audited yourself.

Privacy by Bill Kaysing, Eden Press, P.O. Box 8410, Fountain Valley, CA 92708, $10. Eden Press publishes "underground" books like the infamous *Paper Trip*, which tells you *illegal* ways to get new identification. Only for "deep cover" situations. For the rest of us, pure entertainment.

Harry Browne's Complete Guide to Swiss Banks Kephart Communications, Inc. 901 N. Washington St., Alexandria VA 22314; $25. Privacy is of utmost importance to the Swiss—and Harry Browne superbly outlines the services of Swiss banks. The chapter on privacy is well worth reading.

Privacy, How to Protect What's Left of It, by Robert Ellis Smith, Doubleday, 245 Park Ave., New York, NY 10017, $10. Highly recommended. Smith has specific advice about records maintained by banks, credit bureaus, consumer investigative firms, employment, federal government, insurance companies, schools, social security numbers, etc.

Other Books by Mark Skousen

The Insider's Banking and Credit Almanac. This is a consumer's guide to the "unseen revolution" in banking and credit. *The Almanac,* updated each year, reveals the inside secrets of personal finance—"The Perfect Loan" (how to borrow $25,000 overnight), high earnings on your checking account and savings accounts, foreign bank accounts, smart ways to take advantage of credit cards, how to start your own bank, and how to determine the safety of your bank. Also included is a state-by-state survey of consumer banking. Available for $14.95 from:

> Alexandria House Books
> 901 N. Washington St.,
> Alexandria, VA 22314

Playing the Price Controls Game. This book deals with the number one problem facing our country today: government control over prices, wages, rents, and our financial lives. This book, already in its second edition and selected as the book of the month by the Conservative Book Club, offers practical advice on how to prepare for and even profit from coming wage and price controls. This book is available for $10.95 from:

> Arlington House
> 333 Post Road West
> Westport, CT 06880

The 100 Percent Gold Standard. This book is the only volume on the market today that describes in detail the history of the hard-money school, those economic thinkers and political leaders who supported a pure gold standard of money. They include such people as Thomas Jefferson, John Adams, F.A. Hayek, and Murray N. Rothbard. This book also covers the economic and political arguments in favor of and against the gold standard. It is available for $11 from:

> University Press of America
> 4710 Auth Place, S.E.
> Lanham, MD 20801

New Profits From Your Insurance Policy . This book covers U.S. and foreign annuities, inexpensive term insurance internationally, and insurance in gold. It's available for $15 from:

> Mark Skousen
> P.O. Box 611,
> Merrifield, Va. 22116

NEWSLETTER

Mark Skousen's Forecasts & Strategies. A new monthly newsletter devoted to the issues of taxes, inflation, government controls and privacy in your financial affairs. It's available for $95 from:

> Phillips Publishing, Inc.
> 7315 Wisconsin Avenue
> Suite 1200N
> Washington, DC 20014

Appendix

DEPARTMENT OF THE TREASURY
WASHINGTON, .D.C. 20220

DEPUTY ASSISTANT SECRETARY

OCT 12 1978

Dear Mr. Skousen:

　　As you requested, we have prepared the following
responses to the questions pertaining to the Bank Secrecy
Act in your letter of September 6, 1978:

Question 1:　A spokesman for the American Bankers Asso-
　　　　　　　ciation has said that the photocopying of checks,
　　　　　　　deposits, etc., imposed on all U.S. banks has cost
　　　　　　　over $1 billion since its inception in 1970. Do
　　　　　　　you feel that this photocopying requirement has been
　　　　　　　worth the cost? Specifically, in what way can you
　　　　　　　justify this high cost?

Answer:　We are not familiar with the ABA statement referred
　　　　　to in your question, and as a result, we are not in a
　　　　　position to comment on it. As you may know, however,
　　　　　the regulations that implement the Act do not require
　　　　　banks to photocopy records. In many instances, banks
　　　　　have opted to retain the originals rather than micro-
　　　　　film. In addition, it is estimated that about 70%
　　　　　of all checks are issued for $100 or less and are not
　　　　　subject to the recordkeeping requirements. While we
　　　　　understand that the majority of banks microfilm all
　　　　　of their paid checks, their decision to do so was
　　　　　at least partially based on other considerations, such
　　　　　as convenience and their need for internal controls. We
　　　　　are aware of one large bank that does not microfilm
　　　　　checks written for $100 or less. Many banks photocopied
　　　　　checks prior to the Act.

　　　　　We know that bank records have been essential in
　　　　　thousands of Federal tax investigations as well as
　　　　　large numbers of Justice Department investigations of
　　　　　narcotics trafficking and other violations of Federal
　　　　　law. Congressional committees have also used them in
　　　　　their inquiries into questionable activities. We can
　　　　　only assume that the records are also useful to state
　　　　　and local governmental authorities for tax, regulatory,
　　　　　and criminal investigations.

-2-

Question 2: Why was old IRS Form 4683 replaced this year by
            Treasury Form 90-22.1? Why is the form sent directly
            to the Treasury Office in Washington instead of IRS
            regional offices?

Answer: IRS Form 4683 was replaced with Treasury Department
         Form 90-22.1 to separate the reporting requirement,
         which is based on the (Foreign) Bank Secrecy Act, from
         income tax returns that are authorized under the
         Internal Revenue Code. As the records of the Commerce,
         Consumer and Monetary Affairs Subcommittee of the
         House Committee on Government Operations hearings of
         March 29 and 30, 1977, and the Subcommittee's related
         report indicate, this change was needed to improve the
         implementation of the Act.

         The forms are sent to the Treasury Department in Washington
         rather than to IRS regional offices to emphasize the fact
         that they are not tax forms and to facilitate processing.

Question 3: Is it true that Americans who file Treasury
            Form 90-22.1 have their names placed on a single
            computer tape, with easy access by authorized
            Treasury agents? What kind of information is
            placed on computer?

Answer: Plans for the utilization of the Forms 90-22.1
         have not been finalized; it is expected, however,
         that some of the information in the reports will be
         computerized. However, specific information will
         only be made available to authorized employees who
         have specific needs to meet specific objectives as
         set out in the statute and regulations.

Question 4: What safeguards have you imposed to insure
            financial privacy of Americans who file the new
            Treasury form?

Answer: The reports are maintained in a secure environment
         under the control of my staff. Specific reports may
         be made available to other Federal agencies and
         Congressional committees only when there is an offi-
         cial need for them, in accordance with the statutory
         requirements. Further dissemination by the receiving
         agencies is severely restricted.

-3-

Question 5: Some investment advisers have suggested that
the new reporting requirements on foreign accounts are
in anticipation of foreign exchange controls. Do you
agree? Whether you agree or not, could foreign account
reporting be used for imposing foreign exchange controls?

Answer: The new reporting requirements on foreign accounts
are less stringent than those formerly in effect when
the report was filed with the IRS.

The change in the reporting requirements was made
without any thought of foreign exchange controls. Since
we have not considered such controls, we are unable to
provide a meaningful response to the last part of your
question.

Question 6: Are you considering proposing to Congress that
it exempt small foreign depositors from reporting
under the Bank Secrecy Act? What other proposals are
you considering?

Answer: Since the Secretary of the Treasury has authority to
grant such an exemption under the provisions of the Bank
Secrecy Act, there is no need to seek such authority
from Congress. Although we are considering such an
exemption for small accounts, it has not received
final approval. If it is approved, we will make a
public announcement.

Question 7: A financial adviser has suggested that if
one checks the box, saying he has more than 25 foreign
accounts, that person would undoubtedly be subject
to audit. Is there any truth to that statement?

Answer: No, the statement is not true.

Question 8: Are there any exemptions to the foreign account
reporting requirement?

Answer: As the attached notices state, some exemptions
have been announced.

-4-

Question 9: What percentage of taxpayers fail to check a
    box, yes or no, on whether they have a foreign account,
    on Schedule B? Is failure to check a box subject to
    a fine or penalty?

Answer: Our office does not have the information requested.
    The questions concerning Federal income tax forms should
    be addressed to the Internal Revenue Service.

Question 10: Why are the penalties so high ($500,000 and
    five, years in prison) for failure to file Treasury
    Form 90-22.1 or filing a fraudulent report? Shouldn't
    the punishment fit the crime?

Answer: The criminal penalties are contained in the (Foreign)
    Bank Secrecy Act itself. The $500,000 fine and 5 years
    imprisonment can only be imposed when a reporting viola-
    tion has been committed in furtherance of another
    violation of Federal law, or as part of a pattern of
    illegal activity involving transactions exceeding $100,000
    in a 12 month period.

    The criminal penalties in individual cases are determined
    by Federal judges; they are generally much less than the
    maximum permitted by the Act.

    Your questions numbered 11 and 12 do not appear to be
related to the Bank Secrecy Act. They should be directed
to the Customs and Immigration and Naturalization Services
for their response.

    I hope that we have been helpful to you. If you
have further questions concerning the Act or the regulations,
please write to me. We will be glad to provide you with
whatever assistance we can.

                            Sincerely,

                            Arthur Sinai
                            Deputy Assistant Secretary
                            (Enforcement)

Mr. Mark Skousen
Editor
Kephart Communications, Inc.
901 N. Washington Street
Alexandria, Virginia 22314

Enclosures

Form Approved
OMB No 45-RO 546

Department of the Treasury Form 90-22.1 (9-78) SUPERSEDES ALL PREVIOUS EDITIONS	REPORT OF FOREIGN BANK AND FINANCIAL ACCOUNTS For the calendar year 19......	OFFICIAL USE ONLY

This form should be used to report financial interest in or signature authority or other authority over one or more bank accounts, securities accounts, or other financial accounts in foreign countries as required by Department of the Treasury Regulations (31 CFR 103). You are not required to file a report if the aggregate value of the accounts did not exceed $1,000. Check all appropriate boxes. SEE INSTRUCTIONS ON BACK FOR DEFINITIONS

1 Name (Last, First, Middle)

2. Social security number or employer identification number if other than individual

3 Name in item 1 refers to
☐ Individual
☐ Partnership
☐ Corporation
☐ Fiduciary

4. Address (Street, City, State, Country, ZIP)

5 ☐ I had signature authority or other authority over one or more foreign accounts, but I had no "financial interest" in such accounts (see instruction J). Indicate for these accounts:

(a) Name and social security number or taxpayer identification number of each owner ____

(b) Address of each owner ____

(Do not complete item 9 for these accounts)

6. ☐ I had a "financial interest" in one or more foreign accounts owned by a domestic corporation, partnership or trust which is required to file Form 90-22.1. (See instruction L). Indicate for these accounts.

(a) Name and taxpayer identification number of each such corporation, partnership or trust ____

(b) Address of each such corporation, partnership or trust ____

(Do not complete item 9 for these accounts)

7. ☐ I had a "financial interest" in one or more foreign accounts, but the total maximum value of these accounts (see instruction I) did not exceed $10,000 at any time during the year. (If you checked this box, do not complete item 9).

8 ☐ I had a "financial interest" in 25 or more foreign accounts. (If you checked this box, do not complete item 9.)

9 If you had a "financial interest" in one or more but fewer than 25 foreign accounts which are required to be reported, and the total maximum value of the accounts exceeded $10,000 during the year (see instruction I), write the total number of those accounts here. Complete items (a) through (f) below for one of the accounts and attach a separate Form 90-22.1 for each of the others. Items 1, 2, 3, 9, and 10 must be completed for each account. Check here if this is an attachment. ☐

(a) Name in which account is maintained

(b) Name of bank or other person with whom account is maintained

(c) Number and other account designation, if any

(d) Address of office or branch where account is maintained

(e) Type of account (If not certain of English name for the type of account, give the foreign language name and describe the nature of the account. Attach additional sheets if necessary.)
☐ Bank Account ☐ Securities Account ☐ Other (specify) ____

(f) Maximum value of account (see instruction I)
☐ Under $10,000 ☐ $10,000 to $50,000 ☐ $50,000 to $100,000 ☐ Over $100,000

10 Signature | 11. Title (Not necessary if reporting personal account) | 12. Date

PRIVACY ACT NOTIFICATION

Pursuant to the requirements of Public Law 93 579, (Privacy Act of 1974), notice is hereby given that the authority to collect information on Form 90 22 1 in accordance with 5 U S C 552(e)(3) is Public Law 91 508, 31 U S C 1121, 5 U S C 301, 31 CFR Part 103.
The principal purpose for collecting the information is to assure maintenance of reports or records where such reports or records have a high degree of usefulness in criminal, tax, or regulatory investigation or proceedings The information collected may be provided to those officers and employees of any constituent unit of the Department of the Treasury who have a need for the records in the performance of their duties. The records may be referred to any other department or agency of the Federal Government upon the request of the head of such department or agency for use in a criminal, tax, or regulatory investigation or proceeding.
Disclosure of this information is mandatory. Civil and criminal penalties, including under certain circumstances a fine of not more than $500,000 and imprisonment of not more than five years, are provided for failure to file a report, supply information, and for filing a false or fraudulent report.
Disclosure of the social security number is mandatory The authority to collect this number is 31 CFR 103. The social security number will be used as a means to identify the individual who files the report.

INSTRUCTIONS

A. Who Must File a Report—Each United States person who has a financial interest in or signature authority or other authority over bank, securities, or other financial accounts in a foreign country, which exceeded $1,000 in aggregate value at any time during the calendar year, must report that relationship each calendar year by filing Form 90-22.1 with the Department of the Treasury on or before June 30, of the succeeding year.

An officer or employee of a commercial bank which is subject to the supervision of the Comptroller of the Currency, the Board of Governors of the Federal Reserve System, or the Federal Deposit Insurance Corporation need not report that he has signature or other authority over a foreign bank, securities or other financial account maintained by the bank unless he has a personal financial interest in the account.

In addition, an officer or employee of a domestic corporation whose securities are listed upon national securities exchanges or which has assets exceeding $1 million and 500 or more shareholders of record need not file such a report concerning his signature authority over a foreign financial account of the corporation, if he has no personal financial interest in the account and has been advised in writing by the chief financial officer of the corporation that the corporation has filed a current report which includes that account

B. United States Person—The term "United States person" means (1) a citizen or resident of the United States, (2) a domestic partnership, (3) a domestic corporation, or (4) a domestic estate or trust

C. When and where to File—This report shall be filed on or before June 30 each calendar year with the Department of the Treasury, Post Office Box 28309, Central Station, Washington, D.C., 20005

D. Account in a Foreign Country—A "foreign country" includes all geographical areas located outside the United States, Guam, Puerto Rico, and the Virgin Islands.

Report any account maintained with a bank (except a military banking facility as defined in instruction E) or broker or dealer in securities that is located in a foreign country, even if it is a part of a United States bank or other institution. Do not report any account maintained with a branch, agency, or other office of a foreign bank of other institution that is located in the United States, Guam, Puerto Rico, and the Virgin Islands.

E. Military Banking Facility—Do not consider as an account in a foreign country, an account in an institution known as a "United States military banking facility" (or "United States military finance facility") operated by a United States financial institution designated by the United States Government to serve U.S. Government installations abroad, even if the United States military banking facility is located in a foreign country.

F. Bank, Financial Account—The term "bank account" means a savings, demand, checking, deposit, loan or any other account maintained with a financial institution or other person engaged in the business of banking. It includes certificates of deposit.

The term "securities account" means an account maintained with a financial institution or other person who buys, sells, holds, or trades stock or other securities for the benefit of another

The term "other financial account" means any other account maintained with a financial institution or other person who accepts deposits, exchanges or transmits funds, or acts as a broker or dealer for future transactions in any commodity on (or subject to the rules of) a commodity exchange or association.

G. Financial Interest—A financial interest in a bank, securities, or other financial account in a foreign country means an interest described in either of the following two paragraphs:

(1) A United States person has a financial interest in each account for which such person is the owner of records or has legal title, whether the account is maintained for his or her own benefit or for the benefit of others including non-United States persons. If an account is maintained in the name of two persons jointly, or if several persons each own a partial interest in an account, each of those United States persons has a financial interest in that account.

(2) A United States person has a financial interest in each bank, securities, or other financial account in a foreign country for which the owner of record or holder of legal title is: (a) a person acting as an agent, nominee, attorney, or in some other capacity on behalf of the U.S. person, (b) a corporation in which the United States person owns directly or indirectly more than 50 percent of the total value of shares of stock, (c) a partnership in which the United States person owns an interest in more than 50 percent of the profits (distributive share of income), or (d) a trust in which the United States person either has a present beneficial interest in more than 50 percent of the assets or from which such person receives more than 50 percent of the current income

H. Signature or Other Authority Over an Account—

Signature Authority—A person has signature authority over an account if such person can control the disposition of money or other property in it by delivery of a document containing his or her signature (or his or her signature and that of one or more other persons) to the bank or other person with whom the account is maintained

Other authority exists in a person who can exercise comparable power over an account by direct communication to the bank or other person with whom the account is maintained, either orally or by some other means

I. Account Valuation—For items 7, 9, and Instruction A, the maximum value of an account is the largest amount of currency and non-monetary assets that appear on any quarterly or more frequent account statement issued for the applicable year. If periodic account statements are not so issued, the maximum account asset value is the largest amount of currency and non-monetary assets in the account at any time during the year. Convert foreign currency by using the official exchange rate at the end of the year. In valuing currency of a country that uses multiple exchange rates, use the rate which would apply if the currency in the account were converted into United States dollars at the close of the calendar year.

The value of stock, other securities or other non-monetary assets in an account reported on Form 90-22.1 is the fair market value at the end of the calendar year, or if withdrawn from the account, at the time of the withdrawal.

For purposes of items 7, 9, and Instruction A, if you had a financial interest in more than one account, each account is to be valued separately in accordance with the foregoing two paragraphs.

If you had a financial interest in one or more but fewer than 25 accounts, and you are unable to determine whether the maximum value of these accounts exceeded $10,000 at any time during the year, check item 9 (do not check item 7) and complete item 9 for each of these accounts.

J. United States Persons with Authority Over but No Interest in an Account—Except as provided in Instruction A and the following paragraph, you must state the name, address, and identifying number of each owner of an account over which you had authority, but if you check item 5 for more than one account of the same owner, you need identify the owner only once.

If you check item 5 for one or more accounts in which no United States person had a financial interest, you may state on the first line of this item, in lieu of supplying information about the owner, "No U.S. person had any financial interest in the foreign accounts." This statement must be based upon the actual belief of the person filing this form after he or she has taken reasonable measures to endure its correctness.

If you check item 5 for accounts owned by a domestic corporation and its domestic and/or foreign subsidiaries, you may treat them as one owner and write in the space provided, the name of the parent corporation, followed by "and related entities." and the identifying number and address of the parent corporation

K. Consolidated Reporting—
A corporation which owns directly or indirectly more than 50 percent interest in one or more other entities will be permitted to file a consolidated report on Form 90-22.1, on behalf of itself and such other entities provided that a listing of them is made part of the consolidated report. Such reports should be signed by an authorized official of the parent corporation.

If the group of entities covered by a consolidated report has a financial interest in 25 or more foreign financial accounts, the reporting corporation need only note that fact on the form; it will, however, be required to provide detailed information concerning each account when so requested by the Secretary or his delegate.

L. Avoiding Duplicate Reporting—If you had financial interest as defined in instruction G(2)(b), (c) or (d) in one or more accounts which are owned by a domestic corporation, partnership or trust which is required to file Form 90-22.1 with respect to these accounts in lieu of completing item 9 for each account you may check item 6 and provide the required information.

M. Providing Additional Information—Any person who does not complete item 9, shall when requested by the Department of the Treasury provide the information called for in item 9.

N. Signature (Item 10)—*This report must be signed* by the person named in Item 1. If the report is being filed on behalf of a partnership, corporation, or fiduciary, it must be signed by an authorized individual.

O. Penalties—For criminal penalties for failure to file a report, supply information, and for filing a false or fraudulent report see 31 U.S.C. 1058, 31 U.S.C. 1059, and 18 U.S.C. 1001.

Currency Transaction Report

Form 4789
(April 1972)
(Replaces TCR-1)
Department of the Treasury
Internal Revenue Service

File a separate report for each transaction
(Complete all applicable parts—see instructions)

Part I   Identity of person who conducted this transaction with the financial institution

Name (Last, first and middle initial)	Social security number
Number and street	Business, occupation or profession
City or town, State and ZIP code	

Part II   Person or organization for whom this transaction was completed (Complete only if different than Part I)

Name	Identifying number
Number and street	Business, occupation or profession
City or town, State and ZIP code	

Part III   Description of transaction (If additional space is needed, attach a separate schedule)

1. Nature of transaction (check the applicable boxes)

   ☐ Deposit   ☐ Check purchased
   ☐ Withdrawal   ☐ Traveler's checks purchased
   ☐ Currency exchange   ☐ Security purchase (specify) ....
   ☐ Check cashed   ☐ Other (specify)

2. Total amount of currency transaction (in U.S. dollars)	3. Amount in denominations of $100 or higher	4. Date of transaction (Month, day and year)

5. If other than U.S. currency is involved, please furnish the following information:

Currency name	Country	Total amount of foreign currency

6. If a check was involved in this transaction, please furnish the following information (See instructions):

Date and amount of check	Payee
Drawer of check	Drawee bank and City of location

Part IV   Type of identification presented in this transaction

By customers:	By others:		
☐ Savings account number..........	☐ Driver's permit	State	Number
☐ Checking account number..........			
☐ Share account number..........	☐ Passport	Country	Number
☐ Loan account number..........			
☐ Safety deposit box number..........	☐ Alien ID card	Country	Number
☐ Other (specify)	☐ Other (specify)		

Part V   Financial institution reporting the financial transaction

Name and address	Identifying number (see instructions)
	Business activity

Sign here ▶ _____   _____   _____

                Authorized signature   Title   Date

| Form **4790** (April 1972) Department of the Treasury Internal Revenue Service | **Report of International Transportation of Currency or Monetary Instruments** Date of currency or monetary instrument activity ...., 19...... | This form is to be filed with the Bureau of Customs |

| Part I | Person Transporting, Mailing, Shipping, or Receiving a Monetary Instrument |
(Items 5 through 11 are applicable to alien individuals only)

1. Name (last or family, first, and middle) or business name	2. Identifying number (see instructions)	3. Check whether the currency or monetary instrument was: (a) ☐ Received (b) Shipped or mailed: ☐ Into the U.S. ☐ From the U.S.
4. Permanent address in United States or abroad	
5. Address while in the United States		(c) Carried by traveler (check applicable block and enter city):
6. Date of birth (month, day, and year)	7. Alien registration card number, if any	☐ Entering the U.S.— City...................
8. Visa date	9. Place United States visa was issued	☐ Leaving the U.S.— City
10. Of what country are you a citizen or subject?	11. Passport number and country	

12. Were you acting as an agent, attorney, or in other capacity for anyone in this currency or monetary instrument activity? . . . . ☐ Yes ☐ No
If "Yes," please complete the following:
  (a) Name of person in whose behalf you are acting ....
  (b) Complete address of that person...

  (c) Business activity, occupation or profession of that person ....

| Part II | Currency and Monetary Instrument Information (See Instructions) |

13. Type and amount of currency and/or monetary instrument:
  (a) ☐ Coins (specify amount) . . . . $............................
  (b) ☐ Currency (specify amount) . . . .
  (c) ☐ Bearer instrument (specify type and amount) ....
  (d) ☐ Total amount (add lines (a), (b) and (c)) . . . . $
14. If other than United States currency is involved, please complete the following:
  (a) Currency name ....
  (b) Country ....
  (c) Equivalent in United States dollars (specify amount) . . . . $ ....
15. Name of person from whom the currency or monetary instrument was received (to be completed by recipients only)...............

16. If the currency or monetary instrument was mailed, shipped, transported or carried, please complete the following:
  (a) Method of shipment ....
  (b) Name of transporter or carrier ....
Under penalties of perjury, I declare that I have examined this report, and to the best of my knowledge and belief it is true, correct and complete.

Sign Here ▶ --
Signature

--   -------------------------------
Title (Owner, etc.)   Date
                                                                        •48—18—81904-1

Index